As Sure as the Dawn

A Spiritguide

Through Times
of Darkness

As Sure as the Dawn

A Spiritguide

Through Times
of Darkness

Patrick J. Howell, S.J.

Sheed & Ward

nihil obstat: Rev. Stephen V. Sundborg, SJ, provincial of
the Oregon Province, Society of Jesus.

Sheed & Ward™ is a service of The National Catholic Reporter
Publishing Company.

Library of Congress Cataloguing-in-Publication Data

Howell, Patrick J., S.J.
ISBN: 1-55612-818-5

Published by: Sheed & Ward
115 E. Armour Blvd.
P.O. Box 419492
Kansas City, MO 64141-6492

To order, call: (800) 333-7373

CONTENTS

In their affliction, they shall look for me;
Let us strive to know the Lord;
as certain as the dawn is coming.

– Hosea 6:1-3, NAB

Part One
A Generation of Seekers

Part Two
Risking Belief

Part Three
In the Presence of Mystery

Part Four
Discerning the Way

Acknowledgments

Grateful acknowledgment is given for copyright reprint permissions as follows:

Excerpts from "Satire III," and "Batter my Heart Three-Person'd God," by John Donne are reprinted from *Selections from Divine Poems, Sermons, Devotions, and Prayers,* John Booty, ed. Copyright© 1990 by Paulist Press. Reprinted by permission of Paulist Press.

Excerpts from "The Center," by William Stafford are reprinted from *A Scripture of Leaves.* Copyright© 1989 by Brethren Press (Elgin, IL). Reprinted by permission of Brethren Press.

Excerpts from "The Waste Land" and "The Love Song of J. Alfred Prufrock" from *Collected Poems 1909-1962* by T.S. Eliot, copyright 1936 by Harcourt Brace & Company, copyright© 1964, 1963 by T.S. Eliot, reprinted by permission of the publisher.

Excerpt from "East Coker" in *Four Quartets,* copyright 1943 by T.S. Eliot and renewed 1971 by Esme Valerie Eliot, reprinted by permission of Harcourt Brace & Company.

Excerpts from "The Wreck of the Deutchland," by Gerard Manley Hopkins are reprinted from *The Poetical Works of Gerard Manley Hopkins,* Norman H. MacKenzie, ed. Copyright© 1990 by Oxford University Press. Reprinted by permission of Oxford University Press.

Excerpts from "Clearances," by Seamus Heaney are reprinted from *Selected Poems 1966-1987,* by Seamus Heaney. Copyright© 1990 by Farrar, Straus and Giroux. Reprinted by permission of Farrar, Straus and Giroux (New York), and Faber & Faber Ltd (London).

Excerpts from *Markings* by Dag Hammarskjold, trans., Leif Sjoberg/ W.H. Auden. Translation copyright© by Alfred A. Knopf, Inc. and Faber & Faber Ltd. Reprinted by permission of Alfred A. Knopf, Inc.

Excerpts from *Crimes and Misdemeanors* by Woody Allen, copyright© 1989 by Woody Allen. Permission in process.

Excerpts from "Blessed the Bread: A Litany," by Carter Heyward are reprinted from *Our Passion for Justice: Images of Power, Sexuality, and Liberation.* Copyright© 1984 by Pilgrim Press. Permission in process.

Excerpts from "For the Time Being. IV.," by W.H. Auden are reprinted from *Collected Longer Poems.* Copyright© 1965 by Random House. Permission in process.

Excerpts from *Run with the Horsemen,* by Ferrol Sams, copyright© 1982 by Peachtree Publishers, Ltd. Reprinted by permission of the publisher.

Excerpts from *Sabbaths, IX,* by Wendell Berry, copyright© 1987 by North Point Press. Permission in process.

PART ONE

A Generation
of Seekers

"Are you a God?" they asked the Buddha.

"No," he replied.

"Are you an angel, then?" "No."

"A saint?" "No."

"Then what are you?"

Replied the Buddha, "I am awake."[1]

Searching

"We are the first generation that grew up without religion, and frankly I'm not very optimistic about how we are doing," a young woman named Denise told me. She added, "For myself I am still ambiguous about God and religion, even my boyfriend! Until recently, I have not been able to find much guidance or any place where I can explore my doubts and questions."

I teach a course called "Your Spiritual Journey." In it students explore their own personal and family history, and in the process they explore their own yearning for meaning in their lives. Like Denise, they struggle with their values, their restless drift, and their love relationships, and they are surprised by their own story and its moments of revelation. They may be working through difficult unresolved issues, such as the death of a parent or the loss of a lover. At times they forget it is a class altogether because we explore issues which touch their heart. Despite bleak, even disastrous periods of their lives, most often they are encouraged by seeing their own resilience.

I find that the students who have faced a crisis are most prone to exploring spirituality. It does not matter whether the crisis is moral, political, mental, or physical; it could be the death of a parent, a personal diagnosis of cancer, a ruptured relationship, the witness of Archbishop Oscar Romero martyred because of his outspoken support for the suffering poor in El Salvador, or the outbreak of war in the Persian Gulf and a sudden awakening to their own complicity in violence. We talk about how a crisis dissolves, at least for a time, whatever framework of meaning and interpretation they had. They often acknowledge that their own crisis allowed them the freedom to search for a new way to bring

coherence to their experience. Though it threatened their identity and self-esteem, it broadened their horizon and allowed a
wider synthesis. It was both a danger and an opportunity.

In an earlier book[2] I traced my own personal crisis. I recounted the story of my mental breakdown and recovery, so I will
not repeat that story here except to draw on it for illustrations
for this current project. Since then, my encounters with both
graduate students in ministry and undergraduates searching for
direction in their lives have informed much of my own life and
have helped to shape these reflections. My work with college
students, many hours spent in pastoral counseling, my own experience with mental illness and recovery, and my own search for
an authentic spirituality shape my own understanding of such
direction. Further, since God acts in relationship with each person
and deals differently with each person, such a Way must necessarily be discovered by each person, with the guidance, encouragement, and support of others.

The response to my first book also motivated me to write a
sequel. People from places as diverse as Zambia, Ireland, Uru-
guay, England, New York, Iowa, North Dakota, Minnesota, and
Washington have shared their own breaking/healing stories with
me. Their letters are filled with appreciation, pain, a longing for
peace, and an implicit question. "Is there something or someone
who could guide me? Is there some purpose which my life might
have? What spiritual resources might help me even if this chronic
illness persists?" Others who have recovered their equilibrium
might ask, "Okay, now what?" Or "I've read Scott Peck's *The Road
Less Traveled,*[3] now where do I go from here?"

They may be groping through the remains of their former
lives now that a crisis has shattered their former coherence.
Though they are afflicted, though they move through the shadows, they attend the break of dawn. They are ready to listen and
wait in the darkness.

A Map for the Journey

The following ten chapters provide a map. They do not have a
linear flow, but rather circle round the quest for truth in an
ascending pathway. Each chapter rises to a larger perspective and

intersects with all the previous points. John Donne, the poet, described this spiral ascent:

> On a huge hill
> Cragged and steep, Truth stands, and [those] that will
> Reach her, about must, and about must go.[4]

So too in our spiritual journey, we "about must, and about must go."

I am not so interested in defining spirituality as I am in suggesting guideposts and indicating some directions. My approach is descriptive, not prescriptive. I offer a structure, but not a system. In each chapter I give a perspective on the journey, share a story of someone's life, and conclude with a stream-of-consciousness reflection.

In Part One, "A Generation of Seekers," we explore the search for meaning by asking three questions: How might the West release its own rich spiritual heritage and be strengthened by its encounter with Eastern spiritualities? (Chapter One) How do we opt for life rather than mere survival? (Chapter Two) And how might our own deepest desires give meaning to our lives and be an avenue to Mystery? (Chapter Three)

In Part Two, "Risking Belief," we continue our questions, but move toward "living the question," as the poet Rilke puts it. Doubts continue to haunt us, but we inch towards risking the unknown. We probe these questions: What is the source from which our deepest desires spring? (Chapter Four) What might our human response be to Mystery, to this Source in my life? (Chapter Five) We then consider the obstacles to our journey. What blocks life from flowing through me? What are the hells which condemn us? (Chapter Six) How does shame and stigma paralyze both me and society? (Chapter Seven) By facing the shadows head on, we are no longer haunted by them. Facing the shadows reveals the truth[5] as truth actually comes to us, not as we would wish it.

In Part Three, "In the Presence of Mystery," we turn to God or God turns to us. It is never quite clear. Our questions fade. Our doubts disperse. Mystery envelops us so that we encounter it from within rather than from without. Radical love suddenly courses through our lives. And all is different, all is new (Chapter Eight).

The next two chapters then ponder this radical turn in our lives and our encounter with Ultimate Mystery. Love moves towards deeper acceptance, even forgiveness (Chapter Nine). And our imagination, now grounded in truth, explores this transformative turn (Chapter Ten).

In Part Four, "Discerning the Way," we examine the mentor tradition. The great spiritual writers and poets realized that the wayfarer needed a guide because even a holy person was subject to delusions (Chapter Eleven). More and more the wayfarer internalizes the mentor's wisdom and makes choices out of discerning love (Chapter Twelve). Finally from this vantage we cast an eye backward to gaze on the ultimate Source from which we sprang and forward toward the destiny to which we flow. By now we see "the way home," and we know, with nostalgia but without regret, that we cannot go home again.

A Dedication

I have some friends who have faced several years of chronic mental illness. Bill[6] has a bipolar disorder; he has had 13 hospitalizations in 15 years. Sharon was probably sexually abused from the time she was three years old. She found a defense against her father by creating three personalities, each with different names. When she became an adult at the age of 40, she chose with great courage to live her authentic, core personality – Sharon. Bill and Sharon and many others struggle, not only with their disease, but most often with their own self-esteem, which has been eroded by abuse, joblessness, broken relationships, the debilitating side effects of psychotropic medications, or by a stigmatizing society. Our care for them is a clear sign of whether or not we can build a city of loving, accepting people. They walk now in the darkness visible. Our prayer is that we all emerge together from the shadows when the dawn breaks. To them I dedicate this book.

So let us begin.

Endnotes

1. Huston Smith, *The World's Religions* rev. ed. (NY: Harper & Row, 1958, 1991), p. 82. The Sanskrit root *budh* denotes both to wake up and to know. Buddha means the Enlightened One or the Awakened One.

2. Patrick J. Howell, S.J., *Reducing the Storm to a Whisper: The Story of a Breakdown* (Chicago: Thomas More Press, 1985).

3. M. Scott Peck, *The Road Less Traveled: A New Psychology of Love, Traditional Values and Spiritual Growth* (New York: Simon and Schuster, 1978). This book has helped many students to acknowledge their own worldview or religion and to accept their need for more interior disciplines.

4. John Donne, "Satire III," ll. 72-81 (1597). *Selections from Divine Poems, Sermons, Devotions, and Prayers* ed. by John Booty. The Classics of Western Spirituality (Mahwah: Paulist Press, 1990).

5. Scott Peck says that much unhappiness arises from not facing reality, and he identifies four disciplines for the journey: 1) delaying of gratification, 2) acceptance of responsibility, 3) dedication to truth, and 4) balancing. The problem, Peck says, lies not in their complexity, but in the will to use them. The *will* to use them is love. *The Road Less Traveled*, p. 18.

6. All names for case studies in this book are fictitious. Each case study reflects my own perceptions based on my pastoral experience, friendships, and working relationships with scores of different people during the last 18 years. Each story is a re-imagined composite. The real stories of real people are much richer than these sketches.

CHAPTER ONE

The Way Home

"The West seems lost. It does not teach its people the traditions of wisdom. It's too bad that it does not have a Way." A holy man from India made this observation to a friend of mine 20 years ago. By his comment the holy man meant, of course, that the West did not have access to a path for wisdom, serenity, and attunement, such as Buddha had taught. My friend felt the poignancy of the loss. Yes, he admitted, the West is adrift. Yes, it has lost its Way. In a similar vein, film maker Ingmar Bergman and novelist Albert Camus depicted the alienation, ennui, and shallowness of a people who had lost their soul. It is this Way which we hope to recover or discover, perhaps both.

What an irony! Up until the Modern Era, the West, whose religious and philosophical inspiration sprang from the lands of Palestine and Greater Greece, had had a long, brilliant tradition of spiritual guidance. In fact, the predominant religious group in the West was known in its beginning simply as people of "The Way."[1] These people recalled the claim of Jesus, "I am the Way, the Truth, and the Life," as an affirmation that they themselves were people of The Way. The early Christians had risked their lives, their fortunes, their souls on The Way.[2]

Jesus taught a Way, and his disciples proclaimed him as The Way itself. Thus the early people of The Way saw his lifestyle, his commitment to the poor, his intimate openness to Abba-God, his willingness to be driven by the Spirit, as an embodiment of the way to God.

Another name for the early followers of the Nazarean was The Gathering.[3] It was only in The Gathering, that is, in the community, that they could recognize The Way and then interpret and celebrate their pilgrimage.

In the last two decades since that Indian holy man first made his comment, two remarkable 20th-century breakthroughs into the inner realms of the human psyche have begun to converge. The first breakthrough, led by Freud and Jung in the 1900s and 1910s, opened the door of the psyche and explored the dynamics of the unconscious. The second breakthrough, in the 1950s and 1960s, involved spiritual teachers from the East who awakened Westerners to deeper values and to the exploration of the inner world of the human spirit.[4] Many Westerners, who had grown weary, then confused, then alienated by their own culture, eagerly greeted these spiritual guides. Thousands risked a turn to depth spirituality, to the realm of ancient spiritual wisdom in both the East and the West. They turned not merely to subjective religious experience, but also to the process of growth in the deepest recesses of the psyche.

These two breakthroughs touch common ground, but the boundaries are unclear. They overlap and interpenetrate. How they do this is a question still being explored.

The exploration of the unconscious and the arrival of gurus and Zen masters were not the only sources for psychic-spiritual revitalization. Vatican II (1962-1965) gave an impetus to the renewed search for spiritual roots for Christians by its call for the renewal of the liturgy and for a retrieval of the roots of the spiritual traditions. Spiritual movements, such as the Charismatic Renewal, gave a freedom of spirit for people to explore their interior gifts. The Retreat in Everyday Life, first mapped out by St. Ignatius of Loyola, began in the mid-70s to flourish in multiple centers. Religious orders, such as the Franciscans, accepted many more lay associates. Often these same groups incorporated Zen meditation or yoga postures into their prayer. This process of assimilation continues yet.

The renewal of spirituality included several phenomena. Some secular psychotherapies assimilated features of Buddhist and Hindu spirituality. Some Protestants embraced the sacramental spirituality of Catholics, and Catholics relished the profound grasp of Scripture by Protestants. Together they explored the classical spiritual traditions and broke open fresh perspectives through interreligious dialogue.

Ewert Cousins concludes that as a result of these two break-throughs into the human psyche, a world spirituality is emerging for the first time.[5] This world spirituality flows from the mutual encounters of Eastern and Western religious aspirations. It embraces a comprehensive, multidimensional spiritual wisdom. It pays little regard to ideology, and it tends to blur all distinctions. Within the West, at least, this world spirituality carries a heightened appreciation for native spiritualities, although at times it simply borrows the outer shell without entering into the asceticism essential to these rites.

American students are tantalized by world spirituality. Often they sense that their own traditions are hollow or too dogmatic or given to fanaticism. They sense that American culture and values are bereft of depth, even as they themselves get caught up in the maelstrom of success, materialism, and consumerism. As I said at the outset, their spiritual journey often begins with a personal crisis. Erik Erikson captures this fruitfulness in a crisis when he calls it "a turning point, a crucial period of increased vulnerability and heightened potential."[6] A crisis strips away comforting delusions and sharpens blurred perceptions. The painter Vincent Van Gogh, for instance, suffered incapacitating waves of black depression. Yet, even in the midst of his darkest turmoil, he painted landscapes pulsing with color and vitality. His intensity conveys to us a deeper dimension to life with unjaded freshness.

Whenever students confront their own destructiveness or most often when the bottom of their lives falls out, they face their own mortality and question whatever fragile meaning has held their lives together. In a crisis, it is not surprising that they cast about for an anchor.

My students writing their life stories are often surprised at how a crucial event or a key person in a traumatic situation made all the difference. "How could I have done this when I was only eight?" "How could I have taken care of my mother when she was dying of cancer?" "Thank God, for my junior English teacher; he really understood what was going on and helped me straighten out my head." At times they feel their vulnerability and weakness more than their strength. They may observe, "I just did what I had to do."

As they describe the patterns of their lives, they may seek to explain the continuities. They intuit that divine guidance, or good fortune, or an encounter with God is at work, even though they may be reluctant to call it that. Mystery eludes them. Of course, some feel they have just had to "go it alone." Nobody was there for them.

Writing their story forces them to make decisions and sharpens their own focus on what their history means now. As they face the pain of these times, rather than escaping it with overwork, or with one more trip to the mall, or a weekend kegger, or numbing out in front of the boob tube, they penetrate their own murky shadows and behold their real selves. They often feel a creative spirit, a nameless power, a caressing touch, a refreshing wellspring rising within them.

I share with the students the healthy caution of dramatist Lillian Hellman about childhood memories. Hellman said: "I'm always suspicious of [them] because they are so conditioned by how a person feels now." Hellman can be read ironically, as if she simply dismisses childhood memories, but her comment also provides an antidote for sweet nostalgia or for bitter recriminations. She underscores that we can choose how we relate to our earlier memories. We do select. We are influenced by where we are now. By caring for our affectivity *now,* we can shape our view of our earlier history.

As students seek understanding for their own spirituality, they may examine traditional religions, but often their previous experience with immature, oppressive forms of religion blocks them from openly exploring religion. Or as T. S. Eliot might explain, "We had the experience, but missed the meaning."[7] They could benefit from good mentoring, from adults or peers who took their experience seriously. They value such people who can help them explore their deepest questions and help them explore their experience and its meaning. They seek guides who will not immediately impeach their logical or even illogical arguments against religion.

Admittedly some students operate out of a vague, "one-religion-is-as-good-as-another" mentality, which, in practice means: "Since that's true, then I don't need to commit myself to any particular direction." Or others admit, "I believe in God, but religion is so contradictory, so filled with hypocrisy. Look at Jimmy and Tammy Bakker." Or others charge, "Religion has caused a lot of wars. Look at the Serbs and Croats and others at each others' throats. The Greek Orthodox, the Catholic, and the Muslim leaders are all stirring up the war." These are, of course, honest

critiques, but they can also mask their own ambiguity and vulnerability. Some may write off religion as irrelevant, especially if they
have never had their own religious and deeply spiritual experiences listened to and valued. They *are* interested in some form
of spirituality. They seem to need a place apart to attend to their
own experience, to explore its meaning, and to let go of some
cherished stereotypes. Most welcome the group support for their
explorations.

Those who turn to Eastern religions as a direction for their
lives discover that in India, as in the rest of Asia, several "ways"
or *mārga* pervade the cultures. *Mārga* leads the disciple to enlightenment and inner peace, but it is a way unique to each person.

Those who examine the fresh portrait of Jesus in a book
such as Albert Nolan's *Jesus Before Christianity*[8] find Jesus an attractive man of passion, filled with a yearning for justice, siding with
the poor and the outcast, given to parties that scandalize the
stiff-lipped religious leaders, coming among them as a friend,
enjoying life so much that he earned a bad reputation among
religious leaders as "a drunkard and a glutton."[9] They see Jesus
was attuned to the beauty of fields, songbirds, and lilies around
him and broke down the religious and chauvinistic barriers to
human solidarity. "Why haven't the churches ever preached about
this Jesus?" they ask. They are eager to hear more about a Jesus
who castigated the trappings of religion and stripped the hypocrites of their pretensions so that a genuine spirituality might
thrive.

Before we explore these ways, I would like to share a portion
of my own journey as a limited example of how a personal crisis
jarred my own comfortable, though destructive assumptions, and
precipitated a journey without any known markers or boundaries.

My Own Story

In 1975 I suffered an acute psychosis[10] or mental breakdown.
Initially, it flattened me. It destroyed "my religion." How could
this horrible thing happen to me? How could God allow this to
happen? Would I ever be well again? Eventually, it led me to a
richer, fuller appreciation for life, for friends, for family, and for
the spiritual wisdom in my religious tradition, until then largely
locked up. The crisis tapped in me a deeper awareness of life

flowing through and around me. It taught me to breathe larger drafts of life and to discover afresh that "whenever you breathe, God comes in."[11] The episode and my time in the psych ward and in the psychiatrist's office radically shaped my own journey.

At the time of the breakdown, I was 35 and had just completed one year as the principal of a Jesuit (Catholic) high school. Until then, except for some chest tension pangs in the spring, I had felt fine physically. The unraveling started during an eight-day retreat in July.

At the beginning of the retreat, I started to unwind from the tensions of the school year, did some jogging and stretching every day, and found that scriptural images drew me down to a deeper place within myself. After a few days my dreams took a dramatic turn: At night I woke up startled. A beetle, "Beelze-bug" threatened me. I felt suffocated by a demonic creature. I jumped up shaken, looked toward the window. On the screen was an ugly, buzzing bug – perhaps four inches in diameter, but it loomed even larger in my imagination. I shook. The dreams plunged deeper. Bright tropical colors surrounding the death struggles of baboons. A phrase floated through me, "I am the Way, the Truth, and the Light," or was it "Life"? I couldn't keep it straight. These subconscious images floated upward. I moved from high tension to deep peace and back again. By the end of the retreat, my imagination was firing away with images, insights, a spinning merry-go-round of feelings within me.

Praying one afternoon, I smelled a roomful of lilies – an olfactory hallucination I realized later. The more I prayed, the more rapidly the images fired. Fear and anxiety deepened. I thought these wild images would never end. After a few more days I started to live out my imaginings as if a person not myself were walking through my dreams. A few friends noticed my intensity and some of my bizarre behaviors. They sought professional advice and had me hospitalized on July 18, 1975.

The psych ward was a relief. The ward's environment was staid and neutral. It calmed me. A psychotropic drug, named Thorazine, stoppered up the geyser of my emotions. Then a wave of new fears engulfed me. I wondered whether I could continue my job as principal. I was fraught with anxiety that the psychosis could recycle. I dreaded having to tell my parents and other friends. I feared the stigma.

I dimly heard the doctor say, "It takes time. We don't know how long it will take. Six months is the usual recovery time from the acute phase." From ten fathoms deep I barely heard him.

The medications and the milieu provided safety and relief. Gradually I let go of whatever was going on out there in the real world. After a few days, a simple chant arose from within me, "Trust. Trust and listen. Trust." Perhaps from God. But now my dread of God threatened to plunge me into a fresh abyss. "Stop it!"

"Trust." It was a soothing rhythm.

"Trust the doctors."

"Trust the nurses."

"Trust the time." A healing mantra. A simple gift.

Numb, ambulatory, and edgy, I could simply be. My psychiatrist measured the Thorazine to a fine balance. He sought a proper dosage which would, on the one hand, forestall the whirling, random firing of neurons by blocking the neurotransmitter dopamine, and at the same time allow sufficient psychic space for me to realize and work out my problems. I was never subject to promiscuous prescribing of these potentially dangerous tranquilizers. I had excellent care.

Though a safe place, the ward was not a wonderful, bucolic setting where the patients frolicked in the sun and danced with the flowers. Nor was it an idyllic romp like the playful cavorting of the asylum inmates in the movie "King of Hearts." It was all too real. The medications three times a day quelled most of the raging bio-chemical imbalances within the patients, but from my room I could hear one of them chanting the name of the nurse, "Mary Lou, Mary Lou, Mary Lou," over and over again like a needle stuck on a record. I found out her name was Sarabel, a compulsive woman. Sarabel looked bruised and beaten. Her tiresome voice filled the hallway. It had the fever of a tribal dance, but without the passion. No coursing blood, no dancing. Only the isolated cry, like a bewildered, three-year old wailing for her mother. Twenty minutes on end. It drove all of us crazy!

Wailing, blubbering, bellowing. She went on. My mind flashed to an episode from William Faulkner's novel *The Sound and the Fury*. A central figure of the novel is Benjy Compson, a thirty-three-year old "idiot" who has the mentality of a three-year old. The last in the line of the chivalrous Compsons who helped settle the South, Benjy narrates the first section of the story in a stream of consciousness without any historical sense, shifting back and forth through images as portals to a 30-year timeless period.

Luster, one of the many Blacks in the Compson household who give some cohesion to this decaying family, often cares for Benjy. At the conclusion of the novel, which occurs on Easter Sunday,[12] Luster drives Benjy to town on an old buckboard:

> Ben quit whimpering as they began the ride toward town. He sat in the middle of the seat, holding the repaired flower upright in his fist, his eyes serene and ineffable.

As they approach the square, "where the Confederate soldier gazed with empty eyes beneath his marble hand in wind and weather," Luster takes a notion to show off to the young Black bucks who are watching. Rather than taking the customary turn round to the right, he switches the horse Queenie to move toward the left of the monument.

> For an instant Ben sat in an utter hiatus. Then he bellowed. Bellow on bellow, his voice mounted, with scarce interval for breath. There was more than astonishment in it, it was horror; shock; agony eyeless, tongueless; just sound, and Luster's eyes backrolling for a white instant. "Gret God," he said.

Ben's ne'er-do-well brother Jason sees what is happening, jumps on the wagon, slaps Luster around, straightens out the wagon and runs it round the *right* side on the monument.

> Suddenly the bellowing stopped just as soon as it had started and the broken flower drooped over Ben's fist and his eyes were empty and blue and serene again as cornice and facade flowed smoothly once more from left to right, post and tree, window and doorway and signboard each in its ordered place.

The scene portrays the disruption of order. Ben cannot fathom it, but neither can the rest of the South in the 1930's, which still clings to the monuments of the Civil War and the genteel, slave-owning past. It echoes Shakespeare's line in *Macbeth* that life is "a tale told by an idiot, full of sound and fury, signifying nothing."

For Faulkner the Compsons were a symbol of the decline of the South and its delusional clinging to an ordered past. The South had lost its soul to a new breed of entrepreneurs. It strove for a restoration of the old ways – going the right way around the old Confederate monuments and for a time it gazed out peacefully, with eyes like Ben's, empty, serene, and blue. Faulkner portrayed a whole generation unredeemed, a culture, a country, which had lost its structured, aristocratic ways and was still clinging to the right way around the Civil War monuments. Lost in time.

Back on the ward, the bellowing of Sarabel ceased too. She did get better. At least her cries subsided. Empty, serene, blue. Perhaps her rituals fell back into place. In this austere place with its locked doors and wired windows, she found a peace that she could not find at home. Removed from the anxiety and discord of her previous world, she emerged from the nameless darkness coursing through her. Like a child sent to her room, her rage quieted. In this orderly detention, her only duty was to get well. But out of the bellowing and the blue-eyed serenity, questions arose for me.

Who's mad? Who's the idiot?

Is it all sound and fury signifying nothing?

Does the mad woman bellow for a declining society, for an society emptied of values, faithful only to empty rituals?

The psych ward taught me some basics about spirituality that I was not aware of until years later. They have come to me during these last 20 years as I drew upon my experience while interacting with university students and with others through lectures, retreats, and seminars. My earlier emptiness was not so much filled, as touched. It gave way to a surprising fecundity. I resonated with those who struggled with mental illness or severe loneliness or post-traumatic stress from Vietnam or with social injustice. My candor seemed to open doors to people's traumas or to the creativity of their own lives.

Some acquaintances came to know me as "the priest who knows about mental illness," and they sometimes connected me with people undergoing mental illness. Referring to the title of my earlier book, they might tell me, "She's having one of those whispering experiences." They might even be whispering themselves, as they confide in me. And I know from their conspiratorial tone, "the whisper" is about the waves of psychic delusions sweeping through her, paralyzing her.

I do not offer any more than any one else could offer: Hope. A listening ear. A quiet reassurance. An expectation that things will be better. A referral to professionals. A prayer. At times a hand to hold. And a spirituality, more humane, more grounded, more in touch, than any airy delusions.

Ultimately we each seek love and are healed by Love itself. The medieval teachers said that "Love is diffusive of itself." It spills over; it fills its surroundings. A person radically accepted by another naturally wishes to share that acceptance, that gift of love with others. Love pervades a community which breaks bread together, which shares forgiveness and seeks justice in the face of evil together.

A healing spirituality is not remote from the world, but engaged in it. It enables people to be aware of their own unique gifts and is passionately committed to a better society. It respects human dignity. It fosters a favoritism for "little ones," for children, for the abandoned, for the poor, for the mentally handicapped, for the homeless. It will lay the foundations for a just society.

On this journey together, we need to keep reminding ourselves of the questions: What are my deepest desires? What is the source of my creative spirit? What blocks my creativity? What hobbles my life? Which of my habits or attitudes are destructive? With whom do I take up and continue the journey? In fact, these questions will underlie the next chapters.

As we glimpse our ultimate Source, we catch our breath. We know that the gift received was not our own doing. We see the way ahead. We know we have just begun. We are no longer at ease in the old dispensation. Now a healing, compassionate, mystical spirituality leads us onward into the enchanting mystery of life. We are on the Way. We are awake.

Who am I to quote the Buddha? We're not even acquainted. How's my approach any different from the instant spirituality advertised on every telephone pole at Berkeley? Americanized, sanitized, commercialized, so that the Eastern original can hardly be recognized. It's taught in a class to hundreds. It's graded and sifted and evaluated as if it were on a par with microbiology or Western Civ.

American gyms offer yoga as a good workout or a means of enhancing one's sex life; yoga stripped of interior discipline, cut loose from attending to wisdom. How can the body teach when it's harnessed to a machine?

I grow old, I grow old. I hug my confusion, lest the truth pain me. I wander through a park and find peace. I scurry round a mall and lust for more. I flee from my friends lest I be burdened with love. At nights I awake and tremble momentarily, then drift on and on. So who am I?

Endnotes

1. Acts of the Apostles 9:2; 18:26; 19:9,23; 22:4; 24:14,22. It was in Antioch, 15 or 20 years after the death of Jesus, where "Christians" received that name.

2. Classical spiritual writers described four major Ways. They were *the via positiva, the via negativa, the via creationis,* and *the via transformationis.* These are not four separate ways, rather they intertwine with each other, though at any one stage in a life one of them will predominate. The via positiva is a path of awe and beauty, of generosity and hospitality. The via negativa is a path of the cross, a path of suffering, pain and anger. The via creationis calls us, as an image of God, to co-create with God. It calls us to dwell in the darkness and to bring creation out of chaos.

   Finally, the via transformationis evokes action, a prophetic path, which asks us to question existing structures and to transform society – just as we ourselves are transformed and are being transformed.

3. In Greek *ekklesia* means assembly or gathering. Unfortunately, ecclesiastic now indicates the institutional Church, rather than a communal gathering and sharing of God's presence among us.

4. Ewert Cousins, "States of Consciousness: Charting the Mystical Path," in *The Fires of Desire: Erotic Energies and the Spiritual Quest* edited by Fredrica R. Halligan and John J. Shea (New York: Crossroad, 1992), p. 126. One example of how the Eastern disciplines impacted the West would be Eugen Herrigel's little masterpiece, *Zen in the Art of Archery,* trans. from the German by R.F.C. Hull (New York: Pantheon Books, Inc., 1953).

5. *Ibid.,* p. 127.

6. Erik Erikson, *Identity: Youth and Crisis* (New York: Norton, 1968), p. 96.

7. T.S. Eliot, *The Complete Poems and Plays, 1909-1950* (New York: Harcourt, Brace, & World, Inc., 1971), p. 37.

8. Albert Nolan, *Jesus Before Christianity,* 2nd ed. (Maryknoll: Orbis Books, 1978, 1992).

9. Luke 7:34.

10. An acute psychosis indicates a temporary condition in which the person loses contact with reality. A chronic psychosis indicates a prolonged illness with regular or episodic loss of contact with reality. For an informative booklet see "The Church and Serious Mental Illness," *Church & Society* (Jan./Feb., 1991) published by the Presbyterian Church (100 Witherspoon St., Louisville, KY 40202).

11. William Stafford, *A Scripture of Leaves,* "The Center" (Elgin, IL: Brethren Press, 1989), p. 52.

12. William Faulkner, *The Sound and the Fury,* corrected ed. (New York: Random House, 1929, 1984), pp. 319-321.

CHAPTER TWO

Surviving a Crisis

At the breakfast table my third day in the psych ward I could see the bandages on Betty's wrists where she had slit them. Her husband had found her. Dark blue shadows marked her eyes, but she was pleasant, animated, witty. How could anyone wish to kill herself?

Well, I did know that people in mental crisis can be racked by raging torments. Some years later novelist William Styron in his autobiographical book *Darkness Visible* described the inner turmoil of depression very well for me. "Depression," Styron said, is far too tame a word to describe the black storm within. The word suggests something altogether too bland. So what? Everyone gets a little depressed now and then. "Nervous breakdown" would not do either, Styron protested. It is nondescript; it also insinuates a vague spinelessness. "Melancholia," an older term, aptly portrays the blacker form of the disorder, but is too archaic. The most appropriate word, Styron concluded, would be "brainstorm," but it had already been preempted to describe intellectual inspiration. Only brainstorm, however, genuinely described the howling tempest within his brain.[1]

Crisis Theory

It might be well at this point to pause and to broaden our view of what constitutes a crisis before we consider more fully the spiritual resources that might assist a person in the aftermath of such a crisis.

Crisis theory emphasizes the individual's reaction to a stressful situation.[2] A crisis, therefore, is a disruption such that an individual is unable to maintain normal functioning and must resort to new strategies or modes of coping. Such a state may yield some resolution, or it may result in chronic dysfunction.

We can identify stages in a crisis reaction. The first is marked by a sharp rise in tension, followed by feelings of helplessness and confusion. Individuals in crisis do not know how to think about their problem, nor how to evaluate the crisis, nor how to evaluate the reality of the situation. They cannot marshal problem-solving resources.

In the second stage individuals use new or unusual problem-solving mechanisms. If they achieve no resolution, disorganized thinking and apathy result. If, as often happens, they achieve a new coherence in their lives and an increased ability to face their own reality, then joy, meaning, and life purpose mark their lives.

Crises come in two varieties: *maturational* and *situational*. *Maturational* crises are normal processes of growth and development. They usually evolve over an extended period of time, such as the transition into adolescence or through middle age, and they frequently require that the individual make character changes. *Situational* crises, on the other hand, arise from external sources, such as the death of a loved one, severe physical illness or debilitation, an unexpected pregnancy, opting for an abortion, or divorce.

In recent years communal crises such as the bombing of the Federal Building in Oklahoma City, massive unemployment in Detroit, starvation in Somalia caused largely by warring political parties funded by the superpowers, sudden death of 4000 people by a tsunami in the Philippines, the purging of ethnic groups in Bosnia Herzegovina, looting and burning riots in Los Angeles, and post-traumatic stress from Vietnam or the Gulf War have created both individual and social dysfunction. These situational crises naturally aggravate the maturational crises for each individual. For instance, children of unemployed or addicted parents face a tougher road in their own maturation.

At some stage in a crisis a person begins to ask: What possible meaning could this tragedy, this turmoil, this chaos have in my life? How could this happen to me? What have I done to deserve this? Is there some possible providence or divine hand working through this? These are the questions that Job wrestled with. The answers that Job's friends offered ran the range from superficial and judgmental to distancing or moralizing. In the end no rational answer would do. Nor would the pain, the loss, the total upheaval of self, the mystery of life and death itself yield to the mouthing of banal pieties. Job was patient, Job was silent, Job was angry, Job was long-suffering. In the end a divine power swept away all the arguments (Job 40:1-42:6).

A severe loss of self-esteem lies at the center of a psychological crisis. A storm rages. Boundaries collapse. Old meanings wash away. A person grasps for moorings and meaning. The point where we are on the very edge between hope and absolute despair, between life and death, often darkens or illuminates the rest of our days.

In order to delve into this borderland of despair and hope, I would invite you to listen to a story as we explore some of the underlying causes of existential angst and the loss of meaning in one's life.

Bill's Story

I referred earlier to Bill who suffers from bipolar illness or manic depression. When I first met Bill eight years ago, he had been suffering from his illness for 12 years. He hoped I might help him understand why this terrible thing had happened to him. "Where was God in this?" he pleaded. With some encouragement, he told me his story.

When he was 18, he had had a peak experience. He had hiked up a mountain, and while he was gazing out over the lovely valleys an incredible, powerful, ecstatic rush came over him. "I was rapt over into the seventh heaven, or something like that," Bill said. "I don't have words to describe it." But the rushing didn't stop; for the next two weeks his mind was racing with God, with this overwhelming power, with his own sweeping feelings of having a special mission. He could not sleep, he grew disheveled, and started acting out his visions. Later, friends helped to hospitalize him, the first of many hospitalizations. Thereafter, about every 18 months, he would go on a manic binge, traveling to distant places, breaking a store front window in one instance, wandering the streets in search of his mission, and landing in jail where at last he would find peace and security.[3]

After his mania subsides, Bill riddles himself for the fool he has made of himself during his manic period. He spins along attacking who he is. His fierce self-attacks are, of course, just as crazy as the mania. In fact, they may increase the pressure for the next eruption of mania. Thus his elation and depression form an unpredictable cycle. The collapse of his elation plunges him into depression. Then in his depression, Bill feels overwhelmed by hopelessness. His body sags. His loss of self-esteem squeezes the life juice out of his core. He feels helpless. Then he has an urgency to cling to others, then this dependency gives way to infantile dread. He says he fears the loss of all things, all people close and dear.

One day when we were visiting, he said with a weary anger, "I don't understand it."

"You've been through a lot." Then I paused. "Can you come down from the mountain?"

"I don't understand," Bill looked at me quizzically.

"Can you come down from the mountain?" I repeated.

"Oh, I get it. Can I come from the mountain? Can I give up my mania?"

"Right. Can you give up the vision? Can you give up the surge, the tremendous high? Can you live down here on the ground?"

"Yeah," Bill replied reluctantly. "That's what I need to do. I feel great when I am manic, but it destroys everything."

"That's it," I added. "Can you give up God, or at least can you give up scrambling for God on the mountain top?"

We talked about how he might be unconsciously seeking this powerful rush, especially when he felt depressed, thus setting himself up for a new round of mania. Perhaps he could find God in the day-to-day, humdrum choices that he needed to make: finding a job – even a menial job, working out his housing arrangements, getting his Social Security benefits straightened out, making certain his medications were suitable. Maybe God wasn't so far off?

Bill did "come down from the mountain." He made several humdrum choices which were suited to his needs. Over a period of the next three years, he would drop by to see me every two or three months. He was beginning to recognize his rage for the lost years – rage at God, at himself, at the system of mental health services. In both his manic and normal state, he often wrote poetry. He told me with more heat than clarity: "Writing in an angry state – I feel I can elucidate, numerate myself in its truest self. I've suppressed so many feelings. I realize the rage of this storm. I feel like Job. I want to communicate my despair." Bill's phrase "To numerate myself" meant for him to dissect the causes of why he felt so devastated. The "numeration" protected him from his loneliness and his inner strength.

His rage also blocked others from responding to him in a way he could accept, but his poetry tapped into this rage which lay seething below the surface. He talked about "this rage" abstractly, as if it were separated from himself.

For Bill, there was a twofold danger in facing the rage. First, it could so overwhelm him that he would give up his choices for day to day living. Second, he could become so frightened by the power of his anger that he took flight into mania. It was a risky step for him to touch into his rage.

I began by asking him whether he could face into and touch his pain and his rage.

He paused and physically shuddered: "When you say I need to touch my pain, I feel I'm going to lose myself. It's like I'm looking over the rim of a huge black hole, and if I fall in, I'll fall forever."

He paused for a long time. Perhaps ten minutes of total silence. I think he started to sense his own inner vulnerability, his own deepest core. It was a dreadful, shaky moment. And he trembled.

Rather than trying to "numerate his truest self," as he put it, he began letting go of his fear of anger and allowing his inner self to be touched and accepted. Bill grew somewhat better, though he was not cured. He will undoubtedly always live with this bipolar disorder. That's his reality and his challenge – to accept the fact of his disease without letting it drain him of hope, to imagine a future which makes his daily choices possible. He called me one day in late August, "Today's my anniversary. It's the first time I've had a job for a full year!" He is dating a woman who apparently is interested in him. He may get sick again. He knows that. He's made some provisions should that happen so that a close relative could intervene before the cycle of destruction unleashes its fury.

His view of God is changing. Perhaps God isn't punishing him, he admits. "I don't have to look for God; maybe God will find me some day," he smiles wryly.

Grounding in the Body

A greater grounding in the body may be a remedy for the wild swings between mania and depression that Bill experiences. The mania, some psychologists say, results from unsatisfied needs as a child, but no amount of substitute mothering can give a person the security they failed to get in childhood. "The ego struggles to get free," Alexander Lowen says, "and when it does, it rises triumphant like a gas balloon released from the hand of a child, becoming steadily more inflated as it goes upward."[4] The increased excitation, however, is limited to the head, where it produces hyperactivity and exaggerated verbosity. The flow upward, rather than downward, does not lead to discharge. It serves instead to focus attention on the individual and represents an attempt to restore the sense of infantile omnipotence that was prematurely lost. As an adult, such people must find this security within themselves. No matter how much attention, admiration, approval or love one gives such people, it does not fill their inner emptiness. They can achieve their fulfillment only on an adult level; that is, through love, through work and through sexuality.

Healthy persons do not suffer such dramatically wild mood swings of elation and depression, Lowen says. Most of the time they have their feet firmly planted. They are grounded in their bodies. They may become excited by some event or prospect which brings energy flowing to the head, but their feet never leave terra firma. They may feel pleasure or joy, but rarely unbridled elation. If they are disappointed, they may be saddened, even dejected, but not depressed. They do not lose their ability to respond to new situations.[5]

Healthy spiritualities enable us to appreciate our own bodies. They encourage us to accept love. They do not allow us so much to pamper ourselves as to accept all of who we are: the body in its physical maturation; in its daily cycles of eating, nourishing, sleeping, sexual reproduction. Healthy spiritualities are suited to a person's age and rhythms of life, including the crises which inevitably occur. New Age spirituality began by fighting a rearguard action against earlier tendencies to repress the body. Although it may have destructive features, such as reinforcing narcissism, its primary strength arises from its appreciation for the human body and for the environment of the Earth.

Dread of Abandonment

I do not know what childhood traumas Bill faced, but the repression of the body can occur because of a child's dread of rejection. Bill seems to have had caring parents, but his illness, like any other illness, may also have cultural and social sources in addition to biological ones.

The child psychiatrist Alice Miller has shown how the fear of abandonment, even in the first year or two of childhood, structures our personality.[6] A child will do anything, Miller says, rather than face abandonment. So she does what it takes to draw the mother's affections to the self, even when that involves hiding or crippling her very self. Later, if a grown person undergoes a severe crisis, the new situation plunges her right back to this state of infantile paralysis. She returns to those horrifying feelings of total helplessness, and this regression often exacerbates the crisis.

At times I sensed that the ultimate dread for Bill was the fear of abandonment, that he would be so ostracized that he would be further excluded from any possibility of acceptance for who he is.

During my own recovery period, the psych ward momentarily staved off my own dread of abandonment. Within this safe, structured environment, I could make simple choices. Hospitalization provided me a harbor from the howling storm of my confusion. Seclusion and time, appropriate medication, the caring touch of nurses, and even the black humor of the patients were the healers. The ward was a place where the fragments of a person like Betty or Styron or myself could begin to coalesce again. From thence began a journey, uncharted, but certainly resembling the pattern of thousands of others.

Life or Death

The main bulletin board outside the nurses' station read: "Today is Saturday, July 25, 1975." Very basic orientation. It declared in

effect: You have started another day. Here you are. What are you
going to make of it? Along side it I would have hung two other
texts. One from the book of Deuteronomy: "Today I set before
you life and death, choose life."[7] And the other text from the
beginning of Dante's *Inferno:* "Abandon all hope, ye who enter
here." Life or death. Hope or despair. The choice was that stark.
But we were too numb to know it. I think that in some raw,
untamed place, I chose life in its smallness, in its concreteness,
in its daily security. Just by being there I was making a beginning.
I was surviving with the barest glimmer of hope.

A choice for freedom is never just a personal choice; it is
also a choice for others. It is a choice in community. An observer
could see this in the aftermath of Hurricane Andrew in Florida
in August of 1992. The survivors prayed for deliverance; they
banded together to protect each other, to share whatever food
they had, to drain the water from their homes, to protect their
children from fear and from disease. Their small daily efforts
were choices for life.

When I left the psych ward after 30 days, I was stable, though
tottering. I was not grounded, nor healed. That would take longer.
The process had no definable end. Had it ended in the midst of
these chaotic days, I would have had no story to tell. Someone
else would tell the simple facts: another casualty, one more of the
33% who showed no improvement, documented by a series of
check marks on a medication chart.

Initially the facts of my case appeared grim. An acute psychosis, such as I had, could last for a month, half a year, a year,
or perhaps forever. The prognosis for a second hospitalization
runs about 75%. Indeed I entered the hospital once more, nine
months later. My psychiatrist Dr. Z. left my diagnosis rather vague,
"You've had an acute psychosis. Acute as opposed to chronic.
Occurring once rather than repeatedly. Other diagnoses probably
aren't that helpful to you and, frankly, people are too complex
to fit any one label."

A few years ago I searched through the American Psychiatric
Association's *Diagnostic and Statistical Manual* and concluded that
a diagnosis of "reactive psychosis" or "atypical psychosis" seemed
probable.[8] Either would describe a short-term, disorienting episode with considerable emotional turmoil and hallucinatory behavior.

Our therapeutic culture has a tendency to reduce everything to psychological explanations. Such a narrowing, which precludes the realm of the sacred or the transcendent, likewise precludes a full recovery. Religions may also reduce interior disturbances to spiritual causes. Such a reduction, which denies psycho-physical causes, implicitly denies the body and God's grace which courses through all things. Both tendencies reflect a need to control reality and define it within accepted limits. Both perpetuate a dualism which feeds the psycho-spiritual illness. As we move on our journey, the unity of sacred and profane, of body and spirit, or personal and communal, emerges with increasing clarity.

I was "all better" after a relatively short two years. By then I was stable, coping, and capable of creating my own future. Shortly thereafter, in 1978, I began a successful term as a principal of another school. By then I felt psychically stronger than I had before the breakdown. Two years later I made a 30-day retreat in which I experienced the renewing balm of God's touch. I grew more grounded, more in tune with my body, more sensitive to my psychic makeup, and eventually more courageous in risking my desires for mystery.

The Search for Meaning

Three authors, in particular, have been helpful to me in identifying islands of meaning in a sea of confusion. They do not give the answer, but they frame the questions. The three are Albert Camus, Carl Jung, and Viktor Frankl. Each looked at the edge between destruction and creation. Each was a journeyer himself. Each had an internal journey that went counter to those around them. They helped me in achieving an intellectual framework for the journey. This framework has three movements: a) how do we discover vital motives for choosing life? b) how do we face the darkness and the confusion of our own heart? and c) how do we imagine a possible future which gives us meaning and purpose for our daily struggles? Any framework is tentative and needs to give way to the reality that "life is a mystery to be lived, not a problem to be solved," as Gabriel Marcel once put it.

Why Not Suicide?

Camus sifted the tragedies of life for meaning. Why go on at all?, he asked. Camus made the startling announcement that there is "but one truly serious philosophical problem, and that is suicide." Right after World War II, when Camus was writing, humanity seemed set adrift in an alien universe devoid of any ultimate meaning. Camus observed a whole civilization brought to its knees. French intellectuals, in particular, despaired of finding any ultimate purpose. Reality seemed absurd. People had lost touch with a sense of meaning, and intellectuals especially moved toward a radical alienation. Camus claimed, pessimistically but honestly, that, "A person who has learned how to remain alone with his suffering has little left to learn." Hence he contended, "There is but one truly serious problem, and that is . . . judging whether life is or is not worth living."[9]

In 1975, I encountered a person who had faced such a choice at the leper colony at Kalaupapa, an isolated peninsula on the island of Molokai. The village had a small population of 200 people with Hansen's Disease, popularly but inaccurately called leprosy.[10] Through the heroic labors of Fr. Peter Damian beginning in the 1880s, the people at Kalaupapa had dug trenches to bury the dead, learned to care for and support each other. Since World War II, with the advent of sulfa drugs, the patients could now be treated as outpatients in the city, so the current villagers were mostly elderly.

I visited for a while with a mild-mannered woman in her sixties. I saw that her fingers looked chewed away by the disease. Actually she had probably lost portions of her fingers through injuries, because the disease erodes all feeling in the extremities. She told me how she had arrived on the island in 1920, when she was nine. In those days, she explained, the boats came within a quarter mile of the island and then dumped the patients and supplies overboard into the sea. "Out there in the sea by myself, the first thing I had to decide was whether to swim or not."

Each of us needs to ask, "Why?" Not in the desperate situations that some people face, but desperate enough. Why go on living? Our decision is the first and ultimate choice.

The second thinker that helped shape my thoughts for this inner journey is the Swiss psychologist Carl Jung. Jung argued that a religious outlook was necessary for psychic health. He said that in his 30 years of treating patients in the second half of life, that is over 35 years of age, every one of them fell ill because he or she had lost that which the living religions in every age have given their followers: a meaning for life. None of them was fully healed who did not regain their religious outlook.[11] "The opening up of the unconscious always means the outbreak of intense spiritual suffering,"[12] Jung observed. People are not helped in their suffering by what they think for themselves, but only by revelations of a wisdom greater than their own. Jung stated that only a vision of the infinite helped a person sift the lasting from the trivial.

A year into my own healing process, I needed to revisit my own religious beliefs. My psychiatrist Dr. Z asked me one day, "Where are you taking care of the spiritual dimension of your life? Who do you talk with about that?" I responded somewhat flippantly, "For now, you're it. This daily processing of my psyche is my spirituality for now. You're my spiritual director as well." In time, though, I discovered that psychotherapy would not be enough. It could not in itself provide meaning or purpose. Ultimately I needed to encounter once again the mystery of the Creative Spirit within the present.

Every human being searches for some insight into what it means to be a human being. We search for whatever helps us grow into the deeply centered, loving human beings God made us to be. In a dire crisis, meaning, freedom and love are not very evident. In fact, in the black storm, they seem as remote as the farthest galaxy. No star lights the heavens. All is blackness.

Jung held that a person had to pass through the night, rather than take flight from it. Those who have returned from the black inferno report that that time in the void impelled an openness to a deeper reality, a more profound quest for peace.

An Imagined Future

The third thinker that influenced a deeper integration was Viktor Frankl, a Jewish Viennese psychiatrist. Frankl was suddenly arrested one night by the Nazis, who boarded him and his family members onto a train and sent them to Auschwitz, a death camp in Poland. Except for a sister, the Nazis exterminated all of the other members of his family – children, wife, and parents. Frankl narrated his own survival, his own radical choice for life in *Man's Search for Meaning*.

After a short time in camp, Frankl noticed that he was totally absorbed in day-to-day survival: Should he exchange a cigarette for a bowl of soup? Where might he find a piece of wire to serve as a shoelace? He began to notice that those who survived had a future. They had hope. Shortly, he devised a four-point program for himself:

First of all, to survive.

Second, to help out others.

Third, to imagine a positive future.

And fourth, in order to realize this future, to learn every-thing he could about himself and others even within these absolutely horrifying conditions.

The third point was the most important of the four. He imagined for himself a posh auditorium with comfortable seats in which he was lecturing on the experiences of the concentration camp. Before him sat an audience giving him their rapt attention. Frankl says that an imagined future allows the self to touch transcendent meaning. Without such meaning, the integrating tendencies of the psyche go awry. Without such meaning, the self remains a prisoner of its own troubled ego.

With a positive imaged future in mind, Frankl decided on the fourth point, which was to learn everything he could about himself and others within his present, dire circumstances.

Frankl said, "There were always choices to make. Every day, every hour, offered the opportunity to make a deci-sion, a decision which determined whether you would or would not submit to those powers which threatened to rob you of your very self, your inner freedom; which determined whether or not you would become the play-thing of circumstance, renouncing freedom and dignity to become molded into the form of the typical inmate."[13]

Frankl's four-point model carved out a space for freedom for himself and eventually for others. It made choice possible for him even in the starkest, bleakest, most desperate of settings. Hope was paramount, but it had a structure. It was based on self-care, on altruism, on an imagined future, and on daily choices which made that hoped-for-future possible.

Frankl later found that many of his clients undergoing therapy had good jobs and were successful, but wanted to kill themselves because they found life meaningless.[14] He helped his clients to realize that an imagined future provides a structured hope out of which daily choices may be made.

Frankl recognized that contemporary psychologists and their followers often seek to make a religion out of psychology.[15] He was a pioneer in criticizing potentialism and self-actualization as goals in themselves. Potentialism, that is, discovering the possibilities within one's self, is just the beginning. One must then decide which of a thousand possibilities must be actualized and the rest left unused.

Rather, Frankl offers the way in which a person accepts his or her fate, the way in which they take up their cross, and the way – even under the most difficult circumstances – that they discover a deeper meaning to their lives. Critics of Frankl claim he does not adequately consider those who did not survive, or those who became *Musselmaenner* – the walking dead.[16]

Frankl emphasized that what he learned and taught other despairing people was that what matters is not what we expect from life, but rather what life expects from us. He locates meaning, therefore, in the situations that summon us and call us out. It cannot be invented by the self or even discovered in self-actualization and self-realization, as in the human-potential psychologists, Abram Maslow and Carl Rogers. Rather it must be a product of our openness to the demand of otherness, of what transcends us.[17]

Some Conclusions

Each of these three major thinkers – Camus, Jung, and Frankl – arrived at the foundational question about the meaning of life. Each of their responses was shaped by the obscurity and history of their own unique mix of freedom and compulsions. Each response was grounded in an implicit faith in the human spirit, a claim to something that transcends the moment in such a way that it is compelling for life itself.

Camus sharpens the question of life by asking, "Why not suicide?" Jung asks, "What is the ultimate source for healing?"

Frankl affirms that an imagined future makes possible even the most dreadful day-to-day choices.

Before continuing our exploration of these questions, we might revisit Bill as an example of a person searching for meaning. If we examine Bill's choices in the light of Frankl's model, we could say that Frankl's third point, an imagined future, is still tenuous for Bill, still obscured by the possibility that another manic episode could occur and also by the fact that the disease itself tends to attack the imagination by heightening grandiosity. So far Bill's view of God, although it is becoming less tyrannical, still prevents him from imagining a palpable future. Bill has to rely on the imagination of his therapist or of a spiritual mentor who can help him imagine a suitable job, a caring relationship, and the capacity to manage his own illness. His own imagination needs taming, but the illness itself impedes that.

Not every story has a happy, resolvable ending that fits neatly into human expectations. I wish I could tell you that Bill's illness is in abeyance, that he is happily married, that he has a meaningful job. Bill's positive future cannot be the same as Frankl's, but he has left the door open for healing. He makes small, positive choices and has accepted and plans for one day at a time.

In this chapter we have explored how the will to live, how survival itself, arises out of a hoped-for future. In the case of my illness, my imagination became more grounded, my experience of God grew both more immediate and more mysterious, and my choices for the future became more grounded in the reality of who I am.

Our next step in exploring a contemporary spirituality is to probe the innate desire that all humans have for ultimate mystery and the yearning for union that lies at the core of human existence.

A thin line snakes between sanity and madness. "He's mad," the family members of Jesus feared, and they set out to seize him. (Mark 3:21) Why were some Old Testament prophets exiled? As seers they rattled society. Were they mad? Were they sane? What can we learn?

And the prophet shouts:

"Wanton ways, luxurious excesses, vain piety! Idolatry! A sickness in the land must be cleansed. A scourge will afflict the rich, and comfort

the broken-hearted! Justice will be done. God's poor will be restored and then shalom shall flourish.

"Seared, stripped, scourged. Nothing escapes. If the flesh burns, who cannot speak of the fires. If Life speaks, who can but listen. Tempered for a while, you shall be as a brand plucked from the burning.

"Does a lion roar in the forest, when he has no prey? Is a trumpet blown in a city, and the people are not afraid?

"Hear this word, then, you cows of Bashan who are in the mountain of Samaria, who oppress the poor, who crush the needy, The Lord God has sworn by his holiness. . . . they shall take you away with hooks, even the last of you with fishhooks. . . . And you shall go out through the breaches, every one straight before her; and you shall be cast forth into Harmon. You cows and your consorts shall grind your teeth."

– Amos 3:1-8; 4:11-12, my adaptation.

Endnotes

1. William Styron, *Darkness Visible: A Memoir of Madness* (New York: Random House, 1990).

2. Lawrence G. Calhoun et al., *Dealing with Crisis: A Guide to Critical Life Problems* (Englewood Cliffs, NJ: Prentice Hall, Inc., 1976), pp. 12-14.

3. Police are often the first line of relief for people with mental illness. Many, because of their training, are knowledgeable as well as extraordinarily kind and understanding. Unfortunately society has chosen to make the jail one of the primary treatment centers for this illness. King County Jail in Seattle, for instance, has the second largest population of people with mental illness of any psychiatric institution in the State of Washington. See also "Families, Police Protest Jailing of People Who Are Mentally Ill," NAMI *Advocate* 14 (May, 1993): 1-3.

4. Alexander Lowen, "Grounding in Reality," *Depression and the Body: The Biological Basis of Faith and Reality* (Baltimore: Penguin, 1973), pp. 41-73.

5. *Ibid.*, p. 45.

6. Alice Miller, *For Your Own Good* trans. by Hildegarde and Hunter Hannum (New York: The Noonday Press, 1983, 1990).

7. See Deuteronomy 30:19. "I have set before you life and death, the blessing and the curse. Choose life, then, that you and your descendants may live." *New American Bible (NAB)* (New York: Oxford University Press, 1990).

8. Four possible diagnoses might be considered for my psychotic episode: 1) A brief reactive psychosis, occurring in response to stressful situations, often marked by considerable emotional turmoil, yet with eventual full recovery. 2) Schizophrenia. However, current diagnostic practices require

continuous signs of psychological disturbances for at least six months
before a diagnosis of schizophrenia can be made. 3) Schizophreniform
disorder. The clinical picture is consistent with schizophrenia, but the
disturbance is of shorter duration. 4) Atypical psychosis for a psychotic
episode which does not meet the diagnostic criteria for specific psychotic
disorders such as schizophrenia or when there is inadequate information
to make a specific diagnosis. From my lay position, either the first, third,
or fourth diagnoses seem possible. See American Psychiatric Association
(1987), *Diagnostic and Statistical Manual of Mental Disorders* 3rd ed. rev.
Washington, D.C.

9. Albert Camus, *The Myth of Sisyphus* (New York: Vintage Books, 1955), p.
3.

10. Scholars know now that "leprosy" in the Bible includes a wide range of
skin diseases.

11. C. G. Jung, "Psychotherapists or the Clergy," *Modern Man in Search of a
Soul* (New York: Harcourt Brace & World, 1933), p. 229.

12. *Ibid.*, p. 240.

13. Viktor Frankl, *Man's Search for Meaning: An Introduction to Logotherapy* (rev.
ed.) Original title *From Death-Camp to Existentialism* (New York: Pocket
Books, 1959, 1963), p. 104.

14. Viktor Frankl, *The Unheard Cry for Meaning: Psychotherapy and Humanism*
(New York: Simon and Schuster, 1978), pp. 19-43.

15. I am relying on Maurice Friedman's critique of Frankl, "Religion as the
Search for Meaning: Viktor Frankl's Logotherapy," *Religion and Psychology:
A Dialogic Approach* (New York: Paragon Publishers, 1992), pp. 111-120.

16. For yet another view based on longitudinal studies of Holocaust survivors
see William B. Helmreich *Against All Odds: Holocaust Survivors and the
Successful Lives They Made in America* (New York: Simon & Schuster, 1992).
Survivors had greater success in life than a comparable control group, Dr.
Helmreich says. Many have post-traumatic stress-type problems, but they
had greater marriage stability, practically no incidents of crime, and made
more significant contributions to their communities. In his later book,
The Unheard Cry for Meaning (1978), Frankl made this caution about his
own theories, "Millions had to die in spite of their vision of meaning and
purpose. Their belief could not save their lives, but it did enable them to
meet death with heads held high. . . . Uncounted examples of such heroism
and martyrdom bear witness to the uniquely human potential to find and
fulfill meaning even in an extreme life situation such as Auschwitz." He
concluded with a prayer: "May from unimaginable suffering spring forth
a growing awareness of life's unconditional meaningfulness," pp. 34-35.

17. Helmreich, *Against All Odds*, pp. 112-114.

CHAPTER THREE

Desiring:
An Avenue to Mystery

Many people who seek healing are not looking for healing at all. They simply want relief. They will go through mind-boggling contortions to avoid their problems. Their dodges often gain support from elements of American culture, such as the media and politicians. The media, for instance, seems to urge hard work, hard play, tempered by hedonism. A few years ago an ad for Mediprin showed a series of pain-racked individuals: a woman stressed by the torrid pace of her top-executive job, a rugged guy jack-hammering on a busy city street. Then a soothing voice-over advised, "When you don't have time for the pain, take Mediprin." Such relief only numbs. It does not "restore to life," which is the root meaning of the word *re-lief*. It treats the symptoms so that we can get back to busy-ness as usual.

On a political level, politicians, especially at election time, pour out vast public funds, which tend to treat the symptoms of violence, crime, and child abuse, rather than address the under-lying social causes. They narcotize the pain by promising quick relief. To cite only one gross example: trailing badly in the polls in the fall of 1992, President Bush suddenly approved the sale of F-15's to Taiwan in order to gain the votes of 7000 aircraft work-ers/executives in St. Louis. In doing so, he reversed several years of his own thoughtful, strategic support of Mainland China. Such pandering to the voters only nourishes social violence.

Much unhappiness occurs because people will not face their pain. Perhaps it is because they are less fearful of the enemy they know than of the unknown risk arising from examining the sources of their pain. Consequently, it may take them a long time to confront their pain, to discover what lies beyond it, and to seek help to address it.[1] The pain may have to intensify. Perhaps it finally erupts. People in their forties, for example, often face the reality that "I am no longer doing what I want to do, and I never have done what I really wanted to do." After all the glamour, after all the glittering success, after all the happy formulas of youth, they wake up. They feel an unnamed pang. They discover they have not been following their own deepest desire. They have led a rather addictive life in pursuit of a dream which failed to include their own core self.

The psychiatrist Gerald May writes that "Addiction exists wherever persons are internally compelled to give energy to things that are not true desires."[2] When people confront pain, they name their true desires. When they confront pain, they name their self. They tap into the creative power of who they are. By taking time to explore their own desires and perhaps to discover them for the first time, people in mid-life can shed their addictive behavior, or at least modify it, and have the chance to harness the desires of their heart.

Catherine of Siena, a medieval mystic who also confronted Pope Urban VI to end a schism dividing the church, praised the power of desires. She was a passionate, forthright woman and advised others that our desires are one of the few ways of touching God. God's love is infinite, and only our desires, of all the things human, are infinite.[3] So we most fully encounter God in our desires.

That God's love and our human desire are each infinite is worth pondering further. The word *desire* springs from the Latin *de + sidus*, which translates literally as *concerning the stars*. Hence desire manifests a lunge of the heart toward the stars. The ancients knew that our desires express infinite longings, that starry-eyed lovers expect love to last forever. *Dis-aster*, on the other hand, suggests a star-crossed event. It means *away from the stars*, something out of alignment with the stars, and hence harmful for us.

So desires manifest who we are and how we are aligned with our destiny. In competitive athletics, a good coach knows the importance of desire. He or she not only teaches skills, but inspires desire. Those who excel "have desire." In academics a teacher promotes a desire for excellence, a desire to develop one's talents to the fullest. Friends and lovers know of desires for love, for companionship, for meaning. They know, too, the volatile strength of their sexual desires, but also that sexuality, when it is congruent with self and with another, can wonderfully express who we are in relationship.

A major source of healing is the surfacing of a person's genuine desires, which breaks the cycle of repression. For some people these desires arise in a quiet time apart, a space to await an answer. Still others are shocked, practically forced screaming and kicking by their desires, into a new reality. They must choose not only to face into their own pain but to acknowledge their own helplessness. Once they hit bottom, the drive for survival, the passion for life, may re-emerge. Then they may also affirm their own innate, healthy, and exuberant desires.

The Twelve Step program of Alcoholics Anonymous builds on this spiritual reality. Once such people acknowledge that they need help, they can start to find it. Through the support of a group such as AA, they can reclaim *their own* lives. The mutual witnessing through shared stories helps them to acknowledge the destructive, pain-denying, boozy world from which they have emerged. They support each other and remember their own heart's desires.

The psych ward, where I recovered from my breakdown, had several group therapy activities to put us in touch with what we really wanted and to face whatever habits prevented the realization of our desires. These group activities were innocuous, sometimes diverting, interchanges. One activity was to compile a list of all the things we enjoyed doing. I marked down hiking, playing bridge, jogging, and reading to children. In a second column we were to identify how often we did each activity. Hiking? Are you kidding? I had played bridge *once* in three months. I liked jogging *in theory*. The last time I had read to children was at Christmas time with my nephews and nieces. An obvious gulf existed between my professed desires and my realization of them. Though this exercise, along with other therapy sessions, rested happily in my mind as a break from monotony, the insight changed little. Old habits did not come tumbling down. I still could not or would not face the pain of what had happened.

We may suddenly awaken one day to realize that we have been living out of false desires, in effect, living out of a dream or someone else's conception of who we are. In Buddhism such an awakening begins with the dawning that we live in *maya* or illusion.

It involves recognizing the limits of one's culture and its distortions. It begins a process of detribalization, a leaving of all the familiar and experiencing not only the hardship of a journey, but absorbing new ways of observing, interacting, and shaping ourselves. Like the Buddhist disciple, we then break through conventionality, where most of us remain unquestioning throughout our lives.

When a person awakes, he or see sees how certain traditions, taboos, accepted cultural values, political arrangements have impacted, even warped them. Violence stalks our streets. Consumerism warps our values. Bad things do happen to good people. Some children have lousy parents. Many have been physically and sexually abused. Young adults benefit from a steady guidance which assists them in sifting out the evils that have happened to them and distinguishing those from their own limited choices. Most of all they appreciate help in discovering their own inherent goodness and desires for something more meaningful, more enduring, more spiritual.

A crisis of life-shattering proportions may precede such an awakening. The crisis may be personal sickness; it may be a confrontation with sickness in others. It may be a sudden encounter with death.[4] It stirs the hero(ine) within us from conventional slumber. It confronts all previously held beliefs. But the refusal to follow the consequent journey risks a life of alienation. Once awakened, the hero(ine) within us can no longer be tranquilized by the trivial. If we refuse the journey, conventional unawareness not only re-absorbs us, but can destroy us. An adage from the Gospel of Thomas summarizes this heroic challenge:

> If you bring forth what is within you,
> What you bring forth will save you.
> If you do not bring forth what is within you,
> What you do not bring forth will destroy you.[5]

The potential destruction may be a hydra of many faces. We may be flooded by desires. We may lose track of who we are and what we *most* desire. Rampant fear results. A person may then be paralyzed by desiring conflicting options, or by desiring an object and fearing it at the same time, or by fearing two options, one of which must be chosen. Frustrated by our inability to clarify what we wish, we fear our mixed desires. We fear especially our uncanny ability to get trapped again. Out of fear, we may flatten all desire. At best we grow suspicious of desire.[6]

In spiritual direction I often ask a person, "What do you desire?" "What do you want?" The initial response may be, "Well, I don't really know." or "I haven't given it much thought." or "Do you think it's important?" If they abdicate responsibility for their lives in this fashion, I quell my impatience because I know how difficult it is to surface genuine desires. But if I have established a relationship with the person, I may judiciously express my anger because my directness may sharpen their ability to confront their own professed helplessness.

For someone accustomed to struggling against emotions, the task *to name my desire* might seem impossible. Within a wee voice whispers, "If I let myself experience my emotions, maybe I will go berserk! Or I will lose all control, or I will be annihilated." These are real fears. They are also monstrous, larger-than-life fears. In most situations they indicate how alienated we are from ourselves. When we alienate our own energy, by making it "other" and then judging it negatively, we may come to believe that emotions are dangerous, even monstrous. By treating emotions as autonomous power, we cower at their serpentine strength.[7]

A few years ago a young priest, who had healthy psychological sensibilities, consulted me about a parishioner who was "having visions of the devil." The priest wanted some guidance from me about how he might counsel his parishioner. I advised him not to dismiss it as an illusion, but to take the presenting problem seriously. I suggested, however, that rather than delving into the visions, that he explore with the man how he was feeling.

Sometime later the young priest said to me that an amazing thing had happened. When he asked the man how he felt when he had these visions, the man immediately said he was angry, and then launched into a detailed story of why he was angry, at the end of which he was exhausted but greatly relieved. I understand the visions continued, but the man no longer felt besieged or upset by them. He simply let them pass on through. I am not suggesting by this example that this venting cured the man, but I would highlight three points: 1) Repressed emotions become separated from our self. 2) They then take on a destructive life of their own. They may become demonic, that is, destructive of the human. And 3) they cry out for attention in a manner consistent with the individual's history. If they had been tended to, the imagination might not have provided such devilish solutions.

Often such people do not know clearly what they want, think, or feel. They do not feel they can shape their own destiny in relationship to their circumstances. They are dependent on others for self-esteem and direction. The person who responds, "Well, I really don't know what I want" might silently be conveying to me: "Help me. Do something to make my life better. If you don't, you are incompetent or unloving. I will lose my respect for you." At that moment I need to check my own rising anxiety which signals my need to "prove that I am indeed a good counselor." I scan my own lifetime conditioning to accomplish, to make things better, to please, to avoid anger, to be liked, to be thought of as gentle and intelligent. If I cannot at least acknowledge my feelings, they will inevitably block me from being fully present and allowing me to surface *whatever is* between this person and me.

The ways are legion by which we can deny responsibility for ourselves, but the denial of our own desires is the most lethal. Through the years each of us has learned strategies to avoid them. We protect ourselves. We learn to please others. We use soft language, such as "I am dissatisfied or frustrated" instead of "I am angry." We have grown accustomed to depending on others to shape our actions, or we have washed our sorrows in alcohol or drugs so that we do not need to face the pain of thwarted desires. Whatever the reason, we bury our desires and thereby bury our true self.

Habits of Repression

The habits of repression begin early in childhood. Alice Miller, the Swiss psychotherapist and philosopher, tracked how children are taught to repress their desires and are punished "for their own good." She says that this well-intended punishment creates a cycle of violence, which begins in childhood and continues every time an adult takes revenge on their own parents by taking it out on their children. Of course, adults are not aware of this revenge cycle, because they repressed their pain and anger when they were beaten as children. Every act of cruelty, Miller says, no matter how brutal, no matter how shocking, has traceable antecedents in its perpetrator's past.[8]

Some people will protest, Miller says, by claiming, "I am living proof that beating [or spanking] children is not necessarily harmful, for in spite of it I became a decent person." Nonetheless she says, spanking continues the cycle. Although people consider spanking a less severe measure than beating, the line between the two is a tenuous one. Miller cites the example of a member of a Christian fundamentalist sect in West Virginia who spanked his son for two hours. The little boy died as a result. But even when a spanking is a gentler form of physical violence, the psychic pain and humiliation and the child's need to repress these feelings may be the same as in the case of more severe punishment.

Probably the majority of us, Miller says, belong to the category of decent people who were once spanked or beaten since such treatment of children was a matter of course in past generations. We can all be numbered among the survivors of poisonous pedagogy, she says. Even if we, as survivors of severe childhood humiliations – which we are all too ready to make light of – do not kill ourselves or others, or are not drug addicts or criminals, we will continue to infect the next generation with the virus of poisonous pedagogy as long as we claim that this kind of upbringing is harmless. The claim that it is "for your own good" is pernicious and abusive, Miller avows.

She contends that it is not permissive methods of child-rearing that are responsible for the marked increase in crime and drug addiction, but rather the violence and abuse wreaked on children who are defenseless and who automatically defend their parents whom they know to be, and who most often are, loving. King Solomon's mistaken belief – if you spare the rod, you will spoil the child – is still accepted today in all seriousness, she says, as great wisdom and is still being passed on to the next generation.

Miller envisions a day when we will regard our children not as creatures to manipulate or to change but rather as messengers from a world we once deeply knew, but which we have long since forgotten. Children can reveal to us more about the true secrets of life, and also our own lives, than our parents were able to. We do not need to be told whether to be strict or permissive with our children. We do need to have respect for their needs, their feelings, and their individuality, as well as for our own.

The more we idealize the past, however, and refuse to acknowledge our childhood sufferings, the more we pass them on unconsciously to the next generation, Miller says. A decisive change could well come about in our culture if parents would stop combating their own parents in their children, often when the latter are still infants. This change would also overturn a one-sided interpretation of the Fourth Commandment which endows such child-rearing with unwarranted divine authority.

As long as the child within the adult is not allowed to become aware of what happened to him or her, part of his or her emotional life will remain frozen, and sensitivity to the humiliations of childhood will be dulled.[9]

Miller cites several examples in support of her thesis, but perhaps the most ominous is drawn from the life story of the commandant at Auschwitz, Rudolf Hoss,[10] who obediently sent thousands of people to their deaths: "It was constantly impressed upon me in forceful terms," Commandant Hoss reported, "that I must obey promptly the wishes and commands of my parents, teachers, and priests, and indeed of all grown-up people, including servants, and that nothing must distract me from this duty. Whatever they said was always right. These basic principles by which I was brought up became second nature to me."

Jenny's Story

Not all severe upbringings, of course, have such dire outcomes, but nearly all adults seem to emerge from childhood with some wounded emotions. One of my graduate students, Jenny, described her own childhood during World War II as a time of confusion, loneliness, some bliss in solitude, and an awakening because of the kindness of some adults.

"Solitude ran like a common thread through my life," Jenny recalled. "In my childhood I often felt alone; at first the aloneness felt negative. Sometime later it shifted. Solitude became a warm and yearned for place. It was where I made meaning out of what was happening.

"I was born in the East, the middle child of a white, Irish-American, Catholic family. We grew up on a small farm, surrounded by corn, tomatoes, green beans, sunflowers, and hollyhocks. My precocious sister was two years older than I. She read the Bible by age five. She could not be bothered with me, though I was only two years younger than she. Even today she says, 'You were such a little kid.' She was always involved with reading or with friends and visitors who mysteriously came and went. It didn't make sense. I felt I was lacking something. At five I tried desperately to find someone to teach me to read. I pulled out the Jack and Jill, Spot and Puff book. Reading, I thought, was going to be the door out of this loneliness.

"My brother was born when I was about three. Later I attended 1/2 year of kindergarten and got the chicken pox, thus wasting the tuition money.

"Still later we lived in the mountains. I became aware of secrets and mysterious goings-on, such as a quick trip to the Midwest by my father and the confiscation of the paper dolls – a devastating and bewildering event. My sister and I were in the Brownies for a short time, but then that abruptly stopped. Forty years later, my sister told me that she had been sexually abused by the Brownie leader and that was the end of the Brownies. She also explained to me that the paper dolls were rather sexually explicit, and that she and her girl friend had been into playing doctor with the paper dolls. So the dolls were confiscated and the girl friend banished. I recalled how they were all swooped up, but it was strange because no one explained any of these things to me.

"My grandmother moved into the apartment in our house. She was given the radio; she invited only my sister over to drink tea and to listen to the radio. But one day she invited me. I sat at her table drinking tea out of her very nice teacup. Then she told me, she didn't like me. I would not be coming to her apartment again. I was stunned. When I told my mother about it, she wasn't interested. From then on, I discovered a fierce streak in myself. I told my grandmother, more than once after that, 'I didn't need you or want you or anyone. You can't hurt me.'

"She would laugh and say, 'You're just like me.'

"'No, I'm not. I'm going to be taller than 5'. You just wait and see.' And I went through stretching exercises alone in my room to make me taller.

"I accepted the lonely seclusion," Jenny commented, "and transformed it into my friend. Alone, I would play, and live and be comforted.

"The next years were confusing. From five to eight I have few memories except of being alone and different. I attended five schools in five years. Things changed when I was nine. I attended a long vacation Bible school. It was so much fun. The Sisters seemed to really care about us and a wonderful new priest drove us in the school bus. When I made my First Communion, my image of God was all tied up with that young priest. God was just as warm and open as the priest and the sisters. God was with me in my withdrawal into solitude.

"Our parents instilled respectability in us at an early age. I was to achieve it through education and left brain work. No time or money for flaky luxuries like a visit to the art museum. I could not make any mistakes. I knew their approval was crucial. If I succeeded, I would be loved. Only in solitude could I cry, admit my mistakes, and make sense out of the task assigned. Here I was good enough. I took myself in hand, I stood up to my grandmother, but I also internalized the drive for respectability so that I would be acceptable in my parents' eyes. I became my role."

Jenny, like most children, was sensitive and alert to most events that took place in her world. Children think very concretely and may misinterpret some events or at least not understand why something happens. But like Jenny, they know when something is bothering their parents or siblings. They overhear something, notice the difference in tone of voice, feel tension in the air, and sense the hurt or fear. They do not know exactly what to do about it, so they cope in ways adults can misunderstand. Their laughter, shouting, and other merrymaking does not indicate they are unaware of the seriousness of what is happening.

Children experience fears, anxieties, embarrassments, self-doubts, blows to self-esteem, heartaches, grief, guilt, shame, resentments, and other inner turmoil.[11] They need help in facing the crises and are more harmed by the silent secrets, by the unexplained traumas that every family faces. Adults, on the other hand, may avoid these secrets because they recall some painful incident.

For many years Jenny, a competent supervisory nurse, had great difficulty claiming her talents and what she wanted. She would defer to the system, defer to her husband, defer to her elderly mother, defer to her older sister. She was a constant and faithful care giver. Her neighbors saw her as a strong, able person; many confided in her when they were going through a crisis themselves. She was a patently good and generous person. She diminished herself, however, because her voice, her desires were often outside herself. At an early age, she had gone underground and no longer expressed her feelings to her grandmother, her parents or to others. She started to figure everything out on her own. This interior isolation also stunted her growth because she could not readily draw on the interior experience of others. She spent much of her psychic energy on maintaining a brave front, rather than investing in her own dreams and talents. Finally acknowledging this dynamic enabled her in time to make decisions and choices which were more congruent with her own dreams. Her choices became more liberating not only for herself, but for others.

Distinguishing Genuine Desires

Genuine desire should not be confused with pleasure, its cosmetic cousin. Nor should it be mistaken for cravings for recognition, power, and prestige. Wordsworth, the 19th-century Romantic poet, described these cravings as the "getting and spending" of our industrial age that block our desires:

> The world is too much with us: late and soon,
> Getting and spending, we lay waste our powers;
> Little we see in Nature that is ours,
> We have given our hearts away.
> – Wordsworth[12]

For Wordsworth the industrial revolution alienated the human from Nature. It separated men and women from themselves. He saw Nature as the great restorer of the self and its deepest yearnings.

Strong desires always hint of risk. Such passion, such enthusiasm, such unbridled emotion can overturn the accepted order. Often leaders or geniuses, such as Franklin Roosevelt, Mother Theresa, or Bruce Springsteen are those who have pursued this passion. In doing so, they create a wave which washes out safe arrangements, which had strangled freedom.

Strong desires also commingle with our cravings which arise out of our false self. Desires can free us; cravings enslave us. Desire empowers us to pursue a dream which will benefit others; cravings dissipate our energies. So the theme of desire needs clarification.

When I name my genuine desires, I name myself. I reveal myself. I tap all the energy, vigor, and directional force of which I am capable. For a moment I am wondrously free of the defenses which armor me against the judgments of others. I am even liberated from my own harsher judgments of myself. I am free to become myself. In that moment I both shudder and exult. On the verge of freedom, I know with Kierkegaard that "anxiety is the dizziness of freedom."

To help people to visualize such freedom, I ask them: In your quiet moments, what surges up within you? When you are walking along the Oregon coast gazing out on the swollen waves of the sea, watching the sea gulls glide in the breeze, what do you desire?

On the other hand, when you pause as you trudge through the shopping malls (satisfying your cravings?) what are your thoughts? Where do all these goods take you?

The great spiritual masters knew the importance of holy desires. Ignatius of Loyola, the founder of the Jesuits, urged those making a retreat to ask God "for what I desire."[13] Ignatius spoke of a person being led to a true spiritual freedom so that no decision or choice is made under the influence of a "disordered attachment." A disordered attachment, for Ignatius, was an errant desire, what I have called a craving. It flowed out of our false self. It was disordered because a person clung to the apparent goods of power, pride or possessions to bolster a fragile ego, rather than risking one's self and making choices out of one's true self.

The mystics, such as Ignatius and Catherine of Siena, knew that desire calls us out of our pinched self. It breaks the barriers of our armored self. And it contains fateful choices which both free and enlarge the self.

Yet another source of fear, ironically, is the fear of success. What would happen if we encountered the deepest satisfaction of the human heart, the fulfillment of the most intrinsic destiny of our humanity? Faced with such desires, hoping for such achievement, it is natural that we are tremulous, because we know that their fulfillment will bring the loss of self as we have known it. We may fear that we will be swept away by our desires for God. If we encounter God, all will be changed, all utterly changed.

If a man or woman is called a person of great desires, we do not expect a bloodless, unfeeling soul but someone who is great-hearted with a depth of human compassion. By way of contrast, the enemy of the soul is boredom. Every monk in the desert knew this trial, which they called *acedia*. *Acedia* meant without desire, without juice. It was the noonday devil. It was not some lurid, sexual fantasy, but rather a flatness of spirit. It left the spirit empty. The wise monk knew that a lack of desire was the greatest enemy of spiritual fulfillment.

A healthy person has many desires. People with mental illness, however, have flat affections or a wild mix of cravings. They either desire so little that they are close to somnolence, alienated from the source of who they are. Or they desire so much, really crave so much, that they are overwhelmed by stimuli and after a manic fling put the lid on and shut down.[14] The psychotherapist or spiritual director knows that health arises from trusting a person's deepest desires.

The Jesuit poet Gerard Manley Hopkins wrote an extended poem contemplating the sacrificial life of a German nun who drowned at sea after a shipwreck. In "The Wreck of the Deutschland," Hopkins sought out the raw source of her desire:

> What by your measure is the heaven of desire,
> The treasure never eyesight got, nor was ever guessed
>   what for the hearing?[15]

How could desire engender such devotion? Hopkins asked. How could desire be so great when the treasure hoped for was never seen? His haunting question about desire hovered as a mystery over the sunken ship.

We will need to return to this question later when we treat more fully how our spirituality transcends the immediate, and draws us on toward the Source of all desire. For now, we simply wish to explore the complex realm of desire without being overly concerned about its object. At the same time we recognize that desire without an object is probably distorted or at least more accurately called pining, or yearning, or longing.

Eliciting Great Desires

Edward Kinerk, a Jesuit commentator on *The Spiritual Exercises* lays out several presuppositions about desire.[16] He says that:

1) All desires are not equally authentic. For instance, a person who has been hurt by another might have a desire for revenge as well as a desire to forgive. Her desire to forgive may spring from her genuine self. It is more authentic if it expresses what she wants, even though at the same time her desire for revenge may be more immediate, more intense.

2) Authentic desires move from self-centeredness toward self-donation. They flow from narcissism and self-concern toward transcendence and concern for others. Eventually the distinction between what I desire and what desires I receive blurs. As we reach into ourselves more profoundly, we discover that our desires are simultaneously both our own and God-given.

3) And a paradox exists, according to Kinerk. Though desires are personal, authentic desires are always public. Authentic desires always lead us out of ourselves and into the human community. Desires to feed the hungry, to clothe the naked, and to use our gifts for the service of others become more compelling than private concerns. We can see that Kinerk's guidelines concur with Frankl's critique that self-actualization is not enough. In fact, desires flourish only when they overflow ultimately into service of others.

A final caution. The answer to "what do you desire?" can only be given by you. It cannot be handed down from on high by someone else. Sears does not stock it. Nor will you find it in a book, not even this one. Reading may help, but it will not provide the answer. Reading this chapter may fire your desires, point a direction, offer some guidance, and provide some solace in those empty spaces when you can no longer fathom why you left your secure home base and launched into space with moon craters and pock marks and distant, distorted stars. Ultimately these pages may help you glimpse and return to a solid landing spot on a blue globe, cradled in swaddling clouds, the Earth from whence you sprang.

By acknowledging our own powerful desires, we glimpse a vision of better things. We envision a future of wholeness. Like the star to the star gazer, vision and desire live in increasing mutuality. Vision fuels desire. Desire yearns for vision. As Arnold Toynbee says: Love, which is the fullness of desire, is "the ultimate force that makes for the saving choice of life and good against the damning choice of death and evil. Therefore the first hope in our inventory must be the hope that love is going to have the last word."

We began this section by examining the yearnings for a contemporary spirituality. We looked at a younger generation of seekers who yearn for meaning but often lack guidance. We then delved into the chaos of personal crisis and the quest for meaning that such chaos triggers. Finally in this chapter, we listened to the counsel of the great mystics, such as Ignatius and Catherine, who invited those seeking God to attend to their own desires.

In Chapter Four we will explore the relationship between desire and vision, as well as the origins of desire as a source for vision.

> *Batter my heart, three personed God,*
> *For you as yet but knock.*
> *Father, Son and Spirit breathe, shine, and mend*
> *That I may freely rise.*
> *Overthrow me and bend your force*
> *To break, blow, burn and make me new.*
>
> *Like a walled city, I, laboring to grant you entrance,*
> *am confined,*
> *I owe allegiance to another.*
> *Reason, your ruling ally in me,*
> *Lies captive, often weak, plays the harlot.*
> *Dearly I love and yearn for you*
> *But I am betrothed to your enemy.*
> *Divorce, unbind, untie*
> *Break that knot again,*
> *Seize and imprison me yourself.*
>   *For I,*
> *Except you enthrall me, never shall be free,*
> *Nor ever chaste, except you ravish me.*[17]

Endnotes

1. Peck begins his well-known book *The Road Less Traveled* with a similar assertion and leads the reader through some considerations about "remaking one's maps." See also Daniel J. Levinson, *Seasons of a Man's Life* (New York: Ballantine Books, 1978), pp. 191-200.

2. Gerald May, *Addiction and Grace* (San Francisco: Harper & Row, 1988), p. 14.

3. Catherine of Siena, *The Dialogues*, trans. and intro. by Suzanne Noffke, O. P. (New York, 1980), p. 270, cited by E. Edward Kinerk, S.J., "Eliciting Great Desires: Their Place in the Spirituality of the Society of Jesus," *Studies in the Spirituality of Jesuits* 16 (November, 1984): 2.

4. Robert N. Walsh, *The Spirit of Shamanism* (Los Angeles: Jeremy P. Tarcher, 1990), p. 28.

5. From the Gospel of Thomas, re-discovered in 1945-46 at Nag Hammadi. Reputedly gathered by Didymus Thomas, the apostle, they commingle genuine sayings of Jesus with Gnostic insight.

6. Much of my analysis of desire relies on two sources: 1) Conversations with Richard Ganz, S.J. whose licentiate dissertation at the Jesuit School of Theology at Berkeley was on Eros; and 2) E. Edward Kinerk, S.J., "Eliciting Great Desires," *Studies*, pp. 1-29. For a contemporary expression of the ambiguity, power, and fruitfulness of the desire for God, see the engaging novel by Ron Hansen, *Mariette in Ecstasy* (New York: Harper Collins Publishers, 1991).

7. John Welwood, "Befriending Emotions," *Awakening the Heart* (Boulder: Shambhala Publications, 1983), p. 85.

8. I have drawn the following section from Alice Miller, *For Your Own Good*, pps. xii-xiv.

9. *Ibid.*, p. xvii.

10. Not to be confused with Rudolf Hess, the prominent leader in Hitler's inner circle.

11. Andrew Lester, *Pastoral Care With Children in Crisis* (Philadelphia: Westminster Press, 1985), p. 28.

12. "Miscellaneous Sonnets XXXIII," lls. 1-4 *The Poetical Works of William Wordsworth* (Second Edition) vol. 3 (Oxford: Clarendon Press, 1946, 1954), p. 18.

13. *The Spiritual Exercises of Saint Ignatius* [21] trans. and commentary by George Ganss, S.J. (Chicago: Loyola University Press, 1992), p. 31. Hereafter Ganss, *Exercises*.

14. Scott Peck distinguishes between character disorder and neurosis as disorders of responsibility. "The neurotic assumes too much responsibility; the person with a character disorder not enough. When neurotics are in conflict with the world they automatically assume that they are at fault. When those with character disorders are in conflict with the world they automatically assume that the world is at fault." Peck's distinction on disorders of responsibility illustrates two ways by which people evade their heart's authentic desires and the need for personal discipline in order to discern genuine desires. *The Road Less Traveled*, p. 35.

15. Norman H. MacKenzie (ed.), "The Wreck of the Deutschland," *The Poetical World of Gerard Manley Hopkins* (Oxford: Oxford University Press, 1990), p. 126.

16. Kinerk, "Eliciting Great Desires," *Studies*, pp. 3-5.

17. My adaptation of John Donne's poem, "Batter my Heart Three-Person'd God," Selections from *Divine Poems, Sermons, Devotions, and Prayers*, pp. 81-82.

PART TWO

Risking Belief

I thought of walking round and round a space
Utterly empty, utterly a source.[1]

— Seamus Heaney

CHAPTER FOUR

Naming God

The Mystery of our origins and destiny courses through our lives. It enlivens us. It is the Source of all. By surrendering to this Mystery, we pulsate with the deepest satisfaction of the human heart. We experience what it means to be human.

To encounter Mystery as Source, we need to make a choice. It is a preliminary choice, but at the same time it is a radical choice which will affect all subsequent choices. It is a choice central to human existence. In fact, choice is "too easy" of a word. We are not taking here about choosing between Granola and Raisin Bran for breakfast, or even about choosing between a teaching and a medical career – although that may be involved. Rather we are referring to a life-choice, which summons up and risks our whole being. Our choice for Mystery involves our core existence in such a way that we cannot stand apart from our choosing.

It is the kind of primordial choice that Dag Hammarskjold made when he simply wrote: " – Night is drawing nigh – For all that has been – Thanks!/To all that shall be – Yes!"[2] This "Yes" is both our initial and our final surrender.

This "Yes" is the kind of choice that Mark, 22, a talented, young athlete made a few years ago. A psych grad from a prestigious school, Mark had given up a promising, post-collegiate athletic career in order to join the Jesuit Volunteer Corps (JVC), a one-year commitment to service, to a simple life-style in a community with other volunteers, and to action on behalf of justice. He came to me for "spiritual direction or whatever." As we talked, he explained how the excitement of making a bold, generous leap into the volunteer corps had dissipated rather quickly. Now he felt utterly empty and bewildered.

Mark's volunteer placement at a mental health clinic involved interviewing and treating clients who had addictive, criminal behavior and who had been ordered there by the courts. He was performing well in his work, but feeling listless, envious, and depressed. The Northwest rains cast a bleak, lowering, grayness to the landscape – which matched his own sinking spirits. He had recently broken up with his girlfriend, who happened to be going through a medical crisis at the same time and who had accused him during the breakup of being a self-centered, narcissistic egoist. In addition, his well-to-do parents could not understand how he could waste a year in volunteer work and were convinced that he was stubbornly headed in the wrong direction. For a clincher, he heard periodically from his college friends who had already begun earning fat salaries right out of college.

Mark thought his critics might be right. Perhaps he was an egoist. Perhaps his dedication to his troubled clients was just grandstanding. Perhaps he wanted to be the best, the most generous, the most effective counselor only so that others would admire and talk about him. And wasn't his girlfriend right, that he had deserted her just when she needed him most? And hadn't his college classmates made a better choice? And why would anyone in their right mind live in the gloomy Northwest in the winter when they could be enjoying life – abundant, exuberant life – in sunny California, his home state? And . . . ?

Mark's bleak self-portrait reminded me of Shakespeare's Sonnet 29:

> When, in disgrace with Fortune and men's eyes,
> I all alone beweep my outcast state,
> And trouble deaf heaven with my bootless cries,
> And look upon myself and curse my fate,
> Wishing me like to one more rich in hope,
> Featur'd like him, like him with friends possess'd
> Desiring this man's art, and that man's scope,
> With what I most enjoy contented least.

A serpentine depression gripped Mark, coiled round his interior life, and choked his spirit. A succession of head colds laid him low. When he did feel healthy, he would go on long bike rides which would restore him temporarily. But the gloom soon returned, and he found himself once again "desiring this man's art, and that man's scope."

Mark did have some valuable resources. He was bright, articulate, and above average in emotional sensitivity for his age. He was eager and willing to explore "this interior stuff." The diffused pain from his ongoing depression offered an additional spur.

In the next weeks we focused on the manifest losses he had experienced: the move to a new city, leaving behind old friends, breaking up with his girlfriend, asserting a new independence from his parents, the resignation of a promising athletic career, and the loss of adulating fans. Now in a trusting relationship, he allowed these losses to well up from within him. We kept the focus, however, on exploring this spiritual stuff.[3] Like an errant knight, he was eager to make the quest, committed to whatever interior vigils it took on his part, and looking for some spiritual wizardry as he wended his way through this dark wooded landscape.

Another factor which helped us to stay focused on this spiritual quest was Mark's decision to seek out a psychotherapist, available to him through his health insurance, for six to eight sessions. In psychotherapy he explored the dynamics of his relationship with his ex-girlfriend and early childhood patterns of astute pleasing in order to reduce the tension between his parents.

Before long, he became more active athletically. He took up skiing. Above the clouds, up in the lofty, sunny Cascade peaks, his view of the rainy gloom below dispersed. Talking about his own interior life helped him to clarify his feelings and to discharge pent up energy. Within our relationship he did not have to be the nice guy who took care of others. He could drop his bright smile and let go of his "I've got it all together" mien. He began to track an early pattern of how he could diffuse the anger or tension between his parents by pleasing first one, then the other. In our sessions he could unwind, relax, feel his loneliness and his anger (much harder!). When I said, "You don't have to please me either," he could catch himself and then explore how automatic his response was to please others in order to subdue his own anxiety. He grew to trust himself.

In about three months he was able to look back and see for himself that he had been clinically depressed. "It helps me now in my work at the clinic when people with chronic depression come in," he observed. "I know how hard it is to break the cycle. I know you have to do it in small steps. I know that each dismal day looks like it's going to last forever."

I continued to see him. His confidence and broad smile came easily now. He had a new girlfriend. After his Jesuit Volunteer year, the mental health clinic asked him to stay on in a salaried position.

From the beginning, Mark was distrustful of any "God-talk." He likewise was leery of Bible-thumping fundamentalism and "Jesus saves" preaching. Although his parents had attended Catholic church earlier in their lives, they no longer did so. He thought they felt guilty because they had been married outside the Church. In his work, he saw a lot of people with wacky religious ideas, but he thought that if they could move toward a healthy spirituality, it could be a source of healing for them.

He came in one day – buoyant, bursting with energy. He had been skiing with some friends. After some fantastic runs, as he put it, they were sitting around outdoors in a hot tub at the ski lodge in late afternoon with the sun out and the fog wafting through the mountain tops. "I was with my friends. I was feeling great. I looked up to the blue sky, past the mountains that soared above me and said, 'Thank you!' Thank you!,' and something profound came over me. I don't know what it was. I was filled with a deep joy."

"Was there a response?" I asked.

He was quiet, reflective, almost astonished. "To my 'thank you'?," he finally asked. "No. Well, not in words anyway. Something just swept through me. Yeah, that was it. Something just swept through me."

In time Mark started to call this something "Creative Spirit," or in other instances, "Lifespirit." Actually he preferred not to give this new relationship a name at all. He continued to describe his own reactions and willingness to pursue a spiritual quest as "this interior stuff" or "this spiritual thing." When he gave up the search for the right name, his language was more relational. He described his experience in phrases, such as "being in touch with the Creative Spirit," or even "making decisions that came out of my Spirit center."

Though he did not readily advert to it, I think this experience signaled a turning point for Mark. At some unexplainable level, he began to know he was doing the right thing. His questions about his own egotism or narcissism faded. He admitted that there were vestiges of self-centeredness, moments when he recalled being in the limelight and briefly pined for its return. But his focus took a turn toward a deeper understanding and empathy with his clients. He also made two or three difficult personal decisions, which were congruent with this Lifespirit experience. When he was lonely, he could admit it without filling the hollow or looking for someone else to fill it. In time, he became aware of his own creative center, the richness of his other relationships, and his ability to make decisions which flowed out of this context. His emotional state shifted from depression to freedom, much like the conclusion of Shakespeare's Sonnet 29:

> Yet in these thoughts myself almost despising,
> Haply I think on you, and then my state,
> Like to the lark at break of day arising
> From sullen earth, sing hymns at heaven's gate.
>   For your sweet love remembered such wealth brings
>   That then I scorn to change my state with kings.

We might portray Mark's experience as an epiphany, a revelatory awareness of self, world, and of beauty in a timeless moment of insight. He experienced a revelation – a revelation that comes as a gift, as a surprise, and as an unknown, fresh world of knowledge which beckons and which includes a steady, urgent calling.[4]

It was a gift because it was not something earned or rightfully due. A spontaneous "thank you" response rose up from the depths of Mark's soul and then a "yes" to the moment and all that it implies.

It was a surprise, although the build up occurred over time. "Surprise," from the Latin root "sur-prendere," suggests that something "takes over." Mark was seized with a power, both beyond and within him.[5] He would never have predicted this. At the moment it seemed almost too easy. Later some of its challenges frightened him. He could sense his frailty in the face of the grandness which touched him.

It was a breakthrough in intimacy. It erupted as a profound image in which the majestic mountains pointed to a transcendent, life-giving mystery. It encompassed new knowledge and insight and understanding, which would take time to articulate. Its implications would unfold in time and through ongoing concrete choices.

When Moses experienced this majestic power in the burning bush, the experience stunned and surprised him. It was beyond belief. He was at the same time awed and fearful. He removed his sandals as well as tried to hide whatever talents for leadership he had. "But I am a stutterer," he complains. "How shall I speak to the Pharaoh?" Later the experience empowered his leadership throughout his confrontations with the hardened Pharaoh. Throughout his life Moses was known as the one who had seen God face to face and had lived. Not only that, but he, along with Miriam and Aaron, became the instrument by which God set his people free. Though his conversion was sudden, what made the difference were the subtle, even agonizing, choices he made each day to be faithful to the vision of freedom offered in the encounter with Mystery.

Any revelation inaugurates a new depth, a new intimacy with the ultimate. In the beginning this new dimension may not be all that obvious. Tough decisions still need to be made. Choices, congruent with one's authentic self, shape, define and give expression to this newness.

Just as hope is not hope unless concrete choices are made, revelation is not revelation, unless it is responded to with a "Yes!" and with day-by-day decisions.

Source

Earlier we described how our desires spring from the intimate core of our being. We must now ask what is the relationship between our own desires and this unname-able Spirit that reveals its Self to us. Are we just a knot of desires or do these desires well up from a source, from an ineffable wellspring of life, which is both intimate to us, yet transcendent to us? Are these desires aligned with a destiny, which is one and the same with their source? Even to ask questions implies a willingness to be uncertain, perhaps puzzled or perplexed. To ask questions implies a desire to understand. To ask questions involves a willingness to take a risk. To ask questions implies an orientation towards Mystery. Mark could have avoided such an orientation, at least at this stage of his life. He could have anesthetized his deepest desires by launching a star-studded sports career with glittering rewards.

Emptiness is often the prelude revelation, as the Irish poet Seamus Heaney tells it:

> I thought of walking round and round a space
> Utterly empty, utterly a source.

Utterly empty, then utterly a source. An image bursts through our aloneness and encompasses our total self. Because of the unique relationship of each of us with Spirit, the image uniquely symbolizes the fresh intimacy between persons. Since we need to somehow name these experiences, I use the word *Source.* If we look at its etymological roots, source suggests three dimensions of a current: origin, life stream, and an ultimate rising up. In French *source* means both 1) origin, and 2) water stream. It derives from the Latin verb *surgere,* meaning to lift, to spring up. In addition, *surrectum,* the past participle of *surgere,* from which we derive the English word resurrection, means raised up or risen. So the roots of *source* evoke three meanings. It 1) begins as a spring welling up into 2) the fullness of a stream which flows like life itself 3) toward a final rising up. Thus the image suggests an originating surge of living water which gives contour and direction and an ultimate destiny to our lives.

A stream has a history, its edges etched with time. It has rocks and shoals that narrow its path, speed its journey. It has an ultimate destiny toward which it flows. The water marks its own way, creates its own character, and in time is highly predictable. Our own destiny is similar; it flows out of who we are. We both shape and are shaped. Our waterway has the possibility of unpredictable twists and turns because we have a freedom, with others, to shape our journey and to create, to choose or to reject our destiny.

From our originating *source* surges up our most profound desires. From this source comes the revelation of who I am, the revelation of my own shadowy depths. Contemplating this Source, I become transparent to myself.

The drawback for using Source as a name for ultimate mystery[6] is that it does not capture the encounter of persons, the vulnerable exchange which pervades this communion.

Thus some will prefer the images of Spouse or Mother or Father or Friend. Others might use a word like Creative Spirit or select the traditional word of *God.* Still others might find the example of the Jewish people instructive. In their tradition, the Jews never speak aloud the name of God. They indicate [God] by using the four letters YHWH, the tetragrammaton for Yahweh.

The English equivalent might be G-d. With this reverent practice, they acknowledge that the name of God exceeds all human words. The reality of God cannot be shaped by human tongue nor held by human hands.

Those who have had this awakening struggle to name this primordial experience. They recognize a new-ness, a never-before-experienced reality. They will say, "I can't describe it. I don't even have the words." And when they do tentatively name the experience, they will caution "but I *know* that's not it. It's a lot more than that." Their words come haltingly forth. They can only hint at the depths. Words cannot grasp the abundance. That is why Moses takes off his shoes when he approaches the sacred ground of the burning bush. Holy ground. Who is he to tread on such a space? The bush symbolizes his own interior burning and consuming desire for one-ness with the holy, not only for himself, but for all the nation, for all the peoples who have become enslaved.

In summary, our reflections in this chapter on Source and the last chapter on Desire now converge. Our desires give us a glimmer of our origins and reveal our ultimate destiny. They flow immediately out of who we are. They harken to the tender mutuality between this Source and me. My desires, whenever they come from my center, overflow from this originating relationship. Augustine explains that God is more intimate to me than I am to myself: *Intimior intimo meo.* In those moments my whole being overflows and magnifies my Source. I cannot but exclaim, as Mark did, "Thank you. Thank you."

Places of Revelation

Most of us have had some experience of being rapt by beauty, or by mystery:

> the sweep of a blue sky with bulging cumulus clouds,
> the swelling sea crashing against the rocky coast,
> the loon's haunting call at daybreak,
> the silky stillness of a lake in moonlight.

Spring sunshine, the hush of winter snow, the cry of a newborn baby. Wonder holds us. We encounter an all-encompassing presence, a Source who is prior to us and who transcends all our grasp, even as it embraces us.

We can name at least three other types of encounter with God: 1) in confronting critical choices, 2) in our relationships with other people, and 3) in tragic occurrences.

The encounter with God may occur in our inner depths when we are *confronted with critical choices.* In a moment, in a flash, we receive a gift to seek what is right above self-interest. A woman confronts a sexual seduction even though it will mean the loss of a promotion. Or a young politician refuses an easy bribe. We do not have any idea where this power comes from. We just know it is there. In its wake, we are left discontent with all that is not truthful, not authentic, or not honest. We discover human transcendence, the power to rise above situations and transform them. We are surprised at these inner resources of strength, creativity, and resilience. We experience ourselves as drawn by a power far ahead of us, yet intimately involved, summoning us to be more than we are.

Most of our lives, we are far more conscious of the revelations that open up for us in our *relationships with other people.* In love we discover our own worth and dignity, and this encounter can easily open out on a self-revelation of God who loves us. A mother and father gaze on their newborn child, transfixed, knowing that their own lives are forever changed. Young lovers gaze into each other's eyes, rapt, hopeful, transparent, and catch a glimmer of love itself. Or a native in a strange land provides hospitality when we are all but lost, and the welcome dissolves our own barriers.

The breakthrough may paradoxically occur through a *tragedy.* In my class on Religion and Psychology, an undergraduate wrote that the death of her brother strangely brought her to life. She explained that her brother's presence was always with her. "Through the drug culture, I saw the dark side of humans, but realized as well the incredible and yet untapped power that resides in the human mind and soul. After my brother's death, I confronted this dark side of myself. I broke my connections with friends who were addicted. I somehow realized my own potential. I had a hunger to create, to experience, and to be aware. I became more aware of my own creative talents. I was willing to risk more. Even when I was fearful, I felt a bedrock of courage. Sometimes when I pray now I wonder whether it is to my brother, to myself, or to God, that I pray."

The American culture of rugged individualism conditions how Americans, at least Americans of Anglo-Saxon origins, explain their religious experience. They may tend to express their religious experience as a blend of Carl Rogers (self-discovery) and Ben Franklin (moral perfectionism). They often express their spirituality in "feel good" and "can do" categories. In this, they risk recurring egoism, especially in a culture which measures success in terms of a "material girl" or a number one guy. A spiritual pride of self-perfectionism then takes hold.

Other cultures, such as Hispanics or Afro-Americans or Central American campesinos, and certainly those with roots deeper than 19th century liberalism, may discover this revelatory power in the history and traditions of the *community*. Their religious language describes experiences such as:

> A passage through trials shared with others;
> God liberating the human person *within* community.

> God summoning *sus pueblos* [God's people] to freedom
> out of bondage, giving courage and power to a herd of
> frightened individuals, bringing purpose to an aimless,
> oppressive existence.

The Role of Religion

In past times religion provided the language, symbols, and rituals whereby we could interpret such primordial experiences. Yet today vast numbers of people of good will are repulsed by traditional religion or by its counterfeits. Mark, for instance, was wary of the hucksterism he saw in many religious people.[7] He cringed at the easy assurances of street-corner preachers: "Jesus saves." Their insistent righteousness cast a shadow on their message of love. I challenged him, however, as to whether his fear might not include resistance to encountering Jesus in his own life. What would happen if he risked such an encounter? Did he feel too vulnerable to let down his guard? A stubborn skepticism can simply mask the fear of acting on one's beliefs and actually making a choice for God.

One of my favorite examples of competitive, religious moralism is Cora, a character William Faulkner describes in *As I Lay Dying*. Cora is a God-fearing, Bible-toting woman, who sets about straightening out everyone but herself. Her husband Tull wryly observes, "Cora's always trying to get to heaven ahead of everyone else." Religious righteousness may slam the door on those who might be ready to take a peek and look around.

The reduction of God to one's own image is a constant risk. If we can reduce God to size, then we can control God and maintain the direction of our own lives. It is the mark of an immature religion, according to the psychologist Gordon Allport, to reduce God. If I can assert that "God is precisely who I say God is," then I am also apt to lord it over others.

The religion of maturity, however, makes the simple affirmation: "God is."[8] Pure and simple. God is. Let God be God. The mature person knows that one's life alone does not contain all possible values or all facets of meaning. Other people too have their stake in truth. The Hindu Vedas reflect this insight: "Truth is one; people call it by many names."

The question, "Do you believe in God?" at first blush can apparently be answered by a simple "Yes" or "No." But a deeper analysis lays bare the illusory character of these answers. A great many people imagine that they believe in God, when in fact they are bowing down to an idol of their own creation; and on the other hand, others may think themselves to be atheists because they conceive of God only as an idol to be rejected. Yet in their actions they reveal a profound religious belief. It follows from all this that the answer to a referendum on the question, "Do you believe in God?" ought to be: "I don't know whether I believe in God or not – and I am not even quite sure that I know what 'believing in God' is." Proceeding along these lines, we would be brought to the situation of a quester as one who asks the true questions.[9] The true questions point to a line of direction along which we must move.

A mature religion thus rejects the contemporary tendency to reduce God to a God of human needs, to a God who exists only for our sake.[10] For a mature religion, God must be loved for God's own sake.

A Dialogue

Many Americans appear content to dabble in God. The movie director Woody Allen captures as well as anyone the desultory, American search for God. In his film *Crimes and Misdemeanors* (1989), Allen stands on the edge of any commitment, like an observer of a play in which he is already both actor and author. From the vantage of his characters, he explores the possibilities without making any commitments. The following comments occur in the film:

Professor Levy: When we are born, we need a gradient of love in order to persuade us to stay in life. Once we get that love, it usually lasts, but the universe is a pretty cold place. It's we who invest it with our feelings. And under certain conditions, we feel that the thing isn't worth it anymore.

Mia Farrow: No matter how elaborate a philosophical system you work out, in the end it's got to be incomplete.

Woody Allen: Nobody committed suicide in Manhattan, everyone was too miserable.

Jewish Rabbi: I couldn't go on living if I didn't feel with all my heart there is a moral structure with real meaning and forgiveness, and some kind of higher power, otherwise there is no basis to know how to live. (In a later scene, the Jewish rabbi, who is blind, dances with his daughter at the wedding. He becomes a figure who "sees" even as those around him fumble in the moral, spiritual darkness.)

Professor Levy: We are all faced throughout our lives with agonizing decisions, moral choices. Some are on a grand scale; most of these choices are on lesser points. But, we define ourselves by the choices we have made – we are, in fact, the sum total of our choices. Events unfold so unpredictably, so unfairly -human happiness does not seem to have been included in the design of creation. It is only we, with our capacity to love, that give meaning to the indifferent universe. And yet, most human beings seem to have the ability to keep trying, and even to find joy from simple things, like their family, their work, and from the hope that future generations might understand more.[11]

The characters of Mia Farrow and Woody Allen are mildly interested in the conversation, but not committed to much of anything. Farrow mouths an obvious platitude. Allen, ever the suffering comic, guts out his misery with biting irony. Both borrow energy from the elixir of faith, from others willing to make some commitment, whether it is the Jewish Rabbi, who desperately clings to his faith or from the benign Professor Levy who calls the universe a pretty cold place but has faith in humans to make it habitable because of their ability to love and to give meaning to the indifferent universe. The dialogue continues without resolve. The characters cannot either verify or falsify their hypothetical interpretations of reality because they do not commit to the realities they are trying to interpret.

The dialogue echoes the view of Albert Camus, whose views on suicide and choosing life we considered in Chapter Two. Unlike Allen, however, Camus demanded commitment and had a capacity for beauty. Without risking commitment, the Allen film relies on irony and wit to relieve the absurdity of life.

Absurdity or Mystic Unity?

For Camus the first data of religion and morality were the evil and death that are part of the abiding human condition. Whether or not there be goodness or God is not a primary evidence of human existence. Suffering and death are. Camus said that only after the reality of human evil is given its due does the question of God, and ultimately human submission to or revolt against God, arise. Human evil instructs us first.

The austere message of Camus was that in the absence of hope we must still struggle to survive, and so we do – by the skin of our teeth. We accept the absurd and go forward into life. The choice has the color of verdigris. It offers a mere ledge on the rim of despair.

However, Camus's aesthetic sense at times belies his grim assessment. At times the poet in him catches glimmers of a revelatory experience as the primary data of human existence. In *The Plague,* for instance, Camus envisages the sea as the source and symbol of freedom: "Nous sommes les fils de la mer." "We are the children of the mother-sea.[12] It's out there, out there that we must go. . .We must run to meet the wind. To the sea! The sea at least, the open sea, the water that cleanses, the wind that liberates!" The sea images the human longing for freedom and for communion. Commenting on this hope, however, Camus asserts, "I have the impression that faith is not so much a peace as a tragic hope."[13] Camus's stance reinforces our earlier contention that we choose our world view. We choose whether to focus on good or evil. Out of that choice comes a life direction.

The Russian novelist Feodor Dostoevsky also expresses the absurdity of faith but chooses to move beyond it. Within his own character he discovers personalities which he portrays in his novels: the doubter, the atheist, the crude materialist, and the mystic. Dostoevsky, by his own accounts, knew that all these characters lived in him, that there was something coarse and brutal in his own make up, hence his own desperate straining for love and humility. His character included both the mystic rapture of Alyosha Karamazov, as well as the lust of Dmitri. It held the skepticism of Ivan, as well as the emotional torpor of Stavrogin.[14] As a love-seeker, Dostoevsky was particularly vulnerable to self-torment since he inwardly believed that he had seldom experienced true love. He carried the ambivalence of a neurotic character, torn between embracing God or merely celebrating his own ego, and at times not knowing which was which.

Dostoevsky expresses his mystical foundation with great boldness in *The Brothers Karamazov* in the words which Starets Zosima uttered before the Starets' death:

> God took seeds from other worlds and sowed them on this earth . . . and they germinated. . . . But that which grows lives and enjoys vitality only through its sense of contact with other mysterious worlds. . . . Much on earth is hidden from us, but in exchange we have been given a secret and hidden sense of our living bond with another world. . . ."[15]

For Dostoevsky mysticism was not divorced from the world, but embraced it. Out of this mystic vision, he caught a glimmer of himself and certainly of the saints making their moral commitment to life and to God.

Anyone engaged in the world is inevitably faced with the dilemma of good and evil, according to Dostoevsky, a dilemma from which we can never retreat. In fact, we carry the dilemma within our own character.[16] Yet we know that if we fail to choose the path of good, we necessarily place ourselves on the path of evil.

Both Camus and Dostoevsky, through their characters, made a choice. Their own history, their own culture, their own artistic sensibilities marked this choice. Camus chose to accept life in all its absurdity, rather than suicide. Dostoevsky chose to accept God, but in doing so, he becomes an oddity just as some of his characters were. Both the mystic and the epileptic were oddities in a faithless society.

Reflections

We have examined how some people experience a creative spirit in their lives and the commitment to love which that encounter evokes. So at this point, if you have not already done so, I would invite you to pause. *Plumb your desires. Ponder your own Source: both well-spring and main stream. How and where do you encounter Mystery?*

What do you feel? What do you imagine? What do you think as this Source flows through you? What desires well up within you? How do they both shape and reveal you?

Write your dialogue – with yourself as one of the characters. Are you a Woody Allen or a Professor Levy? A Mia Farrow or a Jewish Rabbi? A Camus anti-hero or a Dostoevskian Alyosha or Ivan? What characters contend within you? What do you desire? Do you have at least the desire for the desire to encounter the Source of all that you are?

You may wish then to ask some further questions: *What destiny flows from my origins? How does my own history reveal myself? Are my choices congruent with my origins, with my self, and with my destiny?*

Do my choices release joy and peace within me? Or do they lead to a biting irony? Do they enable me to harness and channel this energy so that it might be a resource for others? Or do they lead me to observe from a distance the folly and misery of others?

Most of us know people who are congruent with their source, who live in honesty with themselves, with their world and with others, and who have the capacity to make choices which are in harmony with their world view. We call such people wise. We may also call them seers, shamans, counselors, and confessors. Their wisdom is not only for themselves, but for others, because anyone who lives out of their source and makes choices in harmony with their world becomes a re-source for others. Such people are aware too that this source is "not-me," although it flows through them and nourishes and sustains them.

From a person's Source erupts memories, images, thoughts which undulate through the person's life. The Source gives energy and shape to who I am.

Our own depth spirituality bears some resemblance to the practices of the ancient Greek shrine of healing and prophesy at

Delphi. At the shrine a pythoness, or a woman who practiced divination, sat over hot steam vapors and whispered vague prophesies to devotees or pilgrims who came seeking guidance. The Greeks knew that only a wise person could decipher these vaticinations. Without such an interpretation, these free-flowing spirits were at best enigmatic, at worst dangerous. It required wit and will to interpret these images and to make concrete choices congruent with these emanations. Those who consulted these divinations without adequate interpretation remained babbling fools. Our own depth spirituality needs interpretation. It seeks to give tongue to our desires. It longs for unity with our ultimate source. It recognizes the dangers of twisting the divine word into our own image, and it trusts that we have the capacity to recognize God within the uttermost reaches of our self as God truly is.

Believers rely on God even in the grips of uncertainty. At some juncture, they are invited to affirm life, to say "yes," and at the same time to acknowledge that "I myself" am not the Source of life. They acknowledge as a blessing that, "I am not the source of my own being. I am not self-created. I have received who-I-am as gift."

> *In the beginning was the Source*
> *In the beginning*
> *the G[od] of all that is*
> *In the beginning*
> *G[od] yearning*
>
> *moaning, laboring*
> *giving birth, rejoicing*
> *And G[od] loved what she had made.*
> *And G[od] said,*
> *"It is good."*
>
> *And G[od], knowing that all that is good is shared*
> *   held the earth tenderly in her arms.*
> *G[od] yearned for relationship.*
> *G[od] longed to share the good earth,*
> *And humanity was born in the yearning of G[od].*
> *We were born to share the earth.*[17]

Tradition has called our response to God's yearning: faith, which we will explore in the next chapter.

Endnotes

1. Seamus Heaney, "Clearances," #8 *Selected Poems, 1966-1987* (New York: Farrar, Straus and Giroux, 1990), p. 253.

2. Dag Hammarskjold, *Markings,* trans. by Leif Sjoberg & W.H. Auden (New York: Alfred A. Knopf, 1964), p. 89.

3. William Connolly, S. J. and William Barry, S. J., *The Practice of Spiritual Direction* (Minneapolis: Winston-Seabury, 1982). The authors emphasize how important it is in spiritual direction not to substitute therapy for a focus on the person's relationship with Spirit.

4. Cf. Monika Hellwig's description of a revelation in "God Revealed," *Understanding Catholicism* (New York: Paulist Press, 1981), pp. 15-28 or C.S. Lewis, *Surprised by Joy: The Shape of My Early Life* (New York: Harcourt Brace, 1956).

5. The spirit of the Lord "rushed on" David after he was anointed by the prophet. (1 Samuel 16:10-13).

6. Ephesians 3: 4-21.

7. Cf. "God and Money," *Time* (cover story) (August 3, 1987).

8. Gordon Allport, *The Individual and his Religion* (New York: Macmillan, 1950), p. 69.

9. Cf. Gabriel Marcel, *The Mystery of Being: 1. Reflection & Mystery,* Gifford Lectures, 1949-50 (Chicago: Henry Regnery Co., 1960), pp. 14-15.

10. Karl Rahner calls this "anthro-egoism, the most dangerous of all heresies." cf. Harvey D. Egan, S.J. (ed) *Faith in a Wintry Season: Conversations and Interviews with Karl Rahner* (New York: Crossroad: 1990), p. 2. Also Karl Rahner, *Foundations of Christian Faith* (New York: Seabury Press, 1978).

11. Woody Allen. *Crimes and Misdemeanors* (1989). Unpublished screenplay.

12. Literally "sons of the sea." "Mer" carries echoes of "mere," French for mother.

13. Albert Camus, "Actuelles," *Essais.*

14. Irving Howe, "Dostoevsky: The Politics of Salvation," in *Dostoevsky: A Collection of Critical Essays,* Rene Wellek, ed., (Englewood Cliffs, NJ: Prentice-Hall, Inc., 1962), p. 55.

15. As quoted by Zenkovsky in Wellek, *ibid.,* p. 141.

16. V.V. Zenkovsky, "Dostoevsky's Religious and Philosophical Views," in Wellek, *op. cit.,* pp. 130-145.

17. Adapted, with slight modification from Carter Heyward, "Blessed the Bread: A Litany" in *Our Passion for Justice: Images of Power, Sexuality, and Liberation* (New York: Pilgrim Press, 1984).

CHAPTER FIVE

The Courage to Accept Love

It takes courage to respond to God. Courage gives us strength to embrace our total reality and to act on it. Courage is not the opposite of despair, but rather it moves ahead in spite of despair. In fact, the theologian Paul Tillich defines faith as the courage to accept acceptance. It is such courage that we now wish to describe.

Courage flows from the heart. Our English word courage derives from the French word for heart *coeur*. It means to *take heart*. When we are down at heart, friends may en-*courage* us. In doing so, they touch, accept and listen to our *core*, another derivative of *coeur*. In English, we have lost the sense of *take heart*, which is found in en-*courage*ment. Italian and French at least still have this usage. When a young Italian departs for a difficult examination, he friends are likely to cheer him up by saying, *"Corraggio!"*

Without courage, a patient with a serious illness can lie flaccid or inert. We say, "he's lost heart." In a life and death situation, courage may make the difference. It may lend speed to a person's willingness to face death and to be reconciled with his life and his friends. Or it may, on the other hand, rally the body, channel all the remaining energies towards life. Courage makes possible all the virtues of love, fidelity, appreciation, and generosity. My Irish grandmother used to call it "gumption," a gutsy ability to stick through tough times and to stand by her commitments, especially her family, her faith and her values.

Courage enables us to span the chaos between who we are and who we hope to become, between our perceived self and our real self. It energizes us to create ourselves through commitment. In contrast, vegetative life is what it is. It takes no courage. The acorn becomes an oak by means of automatic growth. In the acorn or in a puppy who becomes a dog, nature and being are identical. No gap exists. No courage required. But, a man or a woman becomes fully human only by their choices and by their commitment to them. Thus, Tillich speaks of courage as ontological, as essential to being human. Without courage, we cannot become fully human.

Healers mediate these springs. They en-courage. They offer their presence. They share their tears. Like water witchers, they tap into the wellspring of healing waters because most often they have had to face the darkness of their own doubts.

When Jesus heals, he most often says: "Take courage, your sins are forgiven!" In reading such a passage, we likely glide right by the first injunction: "Take courage!" These simple words bestow encouragement. They offer healing to the forces which hobble us. "Take courage" does not mean that we are to screw up tight every fiber of our body in order to face danger. That is resistance. Rather, courage opens our core to healing. It welcomes the future, even if it frightens us. Often the presence of a friend or of someone that we trust unreservedly makes courage possible.

Courage beats best with predictable, steady rhythms and with anaerobic challenges from time to time. Just as our physical life might combine the aerobic exercise of paddling a canoe on a calm lake with the anaerobic thrill of shooting the rapids in a kayak, so too courage. In fact, we most easily recognize courage when it faces enormous risk. At those moments, when I cannot see or predict the outcome in any rational, logical way and yet am willing to risk my whole life, courage is most evident. Those around us may not recognize the risk, but, by picking up my mat and walking for the first time in years, I may break the paralysis that has gripped me. The road to personal healing occurs when a person risks flowing with the rhythms of one's own unique center.

Rollo May in his little book *The Courage to Create* describes four types of courage: physical, moral, social, and creative.[1] I would like to use May's outline to explore the theme of courage and also add a fifth dimension which I will call spiritual courage: the courage to accept acceptance, which pervades all the other forms of courage.

A. *Physical courage.* May says that Americans take their model of courage from myths of the frontier, war, sport, or space travel.

They celebrate the brute physical courage of a John Wayne. He was a real man, we say! Wayne embodied all the individualistic survival skills: fast gun, self-reliant, capable of enduring loneliness, slow to speak, quick to act, and so independent of women as to view them as a mild nuisance. Stallone in the "Rambo" series takes this frontier individualism to its brutal extreme.

This physical courage, so necessary for taming the West, has lost much of its usefulness, but it now underlies our drive in corporate raids, in the violence in our streets, and in the bombing of Baghdad during the Gulf War. Thirty years ago, boys grew up expecting to engage in fist fights. Unless a boy could "stand up and fight like a man," he was dubbed a sissy. Boys who wished to escape playground violence were labeled "yellow" and could grow up convinced they were cowards. When the U.S. first bombed Baghdad in January, 1991, *Le Monde* in Paris commented that "the American boys" are at it again. The newspaper said Americans were looking for fresh fields to prove themselves and to recover the honor lost in the killing fields of Vietnam.

We need a new kind of physical courage, one that will not require the assertion of power over other people. It will be more vulnerable, more sensitive, more in touch with our own body – in harmony with it, rather than mastering it as a machine. It will respect other cultures and foreign traditions. Perhaps Kevin Costner in "Dances with Wolves" is a good example. Such physical courage will value the body as the means of empathy with others and as an expression of the self's beauty.[2] Another example of physical courage might be of the woman, weighing 310 pounds, who was physically and sexually abused as a young girl. She not only valiantly struggles every day through diet, exercise, and counseling to retrieve her appreciation for her body, but cheerfully cares for elderly patients in a nursing home.

B. *Moral courage.* Rollo May cites Alexander Solzhenitsyn, the Russian author, as an example of moral courage. Solzhenitsyn stood alone against the might of the Soviet apparatchiks to protest the inhuman, cruel treatment of women and men in the gulags. He proclaimed: "I would gladly give my life if it would advance the cause of truth." Such a willingness to face the truth underlies moral courage. It challenges the guardians of lies.

Moral courage also arises out of compassion for human suffering. It flows from an "identification through one's own sensitivity with the suffering of one's fellow human beings."[3] It always has a public value, and it has political consequences although they are not chosen in themselves. It rides the rail between life and death: Anwar Sadat negotiating peace with the Israelis; Corazon Aquino confronting the corrupt Marcos empire; and Oscar Romero siding with the poor against the 14 ruling families in El Salvador. Almost predictably, these courageous people face death. President Sadat was killed by extremists. Archbishop Romero was gunned down by a government thug. These public, political examples of moral courage prod each of us to muster moral courage ourselves.

In the public arena, some religious leaders oppress their followers in the name of salvation. Religious oppression is more seductive than political oppression. Hence, the exceptional, moral courage of Raymond Hunthausen, former Catholic archbishop of Seattle, heartens us. Hunthausen was willing, first of all, to confront the political-economic forces supporting the proliferation of nuclear weapons. In 1983 he described the Trident Missile Base on the Olympic peninsula as the "Auschwitz of the Puget Sound" and said he would no longer pay the percentage of his taxes that supported this. The missile base, he said, with its delivery systems to incinerate the world resembled "the ultimate solution."[4] American public policy seemed to be that when all else failed, we would destroy the enemy and ourselves in a great cataclysmic fire. What is worse is that such incendiary devices drive local and national economies. Boeing competes with McDonnell Douglas for contracts for the dubious Star Wars shields; members of Congress, locked into place with PAC money, scramble to pump military projects into their home districts.

In the summer of 1995, for instance, Congress added $7 billion more to the defense budget than the Pentagon had requested. They added $1.5 billion for the Seawolf submarine, which columnist Clarence Page describes as "a terrific weapon for fighting the sort of major theater wars the United States has virtually no prospect of fighting in the foreseeable future, except in Tom Clancy novels."[5] They also voted for 20 more B-2 Stealth Bombers than even the Air Force requested at a price tag of $1.2 billion each, just days before the controversial plane made news for flunking yet another test. This time its radar showed an embarrassing inability to distinguish a mountainside from rain. The Seawolf secures jobs for Rhode Island and Connecticut. The B-2 contracts not only aid Boeing in Seattle, but are spread around the country in several Congressional districts. Thus does fear, greed, and waste become engrafted in our social, economic, and political structures. Meanwhile, there are scant resources to invest in people and to rebuild the infrastructures; our schools, public transportation, and housing crumble beneath us.

Not long after Hunthausen's denunciation of the Trident Missile Base, the Reagan Government concluded a pact with the Vatican to establish full diplomatic relations, giving the Vatican long-sought recognition with full ambassadorial status. Within the year, the Vatican began an investigation of Hunthausen's ministry in the Seattle Archdiocese, as well as of Bishop Sullivan of Richmond, Virginia, another leader in the peace movement. The Vatican produced a report critical of the Church in Western Washington. But unexpectedly, Hunthausen, who would rather have been fishing in Montana, firmly, patiently and respectfully told the Vatican officials that their judgments were mistaken. He challenged a narrow, legalistic parochialism, and, backed by over 90% of the priests in his diocese, he eventually was restored to full authority.

Other examples hearten us: the moral courage of a teacher of 40 years who, year-in and year-out, challenges her students to the best within them, without hasty compromises to trendy theories; the courage of the Vietnam vets who face the nightmares of war that they carry within them and have sought to wage peace by disarming the forces for war. Each stretches her or his boundaries without calculation of personal gain.[6]

Moral courage is rooted in homey virtues. The *dailyness* of courage testifies to its authenticity. Its *common-senseness* insures that the next step will be done, even when there is no obvious next, because the next has to be imagined and created and acted upon.[7] Common sense conjoins personal truth and reality. It quiets the fear erupting from "it's going to last forever" and creates day-to-day routines even in the midst of crisis. Moral courage buttresses the families of the mentally ill, for instance, who offer hope to their son or daughter when there is no apparent hope – only the hope of tears and of support and of sharing pain.

Knowing there is a tomorrow, moral courage can risk failure. It recognizes that tremulous fears from as short as two weeks ago are now dim memories.

C. *Social Courage.* Rollo May says that social courage is the capacity to risk relationship in order to achieve intimacy. It enables us to give ourselves over to others with increasing and appropriate openness. Intimacy requires courage because risk is inescapable. If one of us in a relationship changes, both of us will change. In relationship we question: Will we grow together towards an unfolding of selves, or will we destroy ourselves together?

May says that the current culture shifts authentic intimacy almost exclusively to the body and makes it simply a matter of physical courage. It is easier for us to be naked physically than to be naked psychically. Easier to share our stripped bodies than to share our fantasies, fears and aspirations.

Social courage, however, requires intimacy on many levels simultaneously. "No wonder," May says, "the meeting of new persons brings a throb of anxiety as well as the joy of expectation; and as we go deeper into relationships, each new depth is marked by some new joy and new anxiety."[8] A courageous person risks movement in relationship, even when the outcome is bleak. Acts and admits one's doubts. In fact, May says, "Commitment is healthiest when it is not without doubt, but *in spite of* doubt."[9]

D. *Creative courage.* The fourth dimension of courage, the one which interests May most, is creative courage. He says that whereas moral courage is the righting of wrongs, creative courage discovers "new forms, new symbols, new patterns on which a new society can be built."[10] Creative courage demands much. For Vietnam vets, for instance, their experience sunders all previous patterns. They must risk a whole new way of becoming themselves. In addition, segments of society have stigmatized them and cast them out from the accepted civic patterns which might have interrupted their wounded experience. Some of them foundered in nightmarish, formless chaos.

Artists, on the other hand, can evoke graphic forms to shape their inner chaos. Gifted with the imagination, they invite us, too, to explore our own darkness, not by talking about it, but by entering into the creative act of dying and rising. When we encounter an artistic creation such as Beethoven's Ninth Symphony, we sense the fleetingness of beauty, the inevitability of death. We feel the poignancy that he was completely deaf when he conducted the premiere of the Ninth. In these moments something unique is born in us, and yet this joyous moment is dying even as it is

born. The form shapes our feelings, allows them to be born and
to die.

Beauty is fleeting and passing beauty beckons to ultimate
beauty. It stirs an ache like lilacs in spring. Was not that the reason
T.S. Eliot called April "the cruellest month, breeding lilacs out
of the dead land"? We yearn to hold on to the brief moment. By
the creative act we reach beyond our own death to shape something beyond us.

Such creativity eludes people with mental illness. Although
their imagination may spin through countless possibilities, they
may lack the stability to focus on a few concrete, realizable hopes
which could propel them toward health. Within their own spinning chaos, they face the challenge to create their self anew. In
the smallest movement, they may grasp their own finite mortality.
Even as they are enraptured by the shimmering beauty of a tree
or a child's smile, they shudder with paralysis at their mortality.
Without the creative courage to risk shaping and forming their
feelings, they wade through the murky swamp of their nightmares.
Fear thrives on darkness, like ghostly rodents scampering through
a darkened alley. Creative courage dispels these shadows, focuses
on the possible, and catches a glimmer of new light.

E. *The courage to accept acceptance.* In addition to these four features
of courage described by Rollo May, a deeper stream of courage
flows through all our choices. It is the courage to give and receive
love. It is the courage to recognize my self with all my gifts and
limitations. It is the courage to accept acceptance from another.
Ultimately it is the courage to accept Acceptance, God's love for
us.

The craving for acceptance can absorb all our creative energies. It is comparable to the physical craving caused by rickets,
a disease which causes a softening of the bones in children who
are deprived of sunlight or vitamin D, which enables them to
assimilate calcium and phosphorus. Children with rickets, especially at the turn of this century, ached for the minerals that their
bodies craved. In some cases, they scratched their bedroom walls
for lime to feed their bones. Similarly, people who are not accepted scratch for acceptance wherever they can find it.

A person who is not accepted acts out destructively: boasting
about accomplishments; pleasing others in a servile manner;
numbing the pain with drugs or alcohol. Such people may be

rigid because they lack the security to risk opening themselves to someone else. Ironically alcohol makes most alcoholics feel like they belong for the first time, but this chemical acceptance is all the more seductive because of its ready availability. Others craving acceptance may be given to sexual abuse to fill the void. Still others may be excessively aggressive or given to exaggeration or to gossip. Such people have a difficult time finding their core truth and acting out of it. Of course, all of us have some of these symptoms.

It takes courage to receive acceptance from another and just be there. To accept all of who I am – my bright, humorous, delightful self, and my brittle, defensive, wounded side as well. I may armor myself because I fear the demands of success or because I feel so vulnerable or because of the emotion and excitement and confusion engendered by my sexuality.

The courageous thrive on humor. They can caricature their fears and laugh at them. Like medieval artists, they can cast their demons as gargoyles on the parapets. Just as these leering grotesques became the conduits of rain water pouring off the roof, fears faced become channels for new energy.

Such courage does not flow from mere approval from others. It accepts applause, but is not paralyzed by it. It acknowledges criticism, but moves on. This courage is what Tillich calls "the courage to accept acceptance,"[11] which he describes as synonymous with faith itself. Through faith I have the courage to receive acceptance for who I am, rather than for what I achieve. This courage risks dying to egotism. It opens the self to love. It accepts the love of another.

A person filled with the courage to accept acceptance surrenders any striving for self-perfectionism. They recognize: "I don't have to do anything to be loved. I don't have to earn love. I couldn't anyway."

Every human person also yearns to be valued. Every one wants to be loved and cared for. Falling in love imparts so much power because it carries with it an oceanic feeling that finally I will be cared for – completely, wholly, and entirely. Such romantic love has the wonderful effect of lowering one's defenses and opening one's self in mutuality to another. But, of course, it is fleeting. And it must be tempered eventually through acknowledgment of the other as they are. This realism enables a deeper love. It paves the way for mutual acceptance of who I am as I am.

And of the Other as who he is or who she is. Then each of us can be valued in relationship for who we are.

We also know the pain of non-acceptance. A baby who is not accepted is damaged at the roots. A student who feels rejected by a teacher does not perform to capacity and the student explains: "Oh, the teacher doesn't like me!"

The deepest pain of the mentally ill is one of non-acceptance. A psychiatrist described this mental anguish and the difficulty for such pained people to love. He asked, "Did you ever have a toothache? Recall how it throbs through every fiber of your being. The pain of mental anguish, likewise, obliterates all other possibilities."

Consider the extent of this pain: One tenth to one third of all people in this country will have some form of mental collapse. Fortunately, most will have a relatively short episode over a period of weeks or months. For the chronically ill, however, they have just begun a lifetime of therapy through drugs, counseling, a quest for elusive medical treatment, for social support and acceptance. Though psychotropic drugs have helped tremendously since they were first introduced in 1953, we now dump thousands of these patients out into the streets and inadequate half-way houses.[12] Research demonstrates that these illnesses are accompanied by or caused by chemical disorders within the brain. Such a mental disorder, which radically shifts mood, makes self-acceptance all the more difficult.

When I was in the psych ward in 1975, a few of us would sit around drinking coffee, making our own astute diagnoses about the "real crazies" about us. We observed one woman of 38. Shapely, cute, she dressed as if she were 20. She could not stop smiling. We called her Barbie Doll. She spent her energy looking right. She could not risk not being a doll, and so was condemned to it. We opined that she needed to "go bananas." We prescribed a crack up so that the rage seething from the fissures in her face could burst and dissipate.

Here we were – one an attempted suicide, another with severe depression, and myself with an acute psychosis – just on the edge of chaos ourselves, fully aware of just what she needed. We laughed at our astuteness. We were implicitly accepting whatever we had gone through and acknowledging that it was okay to crack up.

A radical turning point for me came nine months after my breakdown. After a painful recovery process, I was back to normal. Yet when I stepped into a new assignment, I panicked after a couple of weeks and was hospitalized a second time. I was livid at Dr. Z., the psychiatrist, because he did not know enough to prevent this awful thing from happening. The turning point had two moments.

In the first, I was sitting under a tree in the hospital yard. I do not know how it began, but I imagined myself going to confession to myself. As I finished, I heard myself as the priest gently accepting this penitent and offering kind words of encouragement. I was filled with tears and suddenly realized how gentle I was to others compared to myself. I was filled with a deep self-acceptance.

The second moment came a few days later. I started re-reading Graham Greene's *The Power and the Glory*. Greene described the rage of a frustrated lieutenant:

> He was a mystic, too, and what he had experienced was vacancy – a complete certainty in the existence of a dying, cooling world, of human beings who had evolved from animals for no purpose at all. . . . But he believed against the evidence of his senses in the cold, empty ether space.[13]

I became aware of my own rage. I felt hopeless, suffocated in ether. I exploded, "Well, I had better do something about my sickness, because sure as hell no one else will." How ironic! My anger mobilized me.[14] Then I set about the tedious task again of living day to day, to tending to what I was feeling each day and examining why. I chose once again the path to health – stubbornly, resentfully, but with a degree of courage.

Both experiences – the self-acceptance during confession and tapping my own rage after reading about Greene's lieutenant – were connected. In both instances, I could acknowledge who I was. I could accept where I was, and not mask whatever I was feeling. My anger meant I not only could take responsibility for my own healing process, but that I had to.

The process began, but the healing itself took much longer than a few days or even a few months. Now I could take more risks, engage my emotions and take responsibility for them with increasing effectiveness. Acceptance meant that I was welcome to be myself. I could shout *I do not have to be the person I am not.* It helps to shout when you take a big leap – like the leap off the cliff in "Butch Cassidy and the Sundance Kid." I was well enough now to deal with my normal neurotic self!

We do not, of course, move toward total self-sufficiency. We mobilize some of our resources, we grow in our ability to seek help from others when appropriate, and we discover portions of our self long suppressed. We still crave complete fulfillment. We still yearn for full acceptance. St. Augustine said, "A friend is someone who knows everything about you and still accepts you." This is the dream we all share: that one day we may meet the person to whom we can really talk, who understands us as we are – both the words we say and those we do not – and quietly, simply accepts us. No one person can offer such total acceptance. God alone is the fulfillment and the reality of this dream. God loves me with my ideals, with my disappointments, with my shining cheeks, my big nose, my watery eyes. God accepts my lucid moments and my bitchy tantrums. I believe that is the reason Carl Jung said that all neuroses after the age of 35 need a spiritual solution.

It takes a long time to believe that I am accepted by God as I am. And we all have pockets of atheism: God loves me for everything but this, I whisper to myself. Even after an initial, grounding act of faith, it takes a lifetime to believe that I am invited to love God as myself – as Patrick – not as John, not as Kathleen, nor as Andrea, not as James, but as Patrick.

Self-acceptance can never be based wholly on my own self, my own qualities. Such narcissistic striving undermines the gift of healing. No matter how much I screw up my courage and pine for self-acceptance, I cannot do it on my own. Self-acceptance based only on my self is still self-centered, and it collapses on itself. Radical self-acceptance is an act of faith. When God loves me, I can do no better than accept myself as well.

Now, if you have already realized this depth of acceptance – you can relax, stop working so hard, and let God (or God's mediators – friends, green forests, yawning meadows, a laughing baby) lead you into the ways of God's love. And, if you have not realized this level of acceptance, you can still relax because all of your perfectionism is not going to help one whit.

A Caution

The courage to accept acceptance undergirds the next two chapters. Without it, we are liable to pick at the scabs of our failures. Chapter Six invites the reader to face the darkness of one's own brokenness, and Chapter Seven considers some ways of confronting shame and stigma. But if the reader has not begun to accept acceptance, then he or she may simply be swallowed up by self-pity, rather than be liberated.

> *For the garden is the only place there is,*
>   *but you will not find it.*
> *Until you have looked for it everywhere*
> *and found nowhere*
>   *that is not a desert.*[15]
>   – *W.H. Auden,* For the Time Being

Endnotes

1. Rollo May, *The Courage to Create* (New York: W.W. Norton & Co., 1975). See also Patrick J. Howell SJ, "Psycho-Spiritual Sources of Healing the Human Body," *Suffering and Healing in Our Day,* Francis A. Eigo, ed. (Villanova: Villanova University Press, 1990), pp. 95-131.

2. May, *The Courage to Create,* p. 6.

3. *Ibid.* p. 8.

4. Adolf Hitler referred to the extermination of the Jewish people as "the ultimate solution" and, of course, Auschwitz, where hundreds of thousands were incinerated, was the dreadful tragedy of his meticulous planning.

5. *Seattle Post-Intelligencer* (August 10, 1995), p. A15.

6. Cf. Scott Peck's definition of love: "The will to extend one's self for the purpose of nurturing one's own or another's spiritual growth," *The Road Less Traveled,* p. 81.

7. William Lynch, S.J., says, "People who do not attend to detail are poor in hope." In contrast, Lynch explains, "that an absolutizer will not settle for anything less than perfect." *Images of Hope: Imagination as Healer of the Hopeless* (Notre Dame: University of Notre Dame Press, 1965).

8. May, *The Courage to Create*, p. 10.

9. *Ibid.*, p. 14.

10. *Ibid.*, p. 15.

11. See Peter G. Van Breemen, "The Courage to Accept Acceptance," in *As Bread that is Broken* (Denville, NJ: Dimension Books, 1974), pp. 9-15.

12. Dr. E. Fuller Torrey estimates those currently suffering from chronic schizophrenia number 1.2 million. His book *Surviving Schizophrenia: A Family Manual*, rev. ed. (San Francisco: Harper & Row, 1988) is eminently helpful to families.

13. Graham Greene, *The Power and the Glory* (New York: The Viking Press, 1970), p. 33.

14. I have elaborated these episodes in my book *Reducing the Storm to a Whisper*.

15. "For the Time Being. IV" *Collected Longer Poems* (New York: Random House, 1965), p. 138.

CHAPTER SIX

Naming Evil

We began by saying that the West has lost its Way, that it is experiencing a crisis of meaning, a loss of purpose, and a misdirection. Without a common social vision, it has little basis for appealing to anything beyond self-interest. Witness in American politics the constant consultation of the polls, as if the coalescence of a majority around a couple of questions could create a vision.

Robert Bellah in *Habits of the Heart* identifies this loss of a common vision, which undermines the ideals of personal freedom and liberty. He recalls how separateness and individualism freed pioneer Americans from the oppression of traditional social structures, but now a renewed sense of community, such as characterized earlier American religious communities, is urgent. Community values must balance the value of personal freedom if people are not to self-destruct. Liberalism, advocating the maximum liberty and freedom for the greatest number of people, seeks to secure individual freedom at the cost of all other ideals. Meanwhile the disintegration of common meaning goes unabated. "Without a vision the people perish."(Proverbs 29:18)[1]

In fact, each sector of the world seems to be undergoing a distinct crisis: the crisis of the Third World is economic, the crisis of the Second World is political, the crisis of the capitalistic, First World is cultural. Since the heart of culture is spirituality, we might say that the deeper crisis of each sector of the world is a spiritual crisis. In our own culture, a shared meaning, a shared future, a shared hope are absent. We live out the loss of hope that Dante warned of at the entrance to Hell: "Abandon hope, all ye who enter here." If we are not in hell, we are surely knocking on its door.

Four Modern Hells

Karl Menninger, the psychiatrist, asked some years ago in his book, *Whatever Became of Sin?*, whatever happened to responsibility? The concept of sin, Dr. Menninger explained, acknowledges the importance of our choices and that we are responsible for them. Without a sense of sin, Menninger argued, we can excuse all personal responsibility for destructive choices. He cited the story of Lt. William Calley, the mass murderer at My Lai to illustrate how we can deny responsibility, both as an individual and as a nation. Calley had slaughtered helpless women and babies with the hypocritical justification that they might be carrying explosives. Menninger commented on the public reaction:

> Many angrily disputed the possibility that what Calley did could be properly labeled a crime. Many would not concede he had even committed a sin or made a mistake. He had obeyed orders (they said).[2]

Menninger traced the causes that brought about this decline in responsibility in both society and in the individual. He said the decline began early in this century when a more enlightened view of sexuality and sexual mores threw out the category of sin because it "repressed human freedom." Earlier practically everything having to do with sex was considered sinful, but the new, liberated ethics did not substantially improve the human condition. Rather, by throwing out sin, it did nothing to check human greed, envy, and hatred. In any case, sin, as a helpful naming of the evil perpetrated by human choice, was lost.

Just as Menninger asked "Whatever became of sin?," we could also ask, "Whatever became of hell?" The question underscores the loss of social responsibility. It also shows how each of us shares in and suffers from the destructive choices made in families, communities, or nations. If we cannot imagine hell, then we cannot imagine how we can create communities of justice and peace. As a nation, we are only gradually coming to see how we create our own hells by the choices we make both individually and collectively. Choosing to maximize personal comfort and personal greed has cast us into a hell of our own making. If we choose to maximize profit at the expense of clean water, if we choose to clear-cut forests at the expense of local habitat, then we are surely abandoning hope for the sake of more immediate gratification.

Another dimension of this image of hell is that each of us is conditioned by the evil already structured into society. We may have been born into communities which encourage racism or into a society which maximizes profits to the detriment of justice or into a church which places more value on male dominance than on the mutual sharing of gifts. Our own personal responsibility may be muted at best by the overwhelmingly oppressive conditions of which we are already a part. We may have only slight awareness of how these destructive values condition us to continuing the destruction.

Hell in the medieval imagination meant that choices mattered, especially choices that affected the good of society. However, when Copernicus discovered that the planets revolved around the sun, people could no longer imagine a fiery, eternal place under the crust of the Earth. They were freed from the excesses of "hell, fire, and brimstone preaching," but hell as a symbol for the consequences of our choices lost its place in our spiritual geography. Later in the Age of Enlightenment, scientific reason finally skewered the over-ripe, medieval sense of the afterlife. Science then had no room for a hell, much less for a heaven.

Drawing on the medieval imagination, Dante reserved the most exquisite damnation in the bottom rung of the *Inferno* for three treacherous sins against the common good: the betrayal of God, the betrayal of Christ, and the betrayal of the state. Here Dante discovered a gigantic Satan fixed in ice with three men dangling from his mouth: Cassius and Brutus, traitors to the state, and Judas who betrayed Christ.

> [Satan] wept with six eyes and over his three chins,
>   a bloody froth flowed down.
> With each mouth he was tearing with his teeth,
> a sinner.[3]

In Dante's world, it is clear how Cassius and Brutus betrayed the political community and how Judas betrayed the religious community. However, the great betrayer, the ultimate symbol of a self turned in on itself, is Satan. In his isolation, Satan weeps with rage and impotence. But this slobbering monster conveys no feeling, certainly no responsibility. It dwells in frozen isolation.

Contemporary society has been stripped of its mythic and religious roots; it lacks a simple compass to give it a moral orientation. Its value system revolves around power, prestige, and individual fulfillment to the detriment of social commitment and justice, especially justice for those who are weakest and most vulnerable. It militantly defends its prerogatives through instruments of global war. It spawns anonymous bureaucracies, which maintain its inertia. Through the multinationals, it exploits age-old rain forests, the blue whale, and cascading mountain waters. It feeds on nothing more than old-fashioned greed, but now this appetite for more and more goods and comfort has few restraints. This monster has become globalized.

A good example of a society that had bartered its soul was the grounding of the Exxon Valdez in a pristine sound off Alaska in 1989. The shipwreck created an oily hell that promised death for years to come. It was a typical hell. No one in the upper echelons [who had opted for single hull rather than double-skinned hulls] was responsible. A lowly mate took the rap. And after all, don't we expect accidents to happen? Isn't this the price of fueling the fires of commerce?

As a society, we seem trapped by our greed, by our lust for power, by our fears to protect our wealth against every possibility. Such enslavement constitutes a hell, and our response has been to abandon all hope. Four other hells carry a similar sentence of despair over them: The *hell* of the inner cities, the *hell* of distrust, the *hell* of consumerism, and the *hell* of war. Each of these are quite different types of hell, yet each exemplifies forces that create despair and impair our individual choices: the first hell is a place, the second involves our moral perspective, the third reflects our lifestyle, and the fourth results from socio-political policy. Through each of these hells an all-prevailing smog of hopelessness chokes the human spirit.

To grow up in the *inner cities* of Detroit, Los Angeles, and other urban America areas is to grow up without hope. The inner cities teem with gang violence, drug addiction, a proliferation of guns, and nightly killings. They have become a symbol for wherever shattered dreams, loss of community, and institutional violence strip a people of their hope.[4]

Some parents or a single mother in these hellish places can nourish a flicker of hope for a child, but the lack of opportunity,

gang violence, and ultimately the deadening of imagination snuff
it out. To live in some inner cities is to live under a pall of
suspicion. If a crime occurs, the police, first and foremost, suspect
a Black or a Chicano. Similarly, savings and loans officers, willing
to dole out millions to high-rolling Texas oilmen, look with suspicion on anyone from the inner city who would dare to take out
a loan on a promise of hope. In these cities gangs demarcate the
circles of power, but banks redline the circles of risk.

A subtler hell is the hell of *distrust,* which brings suspicion
on the people we most need to trust for loving and healing:
spouses, ministers, lawyers, and doctors. Spouses become suspicious of each other's friends. Any priest who lingers in conversation around an altar boy gets a second look. Lawyers become
overly zealous about what is legal, rather than what is moral.
Doctors, looking over their shoulders at potential lawsuits, pre-
scribe superfluous tests or overlook a colleague's alcoholism.

In a society which looks out for number one, lawsuits have
become the order of the day. Families suing old friends. Patients
suing doctors. Businesses, schools, and governments bound by a
code of fear: "If we do this, will we be sued?" In a litigious society
every public act becomes an occasion of second guessing, of
cautious, even fearful choices. In this system of distrust, school
administrators are inclined to cover their backside, rather than
inaugurate innovative, out-of-school learning. And in the inner
city schools, eleven-year olds brandish guns, and armed guards
patrol the hallways. Each student and staff member has an I.D.
photo badge.

The distrust extends to the simplest daily acts. In an age of
consumer terrorism J. Alfred Prufrock's question "Dare I eat a
peach?" has become frighteningly pertinent. During the last ten
years we have seen Tylenol laced with cyanide, Chilean grapes
with arsenic, Halloween candy with razor blades, and, as it turned
out, an unfounded scare of syringe needles in Pepsi cans.

In this hell of distrust, gun dealers reap huge profits selling
automatic weapons to whomever walks in off the street. In 1988
the United States had 8,092 people killed by handguns compared
to 8 for Britain, 46 for Japan, and 5 for Canada.[5] By the end of
1991 a national poll revealed that the only institutions that the
public trusted were churches and the military. A curious mix!

A third hell ingratiates its way into every dimension of our
culture. The hell of *consumerism.* Consumer goods are a wonderful

thing. But like every hell, consumerism comes under the guise of the good. Hell would not be hell unless it looked good from the outside. Consumer goods enliven us, they sharpen our appetite, they motivate us to work harder and more productively. Consumerism, however, is the excess. Like an insatiable fire, consumerism leaves us with a craving, not for visions, but for illusions. It shrinks our imaginations down to an abundance of things at the expense of relationships. It would satisfy our hunger for authentic intimacy with a parcel of cosmetics, vacation homes, an extra car, exotic cruises, and closets full of shoes. It leaves us with the taste of ashes.

When I was a boy in Western North Dakota, our family was driving along through the Badlands one Sunday. I saw vast acres of smoke spewing up from the earth. My dad explained how these underground fires began in the lignite coal. The fires could smolder for years, he explained. It wasn't worth the effort to put them out. Such is the underground fire of consumerism in our society.

A fourth hell is all around us: the hell of an undeclared, silent, unending *war* in the name of peace. To enter the hell of *war* denudes the body and soul. War sunders centuries of human endeavor and its terror maims children for generations. Fearful of the enemy, which lingers even after the break up of the USSR, we have, over the last fifty years, assumed the enemy's worst tactics – spying on our own citizens, assisting in destroying a village people in El Salvador, building armed moats on our southern border, tape-recording sermons in churches and keeping on file the names of whoever enters and leaves a given church because they support policies which differ from the federal government's policies. The specific examples of warrish attitudes change from year to year, but the underlying bellicosity remains. Despite the caution even of the Joint Chiefs of Staff, the America public urges its political leaders to do something in Bosnia. By that we mean armed resolution. We are, of course, rightly outraged by the atrocities committed daily, yet impatient with the tedious, messy work of peace. War, we can see, manifests a larger social breakdown. We cannot solve our own problems at home, but we will jump in to set things straight, once and for all, whether it is in El Salvador, Iraq or Somalia, whether the means are moral or not.

In our day a foggy morass wafting up through the belly of these diverse hells winds its deadly way like a yellow mustard gas through modern society. No one is responsible for industrial pollution. No one is responsible for the collapse of the savings and loan industry. No one is responsible for the gluttonous consumption of resources by a military machine. We have given up hope, we have given up responsibility. By losing the capacity to imagine hell, we have taken up our dwelling place there.

The hell of the inner city, the hell of distrust, the hell of consumerism, the hell of war – no enemy could have devised four better hells to destroy our heart, to sap our moral courage, and to mortgage our future. "We have seen the enemy and they is us," Pogo once reminded us. Part of the failure is a failure of imagination; we can no longer see the hells that we have created and, therefore, no one is responsible.

Personal Evil: The Big Lie

To find our way home, we need also to examine ourselves individually for the evil in which we collaborate or initiate. This personal examination carries its own risks. It can be destructive if we approach this reflection with the attitude that, on our own, we can straighten it all out or that I individually could somehow purge myself of my own complicity in evil. Rather, we approach this examination from a stance of faith as *the courage to accept acceptance.* Only if we have experienced some degree of radical acceptance of ourselves and of God's breakthrough into our human history can we face the evil we have wrought. With that crucial understanding, let us proceed.

It is clear, I think, that if we cannot name the evils of racism or of consumerism, or of military exploitation, then we will simply seek adjustment for our own individualized anxiety, guilt or depression. Those who cannot adjust will be called deviants or crazy. At some level we all participate in these social evils and are affected by them. Generally we come to recognize evil by encountering the good and realizing quite suddenly how destructive we have been. Let us trace this pattern.

What are the lures of evil? What are the origins of sin? How does denial of responsibility originate?

At an early stage in our lives, we buy into a lie. It is a lie absorbed initially from other family members who have bought into versions of the same lie. It is spread throughout our communities and institutions. It shapes our legal system. It gives dominance to men over women, straights over gays. It colors our views on people of other color – whether white or black or yellow or brown.

The lie arises from our own limited bodies and from our own limited response to the challenge to grow and to learn and to love. When our parents say, "No" or "You can't" or "You made a mess of things," we may absorb the lie. We take on more than they say and even more than they would ever demand from us.

When we are left behind and feel abandoned, we fear we are no longer loved. When our young bodies flop, we absorb the lie: "You're a failure." "You're not enough." In its virulent form, the lie may expand to: "You're no good." Or in a more cancerous form: "You're no damned good!" It is a lie which wounds all that is human and which fuels the hells around us.

"You are no damned good!" The word damned suggests that there are hellish experiences to which we are condemned and from which we might be redeemed. It suggests a mythic framework, inhabited by evil spirits, goblins and dragons, and dark, fiery places. Underground, threatening, sulfurous. A place where heroes or heroines enter at the outset of their quest for wholeness. When our sense of failure becomes so overwhelming and globalized, we often project our fears onto a screen larger than life.

In his novel *The Exorcist* William Blatty describes a little girl allegedly possessed by an evil spirit. In desperation her parents turn to church officials who summon Father Merrin, a priest paleontologist, from his archaeological digs in the Middle East to perform an exorcism on this ancient enemy with whom the priest is all too well acquainted. In the context of the novel, the evil spirit knows the most vulnerable place of every person. We do not have to believe in the devil to acknowledge the spiritual truth that we are vulnerable to evil at our weak points and that by hiding our weaknesses we can become more destructive towards ourselves and towards others. In *The Exorcist*, Blatty dramatizes this spiritual truth. The Evil One, with deft sureness, attacks Merrin in his pride:

"Prideful bastard, Merrin! Scum! You will lose! She will die! The pig will die!" The demonic entity had returned and raged hatefully at Merrin. "Profligate peacock! Ancient heretic! I adjure you, turn and look on me! Now look on me, you scum!"[6]

To undo Merrin's goodness, the demon casts up Merrin's personal unworthiness, his doubts about himself, his questionable decisions. This demonic shadow darkens Merrin's sense of his own humanity.

Fr. Damien Karras, who is assisting Merrin, asks: "Then what would be the purpose of possession? What's the point?" Merrin ponders the questions and responds:

> I think the demon's target is not the possessed; it is us. . . the observers . . . every person in this house. And I think – I think the point is to make us despair; to reject our own humanity, Damien: to see ourselves as ultimately bestial; as ultimately vile and putrescent; without dignity; ugly; unworthy. And there lies the heart of it, perhaps; in unworthiness. For I think belief in God is not a matter of reason at all; I think it finally is a matter of love; of accepting the possibility that God could love us. . . ."[7]

Merrin's response underscores our point that the lie is a denial of our own goodness. The lie makes us unavailable for love. The lie wounds the heart and spreads its poison through all our choices. It takes subtle forms, shaped according to the character of each person.

How can we best acknowledge the goodness of ourselves and at the same time recognize the evil that betrays us? We need at least a simple shorthand for what we are taking about.

Ignatius of Loyola, a sixteenth century master of the spiritual life, says at the beginning of his little manual *The Spiritual Exercises* that the purpose of these exercises is to lead a person to true spiritual freedom so that every choice or decision be based not on some disordered attachment or aberrant love, but rather on a set of values aligned with God and with God's creation. For Ignatius a "disordered attachment," is any errant desire, any desire that flows out of our false self. The attachment is disordered because we cling to the apparent goods of power, pride or possessions to protect our false self, rather than making choices that are ordered toward our true self.

In psychological terms, we deny our self through one of two destructive patterns: either through a neurosis or a character disorder.[8] To the person with a neurosis the lie says: "You are no damned good, but you have to do it all alone. You're in this by yourself, so you had better prove yourself worthwhile." With the person with a character disorder, however, the lie is even subtler. It nourishes a self-centered complacency: "You are no damned good, but no one knows it [not even you]. So someone else will do it for you" or "They'd better take care of you or you will throw a tantrum." Neither attitude is authentic. Neither is fully human. Neither is bounded by time nor space nor in solidarity with the human. The lie hardens the heart, so that it pumps ever harder against the blockages to the heart's own truth. The lie thus takes on a life of its own. It keeps clogging the flow of personal self-esteem with the neurosis or personality disorder which it has engendered. Or using the language of Ignatius – the self has a disordered attachment which distorts reality.

The Denial of Self and the Denial of Death

The challenge of adolescents who confront their own divided character is to be able to say:

"Aha! This is what I am good at."

"I have a talent for music, for leadership, or for friendship."

"I can write well and edit the school newspaper."

"I'm a great dancer."

"I'm a good soccer forward, or the guys on the team like me."

The young person not only recognizes a talent but receives affirmation for it from peers. An adolescent feels that parents "have to love me, so that doesn't count." But when their peers acknowledge them and like them for who they are, then they can claim, "I know it's real. I accept it. I feel it. I love it. Isn't it awesome!"

Even with this affirmation, the shadow we have seen before lurks. The ancient enemy. The specter of self-doubt. I am not enough. I need more. I will never have enough. We have not yet internalized a love of self.

Of all the things that motivate us, one of the principal ones is our terror of death. Most often we suppress this fear of death lest we become immobilized. Most children seem to become aware of death when they are three to five years old. Some have a flurry of childhood nightmares and then go on to live a healthy, more-or-less optimistic life, untroubled by death fears. Repression, according to Ernest Becker, takes care of the complex symbol of death for most people. But its disappearance does not mean that the fear was never there, Becker says.[9] This denial of death which faces each one of us leads us to repress our self in part. By seeking to escape the mortality of our bodies, we learn that certain dire feelings are unacceptable and must be repressed. Then this repression extends as well to how we feel about our bodies and our body-image.

The contemporary emphasis on the body can provide a welcome corrective and a fresh avenue for the exploration of body-consciousness. It can help us reclaim our sexuality and interrelatedness. Of course, orthodox Christianity has sought to accept the human body by affirming the Incarnation, the birth, death and resurrection of the Christ over against second and third century movements which attempted to deny that God became fully human. Most reform movements within Christianity have had a similar thrust. Francis of Assisi in the 12th century sang of the harmony of creation, the wonders of God's birth among us as human. Ignatius of Loyola in the 16th century shared his great devotion to the Birth of Jesus coupled with a profound appreciation for humanistic education. He saw all of creation as a manifestation of God's goodness and, therefore, it should be reverenced, appreciated, and savored.

Similarly the current feminist retrieval of the Christian tradition leads us to acknowledge the full dimensions of the human body and deepen our contemplation of divinity. Women have asserted that the taboos, prohibitions, and laws that governed their bodies were often a mask for a socio-political agenda of power and exploitation, often within the Church itself.

Of course, we see the excesses too in the contemporary accent on the body. The cult of the body, adrift from any purpose except for displaying sleek, sculpted bodies in the local hall of mirrors. Various diets, health spas, Tai-chi, yoga – you name it, we've got it. Sometimes I speculate that Americans have done for Eastern meditation what they earlier did for Italian pizza – fattened it up and commercialized it. The rush to meditation techniques and body massage parlors can be just another craze, which simply denies our mortality.

A humorous 1988 film, "Moonstruck," explores the link between the denial of death and the human quest for the perfect relationship. It is a film about lovers, "moonstruck" at their nonrational love for each other. Questions such as, What drives us? What is the source of love? Why is love so crazed? drive the film. One of the subplots of the love story centers around an older couple. The husband has taken up with a mistress. And the wife, played by Olivia Dukakis, keeps asking, "Why do men chase women?" She relentlessly pursues the question until her daughter's fiancée responds one evening: "Because they are afraid to die." Dukakis smiles, she has her answer. That night, when her husband creeps in late, she accosts him. "You're going to die." He looks back at her in total bewilderment, as if to say, Where did this come from? She repeats, "You're going to die." He stares blankly. Through some other twists and turns in the plot, he comes to appreciate "family things," his wife's love and other ordinary family things, especially his family gathered around a table. He awkwardly turns to his wife and asks for pardon.

The task of young adulthood centers on the acceptance of my basic goodness. The task includes an acceptance of my body as it is, not as I fantasize it and certainly not as others tell me it should be. Twenty to twenty-five years later, the task of an adult in mid-life lies in the acceptance of all of who I am – broken and whole, creative and destructive, alive and yet dying.[10] The acceptance of our mortality takes the steam out of our illusions.

The human challenge rests in not only accepting our self, but in acting on the good. It lies in opting for the accessible, the ordinary good available now. It means that we choose to be fully human, fully alive, in Philadelphia, in Seattle, in Bangkok, in Nazareth – wherever I am now.

To opt for the attainable good, therefore, is a faith choice for the human good – the limited, the here-and-now good. Limited choices. Achievable good. The insight of Alcoholics Anonymous is that each day I face my addiction. Each day I take a small step toward freedom. Each day I make a faith choice. Over and over again. Can I believe in a higher power? Can I believe in the good which resides in myself? Can I believe that others are there to support me and that I can support them? Can I believe in the mystery of limitation?

A mentor friend of mine went to Frankfurt to study theology in the 1950s. The very first week he dreaded what he had to face for the next four years. He was told that by the time he finished his studies, he would have eaten 120 kilometers of wurst (the German hot dog and its variations). He made it through, one wurst a meal, one day at a time. How this impacted his theology he never said!

Evil, by way of contrast, has no container. It has no limits. Alexander Solzhenitsyn described this unbounded state of evil in his acceptance of the Nobel Prize for Literature: "Violence (read: evil) is less and less embarrassed by the limits imposed by centuries of lawfulness. [It] is brazenly and victoriously striding across the whole world."[11] Evil winds its way through the fabric of institutions and ruptures relationships. It feeds on abused children, impoverished parents, and generational cycles of incest among families. Its parentage is lost. No one seems to take responsibility for such violence. Any person, however, who acknowledges responsibility for their destructive choices breaks the cycle. They also implicitly acknowledge their own goodness: "I made a destructive choice, but I am capable of better."

Dreaming the Possible Dream

It does absolutely no good to imagine hell, of course, unless we can envision a heaven. Because of our interrelationship with other humans and our environment, healing the human heart cannot be hoped for if we have no hope for our planet and for its transformation. Since a dream emerges from hope, we need to examine the anatomy of hope.

We have an odd stance toward hope. When we say a person has hope, we imply that they do not have much else. They are in deep trouble. That is not the hope that I wish to talk about. Hope is vigorous virtue. It imagines the possible.

We have another curious expression that when a person is particularly desperate he or she is hoping against hope. A person hopes without any expectation of fulfillment. This stance may be crucial to hope. Waiting. Just being there. Without expectancy.

This waiting is the origin of hope. This is hope at its starkest; it is hope before the seed bursts to thrust its first sprout. It is hope, but only its dim beginnings, not even the first sprig has stirred yet. And the darkness makes it more palpable, more containable, easier to stay with, though not to visualize. T. S. Eliot described it:

> I said to my soul, be still, and wait without hope
> For hope would be hope for the wrong thing.[12]

Avoid the optimism. Avoid the happy endings. Avoid the glitzy promises by grinning evangelists from the churches or from Miller Lite commercials.

In hoping against hope, a curing, like the tanning of rawhide, occurs. First, a scraping away. Then, a drying and bleaching in the sun. Then stretched and leached with tannic acid. Until it is done. The putrescent flesh is gone and a fibrous hide remains – now supple leather. Scraping, leaching, bleaching, stretching – all that is here. But the image is insufficient, for hope without expectancy lies in darkness. There is no sun here. The only light a vigil. The only act, waiting. Hope awaits the dawn. These are the origins of hope, but hope itself should not be imagined as fragile. It is supple, robust, and enlivening.

William Lynch, the Jesuit poet-theologian who had his own bouts with darkness, describes an essential dimension of hope. It is the vital relationship, which we saw earlier, between hoping and desiring. When we discover what our desires are, we are well on our way toward hope. When we cannot desire, we are moving toward despair. Lynch refers to the Book of Daniel where the angel says to the prophet, "God has loved you because you are a person of desires," and Lynch comments that the human person is a "wishing, desiring being who, in this exalted sense, must at all costs be in contact with his [or her] wishes. Where there is no wishing, there is no hope."[13]

A Vision of Things Hoped For

What are the conditions for a new vision? According to Mary Jo Leddy, such visions are more easily recognized when they are awaited, longed for, and expected.[14] Dwelling in silence at the deeper level of our shared existence hallows the time and hollows out our receptivity. Meaning is not something we can pick up in a workshop, nor is it something we can spin out of nothing. It is something we discover. And we discover it most often in contemplation, in a committed relationship, and in community, because in these settings we let go of our habitual perceptions and risk the other.

What passes for vision at numerous conferences and workshops may be nothing more than the latest formula for survival. A workshop focus on self-care, self-development, self-growth may only extend my self into the future of who I already am. Nothing new breaks through.

A breakthrough occurs when our worldview becomes reconfigured. It occurs, like a revelation, when our view of self, God and world becomes transformed, and we see more clearly and with deeper appreciation who we are. Viktor Frankl, as we saw earlier, built his philosophy on the human person's search for meaning. He explained the need to wait, the need to attend to one's inner spirit, "What counts, what waits in the future, waits to be actualized by you."[15] But if we grant that a shared vision of the future must be discovered rather than constructed, where will it come from? It will come from the deepest level of our lives, from the level where our communion with our Source coincides with our community with others. Thomas Merton called this level the true self, where the self draws closer to others as it draws closer to Source. The great religions record these encounters in their sacred literature, and these texts become avenues for the encounters with primordial meaning which we are describing.

George's Story: Vietnam Trauma

George, a Vietnam vet, shared the story with me some years ago of his warrior experience and the aftermath of nightmares, interior violence, and shattering. Severely wounded by shrapnel, he spent six months in a military hospital where he lost a kidney and, for a second time, came close to dying. Eighteen years later, after a very long road to spiritual, psychological recovery, he wrote this reflection:[16]

"I have come full circle," George began. "My quest has led me back to where I started, within the beauty and horror of my own story as a man. The process of healing shares in the mystery of life itself. It is a process of coming home to oneself. It is to arrive where we started, as T.S. Eliot commented, and to know and inhabit the place for the first time.

"The scattered pieces of knowledge that one gathers along the way do not lead to healing," George reflected, "rather it is the authenticity of the search that brings one back to wholeness in communion with our God.

"When I lay dying in a hospital bed from kidney failure, when my marriage broke up, when I felt abandoned and rejected, I fled God's presence out of fear and anger for the betrayal of my innocent belief in the goodness of life. In my youth, I expected to be loved and cared for. In Nam and afterwards I saw from the inside how life is filled with suffering and felt betrayed by the God who used to laugh with me when I was an innocent child.

"The anthropologist Margaret Mead asserted that warfare is just an invention by which human societies permit their young men either to accumulate prestige or avenge their honor or acquire loot or wives or slaves or land or cattle or appease the blood lust of their gods or the restless souls of the recently dead. It is just an invention, older and more widespread than the jury system, but nonetheless an invention."

George continued, "Another writer, who survived the no-man's land battles of World War I, Erich Maria Remarque in *The Road Back* posed the question: 'Is the reason why wars perpetually recur because none can ever wholly feel what another suffers?'"

Then moving into the heart of his argument, George wrote, "Fathers send their sons to war for the same reasons that they themselves went to war: to protect their culture and to earn a place in the pantheon of god-warriors. If enough men respond and if they win the war, the nation is saved and the warriors return as heroes. If the war is lost, the nation and its people are destroyed.

"I noticed after firefights in Nam that the dying (both the Vietnamese and Americans) cried for their mothers and wives, not for their fathers. Those of us who survived, hide deep inside the dark empty places within ourselves, too wounded and angry to feel any tender presence in our lives.[17]

"As young men, we held a religious fundamentalism that saw evil in the commies. Better dead than red. God was on our side to overcome the dark evil of the other side.

"For me it was the Vietnamese. For my older cousins the Koreans and Chinese. For my father the Germans, the Japanese and Italians. For my grandfather the Germans and Turks. We were tempted to be like the gods who knew what is good and what is evil. We fell. Isn't Grenada, Panama, and Iraq the temptation for this generation?

"In Nam the difference between this and previous wars was that from their own living rooms Americans watched their sons die. They witnessed the agony in between Tums commercials. In this ancient tradition of bloodletting, they met the most primordial religious experiences known – sin, guilt, the fall from grace. As Americans, we lost righteousness. The mythology of war was unmasked. It stood out in all its moral ugliness. It shattered complacency. It opened a wound and the spiritual pain of truth lay opened. We discovered that evil resides in the hearts of all of us.

"War causes an ontological alienation for the warrior, a spiritual crippling of the true self by psychic pain and ever thereafter a fated destiny of trying to find meaning in his life within the narrow confines of a false self.

"The combat soldier," George observed, "is an alienated soul,[18] a tangle of anger, hopelessness, disgust and trauma. Jesus' death on the cross, according to the philosopher Hegel, was the death of God as stranger. Jesus was the first to realize that God reveals God's self to us through reconciliation and sacrifice. War is not part of God's creation. It is an ancient sin rooted in the greed and fear of nation states.

"Thomas Merton believed that we freely choose to reject or accept God's way. In this rejection, we become lost, alienated into the narrow confines of our false self. The ALL of God dies in us and the sterile nothingness of our desires becomes our God. Most men suffering from an estrangement of themselves from others and from God are alienated from the cosmos of life. They are in a spiritual and emotional wasteland.

"Veterans from wars return and wander in aimless search for a spiritual meaning to their lives only to discover that what society tells them has the only meaning: Success can be bought. It is measured in power, control, prestige. But we have been to the bottom. We know the emptiness of these promises, that it is a disappointing chimera. The balladeer Bruce Springsteen hauntingly sings the doleful song of all of the fathers and sons who have gone to war and come home with an empty heart. War has no purpose; it only brings tears to mothers' eyes.

"A strong individualism," George claimed, "armors men against the world, against our selves, and tragically against those we love most. Our spiritual need is to live and grow in a community of people who can love and accept us as we are and see us as sources for grace as well. Such healing liberates us from our inner suffering. It is not some mysterious distant power. It is available daily. It is mediated most of all by human love.

"The veteran in American culture, much like the battered child crawling back to abusive parents, craves the affection of his nation. Like such a parent, America both causes and soothes the pain. On the face of it, America is a "Christian" society. It controls the language, rites and sacraments that are needed for purification and forgiveness. Veterans still wandering the spiritual desert cry out a prophetic 'bullshit' in a society that worships technology and finds the ultimate meaning of life in the pursuit of personal fulfillment, of feeling good."

George concluded his description of the loss of American innocence and subsequent alienation with a question: "How does one actually move from dis-grace to grace?" He suggested that we lament with the psalmist:

> *My God, my God, why do you forsake me?*
> *My groaning does nothing to save me.*
> *I call by day, I shudder in the night,*
> *but you do not answer.*
>
> *You drew me from the womb*
> *And soothed me on my mother's breast.*
> *From all times and all beginnings*
> *I have belonged to you.*
> *Do not be absent, do not abandon me,*
> *My fears explode like rockets,*
> *And no one hears my cries!*
> (adapted from Psalm 22:1-2,9-11)

As the ancients knew, there are tears in the very nature of things.[19] Tears for ourselves, tears for our world. Tears empty us, wash us anew. They halt our wild craving and open us to the source of all healing.

In these first six chapters we have traced a journey which begins with creation: all manner of things are good; we receive the gift of ourselves from a loving, nurturing Creator. We have arrived at a point of profound disorder in our world and in our

own lives. In this chapter we have explored the dodges, subter-
fuges, and guises of evil. We have asked again: What ever happened to sin? and What ever happened to hell? Isn't the denial
of sin and the obliteration of hell actually opening a door to the
demons that haunts us? Our cover ups further the web of evil.

The ancient writers depicted this denial of responsibility in
the story of Adam and Eve. Adam claims, "She did it." Eve count-
ers, "The snake tempted me." These writers portrayed a deep-
seated fear and denial in human experience. In the next chapter
we will try to peel away the masks of this fear and denial and to
explore how stigma and shame operate as cover ups.

Endnotes

1. Literally: "Without prophecy the people become demoralized." *New Ameri-can Bible.*

2. Karl Menninger, *Whatever Became of Sin?* (New York: Hawthorne Books, 1973), p. 13.

3. Canto XXXIV 53-56, *The Inferno* (my own translation).

4. Paradoxically, this hopelessness also extends to adolescents trapped in superficial suburbs. They may turn to drugs to escape from their bland existence. Parents may suffocate them with all kinds of things, rather than providing acceptance, time together, and some flexible structures for work and play.

5. "The Other Arms Race," *Time* 133 (February 6, 1989): 20-21.

6. William P. Blatty, *The Exorcist* (New York: Harper & Row Publishers, 1971), pp. 306-307.

7. *Ibid.*, p. 311. These dramatic passages can easily be misinterpreted. Some people glom onto an image of the personal nature of evil and move rapidly to a fearful, often intense, supposition that Satan can possess a person: "Am I possessed? Could I be possessed? Are my friends possessed?" Such imaginings and projections are understandable among ahistorical, pre-scientific peoples or others with subconscious neuroses. Unfortunately they are often encouraged by priests, ministers, and other literal-minded believers. I have seen no evidence that supports this approach. On the other hand, I think that the metaphors of hell, Satan, and evil spirits enable us to recognize the personal or social evil in which we ourselves

participate. The danger is that we will become stuck in the metaphor and create a fearful idol to whom we pay tribute. Though William Blatty depicts the effects of evil, he also suggests that possession is not aimed at the person possessed, but rather at the discouragement it produces.

8. Cf. my previous explanation of Scott Peck's discussion that these two conditions are disorders of responsibility. The person with a neurosis assumes too much responsibility; the person with a character disorder not enough. (endnote 14, Chapter Three)

9. Ernest Becker, *The Denial of Death* (New York: Free Press, 1973), p. 20.

10. Daniel Levinson describes the four tasks of mid-life as moving toward a paradoxical living out of the polarities of youth and old age, creativity and destructiveness, and so forth. *The Seasons of a Man's Life,* (New York: Ballantine Books, 1978), pp. 197-198.

11. Acceptance Speech for Nobel Prize for Literature. As quoted by Karl Menninger, *Whatever Became of Sin?* (New York: Hawthorn Books, 1973), p. 36.

12. Eliot, "East Coker," *The Complete Poems and Plays, 1909-1950*, p. 126.

13. Lynch, *Images of Hope*, pp. 24-25.

14. Mary Jo Leddy, *Reweaving Religious Life* (Mystic, Conn.: Twenty-Third Publications, 1990), p. 100.

15. Viktor Frankl, *The Will to Meaning* (New York: New American Library, 1969), p. 127.

16. I have edited this original paper to suit my own text limitations.

17. For more on the alienation of sons from their fathers and the civic urgency for healing this relationship see Richard Rohr, "Naming the 'Father Hunger' (an Interview)," *St. Anthony Messenger* (October, 1990).

18. Melvin Seeman, a sociologist, describes the symptoms of alienation as powerlessness, meaninglessness, norm-lessness, isolation, and self-estrangement. Once alienated, Seeman says 1) A person is powerless to influence events that bear on one's major interest; 2) A person is unclear about what he ought to believe and has little or no sense of meaningfulness in his life; 3) The norms of society confuse him. Unapproved behaviors are required to achieve goals because society provides inadequate socially approved means for actually attaining socially approved goals; 4) Isolated, he does not share the dominant values and beliefs of his culture; 5) Estranged from self, he undertakes work or other activities to gain approval or rewards from others, rather than for his own satisfaction or approval.

19. "Sunt lacrimae rerum et mentem mortalia tangunt," Vergil, *Aeneid*, Book IV.

CHAPTER SEVEN

Naming Shame and Stigma

In the last chapter we looked at hell and sin and how deception prevents people from claiming responsibility for the evil in which they have participated. Wispy, sugar-coated lies mask evil choices. In fact, many would claim that evil sounds too harsh. This perspective avows that no one really commits evil. People are merely trapped by their upbringing. They are victims of circumstance. Unfortunately this well-intentioned viewpoint implicitly denies human freedom. It leaves human beings to the whim of family context or the mercy of social planners.

We have seen too how the contemporary person vaguely blurs the origins of evil. Few deny hell or sin, they just don't "see it," or they say that these terms are irrelevant relics of a medieval age. The realities of social injustice, of lying, of leveraging out and then bankrupting trusted institutions, of manipulating a company's equity to destroy pension funds, and of killing upwards of 150,000 Iraqis to protect our "way of life" get swept under the carpet. There these deceptions twist and roil beneath the surface of our lives – hidden. No one is responsible.

The Struggle for Honesty

Karen Horney, the psychologist, stated that each of us has a sequence of ways in which we avoid the truth. We establish a pattern of resistance which we domesticate and which becomes so much a part of us that we resent any intrusions. "The basic factors that no one wants to modify one iota," according to Horney, "are those that concern secret claims on life, claims for 'love,' for power, for independence and the like, illusions about one's self, the safety zones within which a person moves with comparative ease."[1] In fact, she says a major crisis occurs when these factors are challenged and our patterns of resistance collapse.

Classical spiritual writers called this pattern of resistance, *mortifera*, literally a death-bearing pattern. By hiding our true selves, by cloaking our inner selves under the guise of righteousness, by masking destructive behavior with perfectionism – whatever the pattern is – we bring death not only to our relationships, but to our very selves. For this reason Ignatius of Loyola suggested that retreatants should ask in prayer for the grace to feel *shame and confusion* over their destructive choices.[2] Only if we *feel* the disorder, can we be open to healing. Without this remorse, our death-bearing patterns becomes a life-stance by which we close ourselves off from other people. So Ignatius encouraged the retreatant to pray for the grace to *feel* shame. It is an extraordinary request, but it is truly a grace when we take responsibility for who we are and for what we have done. We wish no longer to hide for the evil we have done, but rather to be restored to our authentic selves.

We can easily prettify sin. A mother slaps her child around, but explains, "Well, I was just crabby that day." Or a husband forgets an important promise he made to his wife (for the 10th time): "Well, honey, my computer crashed this morning." Or "I know I was unfaithful, but I've been under a lot of pressure lately." So in our prayer, we ask, "Gracious God, help me to be honest. Take away the perfume, the soft lights, the fancy language – all that cloaks the fact of sin. Disperse whatever chokes off my true self and bring me back to You, the truth and wellspring of my life."

Southern Charm

We should not naively think, however, that simply being honest sets us on the path of healing and holiness. These two words hold a host of complex patterns. To illustrate the complexity, as well as the pathos and humor, in human relationships, we might turn to the novelist Ferrol Sams. In *Run With the Horsemen*, Sams describes the power that a Southern woman held over her normally upright husband who occasionally went on a bender. This gen-

tleman's notorious explosions, occurring in the still frontier-fla-
vored county seat and ignored by law enforcement officers, were
devastatingly embarrassing to the family. The children were deaf,
with as much aloofness as possible, to the snickering comments
of classmates on Monday. Sams describes the infallible pattern:

> The mother's reaction was consistent. She consoled the
> children by blaming these violent manifestations of re-
> leased passions on the War (World War I) and the mys-
> terious tortures their father had endured while "overseas"
> – a distinctly different condition from being "abroad."
> She conquered the father by never evincing the slightest
> show of anger but by being "hurt." This is a Southern
> synonym, usually used by women, for genteel and refined,
> slightly Christian, and very martyred suffering. In the
> hands of an intelligent and artistic expert, it is a formi-
> dable weapon indeed.
>
> It guarantees forgiveness, a condition which the offender
> may not desire but can hardly refuse, and promises a
> fairly immediate return to the emotional status quo, a
> state the offender most devoutly covets. It involves grief,
> but the grief has to be silent, manifested by brimming
> eyes, the wordless splash of a reproachful tear, the very
> slight reddening of a beautiful and aristocratic nose. It
> is a condition which can never be utilized by a coarse-
> featured simple peasant of a female susceptible to aban-
> doned sobbing or other uninhibited behavior. A
> Southern man with any sophistication of breeding who
> hears, "I want you to know that I'm not mad, I'm just
> hurt," in soft controlled tones knows immediately that
> the ball game is over, the race has been run, and his
> shoulders are pinned firmly to the mat.[3]

Sams describes patterns of deception so finely woven that we
should pause to smile and enjoy it before we start tugging at its
threads: the father, we know, will go on other binges; no redemption is possible because the underlying *mortifera* never gets confronted. The mother maintains genteel, aristocratic control by
ever-so mildly shaming her husband. And the children learn the
lessons well by feigning aloofness and ignorance among their
friends at school. We see immediately that the patterns for avoid-
ing the truth are legion. Their attractiveness is that they tempo-

rarily buy a bit of peace. Long term, however, they sacrifice the
self. Let us name a few more:

1) A person may defer to authority – always. If I am a student,
   I am always seeking to please my teachers. I do everything
   they ask me. Even more than they ask me, I anticipate what
   they might want. "He's a good guy so he'll take care of me.
   If I just work harder, everything will be okay."

2) Or a young woman, out of fear of her mother's disapproval,
   becomes enmeshed in perfectionism: "If I'm perfect, if I
   get good grades, if I date the right guy, Mom will finally
   recognize me for who I am."[4]

3) Or a man who always avoids confrontation. "I'm afraid of
   my own anger. I want to be liked."[5] To avoid the anger that
   might erupt from a friend who has a drinking problem, he
   covers up for him. In fact he avoids seeing him because he
   does not want to confront him nor even be reminded of his
   responsibility.

Abraham Low, founder of Recovery, Inc. said that intellec-
tualizing about our problems is complex but easy, while doing
something about them is simple but difficult. Shame-based intellectuals love to discuss and complexify. So this prayer of St.
Ignatius "for shame and confusion" asks for the grace to feel the
discordance, to touch the brokenness. It is salutary for us to be
honest, so we pray for healing to be single-hearted since God is
also single-hearted.

Addiction and Recovering Desire

Gerald May, a psychiatrist, defines addiction as any compulsive,
habitual behavior that limits the freedom of human desire.[6] The
drivenness in any addiction arises from the belief that I must hide
my flaws from others. It is a powerful drive and constitutes another
well-known, defensive pattern, which chokes off our genuine self.
Ironically, the addiction – whether it be overwork, compulsive
buying or gambling – attempts to provide an intimate relationship.
The workaholic with his work, the alcoholic with her booze are
having a love affair. Each avoids loneliness and hurt – however
temporary – which are the underbelly of shame. Each creates

life-damaging consequences which block intimacy and create
more shame.

In addiction, May says, desire attaches to specific objects.
This relationship of addiction and attachment is intricate. For
one thing, the brain never completely forgets its old attachments.
In fact, addictions are able to exist for years completely outside
our awareness. Only when they are frustrated or bring us into
repeated conflict, do we start to notice how attached, that is
defended, we truly are. Our genuine desires are then blocked by
competing cosmetic substitutes. Earlier, in Chapter Three, we
talked about the power of desire and how our genuine desires
put us in touch with our true self, with our ideals, and especially
with our aspiration to union with God. Addictions inhibit these
healthy desires and block the avenue to intimacy because they
arise from my ruptured self.

In May's definition of addiction, behavior indicates that
action is essential to addiction. Narcotic users, for example, talk
about doing drugs. The action encodes both the masking and the
drive. In May's understanding of this dynamic, even images,
memories, fantasies, ideas and feeling states can become such
actions and, therefore, objects of attachment. For example, ob-
sessive thoughts – the worry that refuses to go away – show a
pattern of addiction.[7] Even though there may be minimal external action, a person acts them out internally over and over again.
The first step, therefore, is to stop the destructive action which
becomes possible only when greater values break through or when
a breakdown occurs to interrupt the action.

The Nature of Shame

In order to trace the roots of addiction and of our dishonesty
with ourselves, we need to examine the origins of shame, how it
is distinguished from guilt, and how it is related to the social
dynamic of stigma. We will then identify the gospel strategy of
how the "truth might set us free."[8]

In his popular book on shame, John Bradshaw says that
healthy shame helps us to keep our human boundaries.[9] It lets
us know we can and will make mistakes and that we need help.
It tells us that we are not God.[10] Healthy shame allows the child
to internalize boundaries, to fit into society, to develop friend-

ships, to grow into autonomy, to become self-reliant, and eventually as an adult to mediate the bounds of intimacy. It acknowledges that I did something wrong and I am ashamed of it. The antidote to a bad choice is to acknowledge straight away, "I did it. I was wrong. I'm sorry." Healthy shame is noted for its brevity! It is not drawn out, complicated, or hidden. It sheds a clear, clean light. It is this kind of "shame" which Ignatius encourages the retreatant to ask for as a grace during the *Spiritual Exercises*. Such shame illuminates the goodness of the person who can acknowledge the transgression. I did this, but I know I can do better. My better self has greater capacities.

Since shame touches our identity, however, we cannot learn anything new from more shame. It can, in fact, be transformed into shame as a defensive state of being. As a state of being, shame moves from setting our boundaries to taking over our whole identity. It then creates the belief that I am flawed. I am defective in the intimate core of who I am. In this state, it becomes toxic and dehumanizing. Shame then touches the very identity of the person.

This toxic shame begins to contaminate the core self. It engenders dependent, addictive behavior. It saps strength and self-reliance leading to a disempowering dependence on objects/persons outside one's self. It smothers the genuine self. Inevitably this toxic shaming has sexual manifestations or causes since it touches the most central dimensions of our being.

In toxic shame the self becomes an object of its own contempt. If I am an object that cannot be trusted, then I wish to hide or escape myself. Toxic shame generates its own rack of torture. I have shame about shame. I am isolated and imprisoned in the masks of myself, haunted by absence and emptiness.

Hidden in this darkness, shame festers like a canker in the soul. Oozing woundedness, it subtly draws attention to itself. Beneath the hiding lies the insatiable narcissism of a hurting person. It shudders at the possibility of being touched by anyone. Shame-based persons guard against exposing their inner self to others, but more significantly, they guard against exposing themselves to themselves.

Some religious groups reinforce this toxic shaming. They teach how wretched and full of sin a person is. They distort original sin. They may preach the importance of breaking the child's willfulness rather than beholding the child as a gift of God's abundant love. In a shaming congregation, God keeps score. God is punitive. In a shaming congregation, the human person is a worm, flawed, defective, and barely escaping from the (deserved) fires of hell.

Religious groups in general have not given emotions much support. They have, for instance, been more intent on repressing anger and sexuality than on enabling people to integrate these powerful emotions into their lives. Some churches may resort to shame, rather than helping people acknowledge, interpret and integrate their own volatile instincts, emotions, and desires. Rather than opening the door to redemption, these churches thereby condemn people to a cycle of estrangement from themselves, from God, and from others.

Families, likewise, may never let go of some shameful family secret. At an unconscious level they may contrive a pact never to let out the secret of Mom's mental illness or of a brother's compulsive gambling. They become identified with the shame. Instead of a black sheep found and rejoiced in, each person in the family becomes dead ended around the shameful event. In contrast, the biblical story depicts the good shepherd seeking out the lamb that was lost and returning with it on his shoulders. In actual fact, lambs who become separated from the fold can become paralyzed, so at least in this biblical vignette, the shepherd carries it back. The image suggests that a shame-based group or an individual who is lost does not have the resources to find one's self. It would take the miracle of someone or some group reaching out, finding them, and lifting them up to restore them to the fold.

Carl Jung described how difficult it may be for some parishioners to approach their pastors about the painful details of their sexual disturbances. Jung commented that parishioners rightly suspect that their pastors' moral prejudices are even stronger than their dogmatic biases. To underline his point Jung told a droll story about the American president, "Silent Cal" Coolidge:

> When [Coolidge] returned after an absence one Sunday morning, his wife asked him where he had been. "To church," he replied.
>
> "What did the minister say?"
>
> "He talked about sin."
>
> "And what did he say about sin?"
>
> "He was against it."[11]

People do not feel accepted unless what they perceive as the very worst in them is accepted as well. No one can convey this acceptance in mere words. It can come about only through our sincerity, but especially by our attitude toward ourselves and our own dark side. If we reject or deny the evil we have done or the dimension of our self vectored toward evil, we will do the same with a parishioner, a patient, or a friend. We cannot encourage change in anyone unless we accept them. Condemnation does not liberate, it oppresses. We become the oppressor of the person we condemn, not a friend and fellow-sufferer. This openness certainly does not mean that we must never judge or make decisions in the cases of persons whom we desire to help, but if we wish to help a human being, we must be able to accept them as they are. And we can not do this until we have accepted ourselves as we are.[12]

These perspectives on shame and acceptance permeate cultures. Sports teams may set out to humiliate their rivals. The systematic rape of Muslim women by the Serbs engenders horrifying violence and shame. The Treaty of Versailles at the end of World War I shamed Germans, a dynamic that set in motion the possibility for a demagogue like Hitler to whip up a frenzied reaffirmation of homeland Germany superior over all others: "Deutschland uber alles."

On the other hand, in the simple handshake between Yassar Arafat, the PLO leader, and Yitzhak Rabin, the Israeli prime minister, we see the power of acceptance to break the cycle of shame. Each could acknowledge, even though reluctantly: "You are people, just as we are."

Shame and Guilt

We need to distinguish shame from its younger cousin, guilt. In brief, *guilt* results from something *I do; shame* results from a sense of *who I am.* Guilt flows from an action I initiate; shame happens to me. Guilt arises during what Erik Erikson calls the third state of psycho-social development (three to five years) when the young child develops the polar balance between initiative and guilt. Shame arises earlier during the second stage of developmental life when the child (fourteen months to three years) develops the polar balance between self-autonomy and shame.

Like shame, guilt can have both a healthy and a toxic form. Healthy guilt forms the emotional core of our conscience. It presupposes internalized rules and develops later than shame. It results from behaving in a manner contrary to our beliefs and values. By acknowledging guilt, we also acknowledge that we could have done better. By acknowledging guilt, we reaffirm our values. We repair the damage of our choices and learn and grow from our mistake.

Part of the modern desire to do away with sin was to eradicate shame and guilt as well. A laudable, but fruitless and even dangerous, exercise. Shame and guilt are not so easily rooted out; in fact, the very attempt may tighten their octopal grip. We need not only to name the shame, but then to explore what its sources are. Some of the causes lie well beyond us individually. They arise from neurotic needs embedded in society itself.

A central feature of both guilt and shame is the instinctive response to hide one's self.[13] Hiding, as a dimension of sinfulness, has recently received much attention from women. Hiding not only buries one's gifts, but it obscures the manipulations and petty lies used to hide one's anxieties.

In an important article Susan Nelson Dunfee explains how this mechanism of hiding functions. Dunfee says that a man's underlying sin may be pride, but a woman's underlying sin may be the sin of hiding.[14] Her thesis is complex, but important, if we are to understand how shame and guilt function.

Dunfee explains that a woman knows guilt for most of her life. She is guilty if she is too assertive; she is guilty if she is too feminine and therefore seductive. She is guilty if she is too brilliant, too articulate, too successful. If she becomes pregnant, she is at fault. If she chooses not to have children, she is guilty of denying her true femininity. If her marriage fails, if her husband loses interest and chooses the attentions of another, it is because she has fallen short.

Guilt takes its toll. It etches its way through the secret lives of women who turn against themselves in self-hatred; who lose themselves in alcohol, drugs, starvation diets; or who hide behind the frenetic activity of trying to please everyone else.

Guilt, Dunfee says, directly relates to the way religion names and proclaims the forms of sin. In Christianity, one knows one's sin and one's guilt, but one also is promised the forgiveness and love of God. In authentic Christian consciousness guilt does not

stand alone, for sin is recognized within the context of the forgiveness and mercy of God which leads to regeneration.[15]

But the guilt of woman, Dunfee continues, does not seem
to have known the same redemptive promise. Rather than guilt
leading to confession of sin, the knowledge of forgiveness, and
the transformation into new life, guilt has led woman into a cycle
of bondage. What has gone wrong? Why has woman often not
experienced the reality of redemption?

The key, Dunfee says, lies within the Christian tradition itself.
In its development of sin as the sin of pride, and in its failure to
develop fully the sin of hiding, Christianity has perpetuated bondage rather than broken it. It has encouraged women to confess
the wrong sin and thereby added to woman's guilt and failed to
call her into her full humanity.

Theologians such as Niebuhr, Augustine, Luther, Aquinas,
and John Calvin have focused on pride as the fundamental, primary sin. According to Dunfee, they taught a one-sided truth:
that a person engorged with pride lacks trust in God. A prideful
person turns away from the One in relation to Whom one can
know one's full humanity. Filled with anxiety and faced with
attempting to hold one's life together – without God as center –
the prideful person chooses a god other than God – around which
to focus one's life.

When "humanity seeks to overcome its insecurity by a will-
to-power, when it over-reaches the limits of human creatureliness,
when it pretends that it is not limited, it becomes infected with
the sin of pride," Dunfee explains.

Dunfee adds, however, that humanity can also seek to solve
the problem of finitude and freedom by hiding its freedom and
by losing itself behind some apparent good. Some male theologians, such as Niebuhr, have defined this latter sin as the sin of
sensuality, but in doing so, Dunfee says, they fail to recognize that
sensuality is only one of the many manifestations of the sin of
hiding. By naming it as sensuality, Niebuhr reveals the male bias
of seeing woman as both temptress and seducer. Eve, the seduc-
tress, the carnal, the culpable, earthly one lures man – the spiritual
one – into the sin of carnality.

In fact, however, through the sin of hiding, women escape
their true self. They escape from freedom. Hence the sin of hiding
can just as easily take the form of servile devotion to another. A
person, but especially a woman, may expend her vital energies

not in the acceptance of her own freedom but in running away from that freedom by pouring those energies into the life of another.

Proposing self-sacrifice as the goal of human life creates an added ambiguity. Niebuhr describes self-sacrificial love as the total giving of one's self for the sake of another. But, for a woman, especially, such self-sacrifice can be a religiously approved mask for the sin of hiding. It can be nothing more than an escape from self. For such a woman, the virtue and sin become synonymous. Thus Christianity has ironically encouraged the sin of hiding.

A theology that recognizes only pride as the primary form of sin perpetuates woman's bondage to her hiddenness. It does not call her to emerge from the state of hiddenness. Furthermore, because self-assertion is equated with the sin of pride, women who acknowledge their desire to be a self feel bound with guilt and anxiety.

Cut off from herself, alienated from others, hidden woman lives a submerged existence. She bears the name of evil, fallen woman, when she seeks to fulfill herself in ways other than the role of mother. She is the woman who waits seven years for her husband to decide who *he* is going to be so that she can know who she is. She is the woman who feels guilty for every dollar spent on baby-sitting or continuing education and for every moment spent away from home, and who agonizes over every slip that reveals a submerged motive. She is the woman who apologizes for having her own thoughts and who in guilt hides her creativity because it seems too much like self-assertion.

She has been guilty of the sin of hiding; inasmuch as she has poured herself into vicarious living, inasmuch as she has denied her sense of self in total submission to husband/father/boss or in total self-giving to children, job, or family, she has been guilty of the sin of hiding She has hidden from her full humanity.[16] Rather than show her hand, her "manus," and reveal herself, she "mani-pulates" from shadows. Asserting her selfhood would be threatening because then she would need to emerge from the hidden shadows and be herself.

The question arises, "How can this hiding be a sin, when women are *trained* towards this life? Whose sin?" This question moves us toward briefly exploring the relationship of social and personal sin.

Sin is whatever destroys or blocks our relationships with God, with self, and with others. We are not talking here about personal culpability, but rather destructive forces which we inherit as part of our culture and which govern our lives. Sin comprises death-dealing patterns which prevent the free sharing of our gifts. Theologians used to speak of these death-dealing patterns as original sin, which were passed down from generation to generation. But too often their explanations for original sin were too mechanical, too impersonal. A better term might be originating sin, the choices made by our ancestors which continue to impact us and to erode our God-given dignity. For instance, legitimized slavery, even 130 years after its end, still impacts white and black relationships. The leveraged buy-outs of the 1980s destroyed the pensions for some conservatively managed companies causing workers over the next several decades to live out their retirement in penury.

If we say then that a person has been "guilty of the sin of hiding," it may simply mean she or he has been conditioned to habits of servitude. It may also be an invitation to recognize finally how one has "bought into the system" and to take the first tremulous steps towards a greater degree of personal freedom. Any genuine step towards personal freedom will necessarily challenge the system of destructive relationships.

The God who judges human pride also judges human hiding and passivity. God does not demand a sacrifice of the self. Rather, God invites the contrite heart to seek forgiveness. God then beckons the forgiven self to affirm her full humanity through accepting her call to freedom.

Shame and Stigma

Having delved into the dynamics of shame and guilt, we are now prepared to examine how stigma operates in our society. Shame and stigma share a similar anonymity. Shame thrives in hiding. Stigma, wielded by a society in denial, brands people publicly so that they conspire to hide themselves. By hiding the pain, by muting anger and by burying fears of abandonment, both shame and stigma support a malaise of helplessness. Jews in Germany, Catholics in the South of the U.S., Blacks throughout the U.S., Japanese-Americans on the West Coast during World War II have all shared the fate of the stigmatized. So too have gays and lesbians, people with mental illness, and people with AIDS.

Stigma connects intimately with who a person is. It marks the body in order to control the power and energy flowing out from sexuality, from nonconformist behavior, from any deviancy which society dreads. We can see an extreme example of this marking of the body in the Nazi concentration camps where the Jews, Gypsies, and dissidents were branded on their flesh.

Society uses stigma to set itself apart, to claim, "We are elite, we are special. You are inferior, but so long as you accept our branding iron, we will tolerate you." In Nathaniel Hawthorne's classic *The Scarlet Letter*, the community "brands" Hester Prynne as an adulteress. By hanging a scarlet "A" (for adultery) around her neck, it sets her apart. It not only lays out her sin for all to see, but publicly names her as other. You are "not-us." Much hypocrisy surrounds this stigmatization of Hester, not least of which arises from her partner in adultery, Dimmesdale, who is the popular preacher in the local Congregational Church. The sin of their adulterous love results in a child, Pearl, as in the biblical pearl of great price. Hester bears the child publicly, but Dimmesdale hides his fatherhood. The child, however, breaks silence. Pearl identifies her father with simple and child-like clarity. In doing so, she manifests the grace of love.

Church attitudes toward gays and lesbians reveal the dynamics of a shame-based religion furiously at work. The Vatican and much of the Religious Right in the U.S. have declared that people with a homosexual orientation are fundamentally disordered, but so long as gays hide their shame, they will not be hurt. The Vatican declares in effect, there will be no shame, no stigma, so long as you hide it.[17] The perfect bind. If a gay person accepts the stigma, then the dominant culture need only finger point at the shame in order to control behavior. Of course, coming out of the closet to join in solidarity with others breaks this shaming power.

Until recently Christianity held a similar kind of power over women. Among the many taboos around women's sexuality was the unvoiced assumption that menstruation and menopause were vaguely sinful, certainly unclean, and could not be talked about. At least some women shared their biological realities among themselves but not in public. In fact, wasn't it men's fear that needed protecting? All that blood and darkness. By hiding female body functions under taboo, stigma, and shame, the dominant (patriarchal) culture protected its own.

These same stigmatizing dynamics occur in the hyper-fear, ostracizing, and panic surrounding AIDS. As an infectious epidemic, the disease arouses the primitive urge to expel the sick one. Since the majority of AIDS patients in this country are male homosexuals, the disease arouses homophobic fears which erupt from the incomplete integration of one's own sexuality. Religious fundamentalists, for instance, readily claim that the disease results from God's righteousness. It is the judgment of God on the "sin of homosexuality."

Mental illness falls under a similar stigma. So much fear surrounds this illness that society reverts to its most primitive form of protection, by branding such persons outcast. It marks, sets apart, and forsakes people with mental illness as different from the rest of humanity. As long as people with mental illness accept the brand of shame, society can control and dispose of them as it sees fit. It can protect itself from involvement. It can cloak the facts of mental illness in mystery and encourage everyone, even family members, to maintain the great silence.

An organization which has helped enormously to break the code of silence and to unravel the binding myths of mental illness has been the National Alliance for Mental Illness (N/AMI). Composed of both family members and "consumers," N/AMI has brought practical, knowledgeable support to families by encouraging them to share their painful isolation and to band together, it has pioneered legislative reform, and through educational programs it has reduced unwarranted fears about this disease.

Since so much guilt has unjustly been laid on parents, N/AMI often begins its sessions with families by having everyone stand up and declare in unison: "Not guilty!" Rather than focusing on fruitless blaming, N/AMI explores the biological causes of the illness and the sociological conditions which prevent a person from receiving medical treatment and spiritual/healing resources. Recently though its Religious Outreach program, it has recognized the powerful role that communities of faith can play in welcoming home and accepting those with mental illness.[18]

A Source of Shame: Broken Mirrors

Infants know who they are through reflective mirrors. Without them they perish psychologically. Mirroring is crucial. Parents who are shut down emotionally cannot mirror and affirm their children's emotions. Consequently when children have shame-based parents, they identify with them.

Abandonment or the threat of abandonment shatters the mirror and creates the fear that I can cease to exist. Out of fear of abandonment, we develop masks (pleasing, manipulative, aggressive, nice) so that we will never, never be abandoned again.

If someone else loves me for who I actually am, my mask melts. It becomes irrelevant. I experience both sorrow and joy. I regret the years lost to maintaining a facade, and I rejoice at the discovery of my self as I am. Now all that energy directed to preserving the mask can be directed toward what I genuinely want to do. This time of revelation can also be a highly vulnerable, fragile time, so the support of a trusted friend or spouse or counselor is often crucial for long-term healing.

Who Shall Deliver Me?

Toxic shame ultimately is a spiritual problem. It flows from spiritual bankruptcy in some part of who we are. For our toxic shame to be healed, we must be willing to come out of hiding. As long as we hide our shame, nothing can touch us. In order to change we must expose our toxic shame, following an adage from therapy: "the only way out is through." Opening up our shame involves pain, which is precisely what we have been trying to avoid all along. Of course, the more we avoid it, the worse it gets. We cannot change our internalized shame until we externalize it within a safe, healing relationship.[19]

When I realized a few days after I arrived in the psych ward in 1975 that I had had a nervous breakdown, I was stunned. I was shocked. I felt that the stigma of mental illness would now mark me forever. For a few days, I wanted to hide. I told the staff that I did not want any more visitors. Before long, however, I knew that I could have a part in how people interpreted my experience. At least some would take their clues from me. "Trust." "Trust and listen."

During the second week of my hospitalization, the attending psychiatrist invited me to speak to a group of Portland police officers for whom he was conducting a seminar on mental illness. I accepted. A bit wobbly, I described what had occurred to me and responded to their questions. From them I learned that they were often not only the arrestors of bizarre behavior, but the first caregivers for the mentally ill. I was impressed with their willingness to learn and their openness to me. A small, first step in interpreting my experience – publicly.

Not long after I left the hospital, I decided to attend a large gathering of Jesuits. Mike, one of my friends there, no doubt sensing my ambiguity about joining this public gathering, asked me a couple of questions about how I was doing. He then asked, "Isn't it hard for you to be here?" Implicit in his questions, I think, was, "Don't you feel awkward, out of touch, even stigmatized in this setting?" I forced myself to respond as openly as I could. I do not remember what I said. I do recall the care and acceptance with which Mike expressed his concern. Another step.

I knew I had a choice. I could go into hiding or I could share who I was. These risks at going public also gave me grist for the mill in my bi-weekly sessions with my psychiatrist.

Silence, fear, and projections lie at the heart of stigma. By breaking the silence, by caring for ourselves as much as we are able rather than projecting our needs onto erstwhile experts, by seeking help from appropriate, competent resources, and by joining with others who are also marginalized, we can break the bonds of stigma.

The Danish people spontaneously understood this power in 1942 when the Nazis proclaimed an order for every Jew to wear the yellow Star of David on their arm. The next day the Danes, led by the King of Denmark, universally armed themselves with the Star of David in open defiance of the Nazi invaders. This stigma became a mark of national pride, of mutual affirmation, and human solidarity. Later in 1943, when the Nazis threatened to round up all the Jews in the country, the Danes organized a massive flotilla of boats to ferry the remaining Jews across the water to a safe harbor in neutral Sweden.

By accepting the stigma of my mental illness, I could explore my own depth experience with others and receive their care and support which could open the doors to friendship and intimacy. Such relationships heal the wounds and build a caring community.

With friends or during solitary walks on an ocean beach, I discovered or coined the psychological and spiritual language to interpret my experience. Stigma, unfortunately, alienates persons from the sources, communal and spiritual, which could wash the shame and pour balm on the pain. It hides the pain so that no one has to deal with it. Most of all, it hides us from the God who heals, the God who touches wounds with loving care and finally transforms them.

If the stigma is opened, touched, and healed, it may become the stigmata, a proud badge of the healing that we have undergone and a source of grace for others.

A More Radical Acceptance

Beneath the shame, beneath the guilt, beneath the stigma, we can see the yearning for acceptance in each and all of us. We can see the foundational need of radical acceptance. Earlier I described how the mantra "Trust" came to me as a chant in the psych ward. Such trust, cleansed of its compulsivity, provides the grounds for healing. It is at the core of faith, which Paul Tillich describes as the courage to accept acceptance. It opens our flinty hearts to the Source who courses through all our life, from whose wellsprings we receive the life-giving waters of forgiveness.

The biblical writer of the Book of Genesis reports God's acceptance of human creatures as we are – with nothing to hide. The nakedness of Adam and Eve symbolize their true and authentic selves.[20] And God said, "it was good." The writer explains, "And they knew no shame." They could be open to who they were. They had nothing to hide. Job later echoes this radical acceptance: "naked I came into the world, naked I leave it, blessed be the name of the Lord."[21] Nakedness symbolizes the unconditional acceptance of our very self which God offers us which God invites us to extend to others.

The biblical writer, all too aware of human failing, violence, and cruelty, portrayed how the refusal to accept our real selves created in the same instance a powerful false self. By seeking to be "like the gods," we deny our human selves and paradoxically fall into destructive ways. This non-acceptance results in a cover up, it erodes the self, and finally chokes off the very intimacy and mutuality with others for which we yearn.

God's enduring care is not simply an add-on in our journey towards union and fullness. Rather God pervades, sustains, and nourishes us throughout each breath and moment of our days. Spirituality describes our experience of this relationship. It enhances and expands life. It embodies growth, newness, and creativity. It frees our spirit by keeping us in touch with the ultimate ground of being, with the holy mystery, with the Spirit through whom we live and move and have our being. Thus spirituality is not an add-on. It is not one more workshop. It is not one more choice among the smorgasbord offerings of the Enneagram, Family of Origins, T-Groups, Men's or Women's Issues, Shame and Guilt Workshops. In fact, a debilitating drawback to all these self-help works is that spirituality becomes simply one more therapeutic technique. These workshops, these "works" to paraphrase Martin Luther, convict us. Without the God Who IS, without the God Who Loves me into being, I am condemned to a non-ending cycle of self-perpetuating "working" to be lovable. That's what "sin" and "condemnation" under the Law were for both Luther and Paul.

Two of the more popular self-help evangelists, Scott Peck, *The Road Less Traveled,* and John Bradshaw, *Healing the Shame that Binds,* seem to suggest spirituality as such an add-on rather than as integral, life-bestowing grace for the journey. In fact, Peck describes grace as those serendipitous moments when nothing else can explain what has happened. He seems to relegate grace to breakthroughs from the preternatural world or to whatever cannot be explained by natural causes.

Bradshaw similarly describes spirituality as one more weapon in the arsenal to unmask shame. The title of his book *Healing the Shame* suggests the self as healing the shame – admittedly in conjunction with other shamed individuals, admittedly through a beneficial Twelve Step Program. He describes a self-centered, rather than a Spirit-centered spirituality. Condemned to healing one's shame instead of receiving Spirit, the individual *works* at his therapy. He or she strives to nourish their inner child, and, of course, attends a host of workshops. Bradshaw does, however, offer an excellent diagnosis of the dynamics of shame, which I have relied on extensively.

In the vision which I am presenting (or giving a glimmer of), Spirit groans within the fiber of our being. Spirit gives birth to the self which images the face of God in loving freedom and freeing love. Spirit, just as a nursing Mother, washes, bathes, and renews us throughout each moment of the day. With an overflow of love, we seek in service to share this abundance with others. My own vision would be more closely aligned with Gerald May who places the emphasis on God's initiative and invites the person to take responsibility within the bounds of one's own gifts and capacities. It assumes a divine-human partnership. It flourishes on intimacy with God which allows a person's creativity to overflow in service and compassion for others.

Bradshaw and Peck, on the other hand, show up regularly in the self-help section. Their work has obviously inspired many people, but, ultimately, I believe that people who follow their approach will become stuck, because in their quest for spiritual wholeness they will rely on the same personal mechanisms which led to destruction in the first place. Nothing breaks the cycle.

Carmen's Story

Carmen, 44, divorced for nine years, was sexually abused by her father over a two-year period when she was eight to ten years old. When her mother discovered the situation, she divorced her husband. The young girl was never told why the parents divorced, but she knew it was her fault because her father had told her that "something bad would happen" if she ever told anyone about what they were doing together. "My parents got divorced and it was my fault," she vaguely remembered.

A year later, when she was 11, Carmen became very chunky. In her late teens she had a boyfriend, but she broke off their relationship when he got "too fresh." At 21, already weighing 250 pounds, she married impulsively a handsome service man, but he "just used me. All he wanted was someone to do his laundry and to keep the home fires burning."

When she came to me for spiritual direction, she weighed 300 pounds, and had been in therapy for eight years. Her weight was damaging her overall health. During our third session together, I asked her how her psychotherapy and group therapy were going and whether she had any goals in therapy. She was reluctant to talk about it, but after a short time said:

"Dr. E. is very good. The group gets down on me to maintain my diet and to keep going to Weight Watchers" (talks on for a while about the group).

"How do you feel about the group?"

"Oh, they're a wonderful group of people, but they don't really know what I need" (starts to talk about each member of the group and their individual problems).

"So how do you feel about them?"

(Pauses) "Frustrated, sometimes."

"Frustrated?" I asked.

"They make me angry."

"Hmmn."

"They don't understand me."

"That must be hard," I said sympathetically.

(Starts to weep lightly, then bites her lip). "Everyone tells me what to do."

"How's that?"

"They don't understand how hard it is. (Sniffles) Dr. E. doesn't either."

"Oh?"

(Then from out of the blue) "I got mad at Dr. E. five years ago and stopped telling him what was really going on with me."

(Now we had something to deal with anyway!)

Carmen had learned several lessons very well. She cleverly maintained several dodges for hiding herself. Early on, out of dread of being abandoned, out of shame, she learned to hide from her sexuality. As the years passed and she continued to stifle her self, she became suffused with undefinable rage. We might also surmise that she encircled herself symbolically with her weight so that she was cushioned against her deepest feelings. After all, her sexuality had "caused" the horrible abandonment by her father and the break-up of her parents' marriage. Her weight covered up these feelings. It became a mark of shame behind which she could bunker in. Well-defended, she could play hide and seek. The therapeutic group, her friends, even Dr. E., could point to her weight and tell her what to do. She could tell them whether they were right or not. They were not.

Her verbal pattern offered another hiding device. She spoke in a verbose, diffused manner, which dammed up her feelings and allowed them to trickle out. Whenever she and I surfaced some emotion or touched the truth together, she started to ramble.

Her teary sadness provided another mask. Her sniffles, the tears of a helpless victim, came from her head, rather than from her gut: "Nobody knows how hard it is. Nobody knows what I am going through." Unfortunately, nothing touched her below the neck. Her tears could elicit sympathy, but not compassion.

Her spirituality also kept her in hiding. Making visits to the church when it was largely empty, she was devoted to Christ in the tabernacle. She clung to the hidden Eucharist.

Developmentally she was stuck at Erikson's Stage Two (learning the balance between self-autonomy and shame). Filled with shame, she turned her power over to others so that they might take care of her. This dynamic led to an endless series of shaming events as she was exposed. So, even though she was an intelligent, well-educated woman, her coping skills were regressive. In fact, she had manipulated her previous therapy by hiding from her psychiatrist – offering apparent cooperation. Not only did she shut out Dr. E, but she could use him against himself, against her self: "Dr. E. says that tears are good," she repeated to me as she dabbed a tear from her eye.

Within the first few months she was fearful that I would leave her like all the others. She brought up her fears indirectly and often in a "hit and run" mode. Toward the end of a session, she might say, "Well, I suppose you have to run off now to see someone else before we're finished." or "I don't suppose you have time to see me next week." When she did this, I expressed my anger to her, even as I maintained my genuine appreciation and care for her. These initial sessions were difficult for both of us, but in time Carmen started to express her fears more directly. She could claim what she needed rather than repressing her dread of abandonment and projecting onto me her needs for a savior figure. Most of all, she needed to be loved and accepted for who she was.

Her prayer was a rich resource and comfort to her, although much of it was tainted and conditioned by her shaming dynamic. Beneath her nice exterior raged the fires of anger at being told what to do by people for whom she had lost respect. She had yet to express any anger toward God (for abandoning her to her lot?).

Fortunately she stayed with her now-focused anger at Dr. E. Independently she arrived at a decision to change therapists. A scary step to leave her therapist of eight years, but a positive one, now that she was conscious of how Dr. E. supported her hiding, shaming behavior. She knew that she could be angry without fear of annihilation. With another psychiatrist she developed a comprehensive program with realistic goals.

She also found a simple formula from AA helpful: **HALT** (**H**-unger **A**-nger **L**-oneliness **T**-iredness). This acronym functioned as a warning sign. It signaled her that she needed to take an emotional inventory. Whenever she was excessively hungry, angry, lonely or tired, she listened to her body and at times sought help from a friend.

Not surprisingly, she found regular exercise the most difficult point of the program. She was ashamed of having people see her body in a swimming pool or in a public gym. She made considerable progress in other areas, especially in being more direct with her anger and thereby less manipulative. She moved gradually to an acceptance of herself with grace, rather than fitting into some stereotypical pattern of who "she should be." Rather than being defined by society or by her ex-husband or by the therapeutic profession or by me, she now had the possibility of shaping her own boundaries.

I had thought that a fuller experience of the Eucharist might augur another transformation for her, but my hypothesis remained unresolved when she eventually moved out of town to take a new job.

Woman with the Issue of Blood

The story of the woman with the issue of blood in the Gospel of Mark exemplifies the breaking of social stigma, taboos, and boundaries.[22] The scripture scholar Karen Barta comments that the Marcan story centers on the human struggle of the woman to express and realize a demand addressed to Jesus, the miracle worker. Opposition to her demands by the coterie of disciples surrounding Jesus provides the tension and boundary which she must willingly overcome. Every reader of this story is invited to break out of a closed world and to demand, to struggle, and to realize a miracle in human life. Observe the opposition she meets in her effort to be cured:

A large crowd followed Jesus and pressed upon him. There was a woman afflicted with hemorrhages for twelve years. She had suffered greatly at the hands of many doctors and had spent all that she had. Yet she was not helped but only grew worse. She had heard about Jesus and came up behind him in the crowd and touched his cloak. She said, "If I but touch his clothes, I shall be cured." Immediately her flow of blood dried up. She felt in her body that she was healed of her affliction.

Jesus, aware at once that power had gone out from him, turned around in the crowd and asked," Who has touched my clothes?" But his disciples said to him, "You see how the crowd is pressing upon you, and yet you ask, "Who touched me?" And he looked around to see who had done it. The woman, realizing what had happened to her, approached in fear and trembling. She fell down before Jesus and told him the whole truth. He said to her, "Daughter, your faith has saved you. Go in peace and be cured of your affliction" (Mk 5:24b-34, *NAB*).

The woman has to overcome formidable opposition. She has to jostle the crowds who surround Jesus. In reaching out to touch him, she has to break Jewish purity regulations since her hemorrhaging (probably menstrual) made her and anyone she touched "unclean." She has to overcome the shame of her disease and the feeling that she had stolen power without authority. She also has to combat the possibility of other's thinking she was attempting to get rid of her disease by passing it on. But her faith prevails. Believing that Jesus is able to absorb her disease without being endangered himself, she reaches beyond the boundaries set by social convention and religious ritual. In so doing, she expresses a faith which transcends the bind of illegitimate, ritual impurity and social stigma. Cured, she immediately owns her experience. And to the disciples' surprise, Jesus commends her bold, assertive faith.

We might ask, how would a modern version of this story read and what would be the general reaction? Would the woman be labeled as self-serving, pushy, unfeminine, too goal-oriented? Would she be considered a woman of faith at all? Of course, these dynamics of hiding and the need to break taboos apply equally to men. Only the content will probably differ.

You might pause again to ask yourself, what taboos constrict
my life? What holds me back from crossing boundaries that enslave? What rewards do I reap from my passivity? What excuses
do I hide behind? What do I hide and what needs touching? When
I have crossed boundaries, what were the results? What specific
obstacles did I have to overcome? What role did my family and
friends play? What lesson have I learned from these experiences?

With a recognition of God as Source in one's life, people
become aware of their own sinfulness as guilt and grieve for what
"I have done." This new awareness flows out of a claim on their
own gifted identity. As they become aware of the God Who IS,
they receive their self in greater fullness which leads – in the same
moment – to spreading the good news. A profound desire to share
the gift of healing flows from their core.[23]

The apostle Peter experiences this calling in an early encounter with Jesus, recorded in Luke 5:1-11. Peter has been fishing
all night and has caught nothing. Jesus comes along, hails the
fishermen, and asks what's up. Hearing that they have caught
nothing all night, Jesus not only tells them but commands them
to cast their nets. "Put out into the deep and lower your nets for
a catch" (Luke 5:4).

Grumbling, no doubt about this carpenter, muttering – "why
doesn't he stick to his wood," Peter does as he is told. He and his
workmates then catch an enormous number of fish and call out
to another boat to help them out. "Astonishment *seized* him."[24]
Peter is touched to the quick precisely in the area in which he
considers himself an expert. Both grateful and grieving, he bursts
out, "Depart from me, O Lord, for I am a sinful man." Peter
intuits that he has been grasped for who he is. He is shaken with
confusion. Aware of whatever sin shadows his life, he repents by
acknowledging holiness itself: "Depart from me, O Lord." This
bright light of love illumines all the darkness of his soul. He
cannot but follow the Lord: "When they brought their boats to
the shore, they left everything and followed him."

This event marks a *first* conversion for Peter: an awareness of
his immediate compelling draw to the Lord. He is seized with
astonishment, with wonder, with gratitude. Within this wonder, he
awakens to all those ways in which he blocks out life itself. Later in
the Gospels we see a *second* conversion in Peter when he claims he
is willing to "go wherever the Lord goes," even unto death. And
finally a *third* conversion when the Lord directs Peter's attention to

caring for others: "Feed by lambs, feed my sheep." But for now we can observe in this first encounter how Peter receives his full identity from the Lord: "you will become fisher of the living ones." The very part which he wishes to suppress, namely his Peter-ity – his fisherman-ness, his sinfulness, all of who he is – lies open before the Lord, who accepts him for all of who he is.   •

Gospel Strategy

What breaks the chain of lying, avoidance, envy, the lust for more, what brings light to *darkness*? The gospel strategy is simple: 1) *Acknowledge* both God and who I am.   2) *Feel* the shame and confusion for my destructive choices, which means I will *feel* the weakness of my self and which may mean some public exposure. 3) *Ask for forgiveness.*

Psychological moderns may muck around in their shame and guilt, which, of course, does not help much. The gospel message is simple, straightforward, encouraging, even colloquial: Yes, you screwed up, don't do it again. Yes, you've had a tough life, now face up to it, accept it, get some help, and move forward. This trait, so rare in American public life, catches us off guard whenever we encounter it. President Kennedy acknowledged up front his blunder at the Bay of Pigs and then moved on. Ross Perot startled the nation with his direct, folksy analysis of the blight that our national debt spreads through the land. Attorney General Janet Reno, after the inferno at Waco, Texas, echoed Harry Truman: "The buck stops here. I'm responsible. I did it. I'm sorry we didn't do a better job."

Few, perhaps none, can walk this path alone. As a vital part of its Twelve Step program, AA recommends getting a sponsor. In Dante's allegorical journey of the soul, for instance, the poet Vergil accompanied him on his tempestuous journey through hell. Later on in Chapter Eleven, we will look more fully at the healing that occurs through a healthy relationship and the need for a spiritguide who cares for us with freeing love.

At the end of this difficult chapter, I would invite the reader to pause and to spend some quiet time, either meditating in silence, or considering where and how toxic shame touches you in your life, or how you hide yourself, or by praying for forgiveness in a destructive relationship.

It may be helpful to consider how the need for forgiveness and the need to forgive others move in tandem. The Christian prayer "forgive us our trespasses as we forgive those who trespass against us" recognizes this linkage.

You may find the following structure for prayer helpful, especially if you pray for the desire to forgive as well as be forgiven:

The Prayer of Forgiveness

Bring to your prayer a person you need or want to forgive.

1. In your own words, tell God[25] what hurt you the most. Share with God, as with a close friend, all of your hurt feelings.

2. Ask God to forgive the person who has/is hurting you.

3. Ask God for the grace to forgive this person yourself. If you really don't want to forgive or can't forgive, ask God to give you at least the grace to want to forgive.

4. Put the person you are trying to forgive into God's hands. Give God all the anger, hurt, resentment that you feel. You do not have to feel concerned if you cannot do this all at once. No one can. Realize that it is okay to have to do this over and over again in your prayer.

5. Make the decision to forgive. Pray: "Gracious God, I choose to forgive_____."

Second prayer time:
 – after the above considerations, you may wish to:

6. Thank God for the experience that caused/causes you pain. Not because the experience itself was good. But because you believe that God will bring something good out of the painful experience you had.

stigma [L. *stigmat-, stigma* mark, brand, fr. Gk, fr. stizen *to tattoo, to prick*] *1. a. archaic: a scar left by a hot iron: brand b. a mark of shame or discredit: stain c. an identifying mark or characteristic: specif: diagnostic sign of a disease*

2. **stigmata** *pl: bodily marks or pains resembling the wounds of the crucified Christ and sometimes accompanying religious ecstasy.*[26]

Endnotes

1. Karen Horney, *Self-Analysis* (New York: W.W. Norton & Co.,1942), p. 271.

2. Ganss, ed., *Spiritual Exercises*, #48, also 63.

3. Ferrol Sams, *Run with the Horsemen* (Peachtree Publishers Limited, 1982), pp. 35-36.

4. Wilkie Au, S.J. and Noreen Cannon, C.S.J., "The Plague of Perfectionism," *Human Development* 13 (Fall, 1992): 5-12.

5. Gary Hankins with Carol Hankins, *Prescription for Anger: Coping with Angry Feelings and Angry People* (New York: Warner Books, 1988, 1993).

6. May, *Addiction and Grace*, p. 14.

7. For an excellent description of the full nature of addiction see May. See also his five point indicator for determining addiction: 1) tolerance, 2) withdrawal symptoms, 3) self-deception, 4) loss of willpower, and 5) distortion of attention. *Ibid.*, pp. 25-31.

8. John 8:32.

9. John Bradshaw, *Healing the Shame that Binds You* (Deerfield Beach, Florida: Health Communications, Inc., 1988).

10. *Ibid.*, p. vii.

11. Jung, *Modern Man in Search of a Soul*, p. 234.

12. *Ibid.*, pp. 234-235. From a faith perspective, as we saw in Chapter Five, such acceptance is possible only because we are ultimately accepted by God.

13. A healthy shame acknowledges that we did wrong. An unhealthy shame hides one's talents out of fear of standing out from the crowd. The author of Genesis recounts the shame of Adam and Eve after their fall from innocence. "And they heard the sound of the Lord God walking in the garden in the cool of the day. The man and his wife hid themselves from the presence of the Lord God" Genesis 3:8.

14. Susan Nelson Dunfee, "The Sin of Hiding: A Feminist Critique of Reinhold Niebuhr's Account of the Sin of Pride," *Soundings* 65 (1982): 316-326.

15. Tad Dunne has said that the traditional Protestant culture of Luther and Calvin tends toward a guilt-ridden ethos. Traditional Catholic culture, on the other hand, tends toward a shame-ridden ethos. The Protestant culture pressures its members to say, "Yes, I did it! I'm guilty," and then offers its members the saving grace of God to cover this heap of ordure. The Catholic culture, on the other hand, encourages people to bury their uniqueness, to cover their pain, to hide their bodies in order that "all may be one." It offers communion within the Church as a sacramental sign of God's saving grace. When shaming techniques fail, then inquisitional techniques batter "deviants" into line. Tad Dunne, S.J., "Guilt and Healing," 42 *Review for Religious* (Jan.-Feb., 1983): 110-117.

16. Dunfee,"The Sin of Hiding," *Soundings*: p. 322.

17. cf. John F. Tuohey, "The C.D.F. and Homosexuals: Rewriting the Moral Tradition," 167 *America* (September 12, 1992): 136-138. In a July 23, 1992

communication from the Congregation for the Doctrine of Faith to American Bishops discouraging legislative support for the non-discrimination of homosexual persons, the C.D.F. declared, "The 'sexual orientation' of a person is not comparable to race, sex, age, etc. . . . . An individual's sexual orientation is generally not known to others unless he (*sic*) publicly identifies himself as having this orientation or unless some overt behavior manifests it. As a rule, the majority of homosexually oriented persons who seek to lead chaste lives do not publicize their sexual orientation. Hence the problem of discrimination in terms of employment, housing, etc., does not usually arise." The inference of the Vatican's message is clear – if you stay in hiding, you will not suffer discrimination.

18. See the excellent video produced by The American Lutheran Church, "A Place to Come Back To," 29 min. (St. Paul: Seraphim Communications, 1568 Eustis Street).

19. Bradshaw, *Healing the Shame*, p. 115.

20. A myth tells a story with spiritual and psychological significance. In interpreting myth, a strict literal reading and application, such as, "we should all disrobe and run around naked in order to symbolize our God-given freedom," would distort the truth which the myth seeks to convey.

21. See "Naked I came from my mother's womb, and naked shall I return there; the Lord gave, and the Lord has taken away; blessed by the name of the Lord." Job 1:21, *NRSV*.

22. See Karen Barta's cogent analysis of this healing event from a feminist perspective in "Healing," *The Gospel of Mark* (Wilmington: Michael Glazier, Inc., 1988), pp. 83-95.

23. A secular version of this dynamic might be: 1) Become relaxed; 2) become aware; 3) become reconciled; 4) become good news.

24. The Greek text reads: *thambos gar perieschen*, a phrase often used for an encounter with divine power.

25. Naturally God is a shorthand word for naming the sacred presence, the Lord, the ground of being, or Source as Life Spirit. I recommend a conversation with God using some personalized name, such as friend, Loving Mother, Gracious Father.

26. *Webster's Third New International Dictionary* (Springfield, Mass.: Merriam-Webster, 1986).

PART THREE

In the Presence of Mystery

Gazing up into the darkness

I saw myself as a creature driven

and derided by vanity;

and my eyes burned with anguish and anger.

— James Joyce, "Araby"[1]

1. *Dubliners* (New York: The Modern Library, 1926), p. 41.

CHAPTER EIGHT

Conversion: Discovering Mystery

Once again a choice. Naming darkness, asking forgiveness. Before the words are half out, light, like shining from shook foil, dazzles us, illuminating folly. Shame long hidden breaks.

"Depart from me, O Lord, for I am a sinful man!"

An angel touches the frozen lips of foolish Zechariah who sings:

And you child will be called the Prophet of the Most High;
Through the tender mercy of our God,
you will announce redeeming love.
Daybreak from on high will visit
those in death's shadow, to guide our feet
into the way of peace. (Luke 1:77-79)

Tongues stutter, babble
fresh wordsong.
Trilling, bursting, spilling music,
then crescendo breathless in the falling darkness,
gashing white
sparkling mystic
in the oneness of the stream.

And after long silence, it is right.

CHAPTER NINE

Forgiving: Sharing Mystery

Conversion may happen in a flash. A sudden, lyrical, transformation. It may jolt us on a journey. It may happen when we see a big smile on the face of a child outside a shanty. It may break upon us in the soft exchange of love or flood in upon us as we walk through a darkening woods and hear the trill of a redbird. In any conversion old patterns suddenly dissolve. We experience radical acceptance by God. We grasp that we are held with care.

This acceptance overcomes division in the self. It unifies us so that our energy flows from our very core outward. Until then, non-acceptance generates interior warfare. We are beside ourselves. We use our energy to hide our self from our self. The experience of acceptance, however, enables us whole-heartedly to accept ourselves and others. Acceptance may carry the meaning better than forgiveness, especially if it includes self-acceptance, a deeper, more vital awareness of who I am, how I uniquely claim who I am, and how in fact I am gifted. Acceptance implies a grateful openness to life, to friendship, to beauty, but in no way a naive surrender to violence. In fact, the very opposite. It embodies a bright, tough resilience, a willingness to confront these dark forces and to protect the gift of self.

Yet at the center of acceptance is forgiveness. If we receive forgiveness, we feel accepted for who we are, rather than for what we have done. And if we grant forgiveness, we accept the other. We love them as we love ourselves.

One day, Peter, the disciple of Jesus, feeling unusually generous, asked, "How often must we forgive our neighbor, seven times?" Pushing his limits, Jesus responded, "Not seven times, but seventy times seven times." Forgiveness cannot be measured; it cannot be doled out. Like self-acceptance, it is an ongoing process. In effect, Jesus says you may need to forgive the person who caused an ancient hurt again and again. In a similar vein, Elie Wiesel, a survivor of Auschwitz, said, "I cannot celebrate the Pasch again (the Jewish high feast) until I have wept to the depths the anguish and the torment of the Holocaust." Years of tears, lamentation, sorrow may need to wash the wounds. Yet, who is to say that these are not the prelude to forgiveness or, more aptly, that the lamentation partakes of the act of forgiveness?

Our concept of forgiveness may be too shallow. As North Americans who emphasize individual rights, we find it hard to let go of our prerogatives, of our hurt, of a talismanic code of an eye for an eye. Furthermore, *working* through neuroses or *doing* our grief work – all worthy endeavors – may set our focus on doing rather than on letting go, on recovery rather than on accepting. In these instances, forgiveness looms as one more monumental task. We may then just want to *do* it, get it over with, or avoid it altogether. The challenge, however, may be to till the ground for forgiveness, and then to sow it, watch how it springs from our spadework as a flowering which we could not have anticipated.

Forgiveness as a Gift

Forgiveness lies both within and beyond the spectrum of our own efforts. Like an ultra-violet light, it has an illumination that eludes our normal range of vision. Yet within the normal range of our capacity, it names the truth, it laments the pain, and it grieves the loss. It affirms: Yes, I was hurt and yes, someone hurt me; and yes, I am now an adult who should be able to let go of these past, even horrible, injuries. Forgiveness involves a risk. For, if I forgive, who will I be? and don't I risk injury all over again? (*a real* possibility for some people). And yet forgiveness does risk the darkness, it does risk the ultra-violet – the light beyond our sight. And it acts. And if it goes well, reconciliation gives an incandescence to my life which was well beyond my doing. If not, I may be hurt again, but perhaps then I will allow myself the space to grow into my own self-acceptance.

Forgiveness resembles the features of revelation which we described earlier: it comes as a surprise; it is a gift beyond reckoning; and it has a power beyond me that not only, reorders, but transforms my orientation towards life. When forgiveness occurs, I begin to see the person who injured me differently.

Is Forgiveness Always Possible?

Many people, especially victims of such heinous crimes as rape or incest, have legitimately asked whether forgiveness is possible or even desirable.[1] The same question needs to be raised by Vietnam veterans, by political prisoners subject to outrageous tortures in shadowy, anonymous cells, and by those silent survivors of our modern day holocausts in Bosnia-Herzegovina, in Iraq, and in Cambodia.

No. Of course not. Forgiveness is not possible in this framing because the question implies that somehow *I* am the one who works the forgiveness. At best, I can ask for the desire to offer forgiveness.

More importantly, by offering forgiveness prematurely people may simply be victimizing themselves. Through premature forgiveness, they may be wounding themselves anew. They may sense that somehow they are responsible, that they are hateful. To let go of the wound, to accept a fresh, renewing orientation, may be possible and devoutly to be wished. But it is also crucial to keep in place that this letting go does not mean that survivors of rape, pillage, or torture let down their defenses. They must not leave themselves open to abuse or to violence all over again. Forgiveness has nothing to do with naiveté. Nor does it imply rushing to forgive people who have not asked for it.

In forgiving we risk who we are. Hearts thumping, our stomach in knots, we *risk* accepting others, even when they have done us grave harm. At the same time we *risk* accepting ourselves now, the way we are, not some idealized version of ourselves. We risk acknowledging that we are not perfect, that we do not have it all together, that we ourselves have injured others. So we no longer simply mouth the words, but enter into prayer with honesty,

"Forgive us our trespasses, as we forgive those who trespass against us."

Forgiveness flourishes beyond the boundaries of my hurt, even beyond my death. It may burst through, most especially, after some years of grieving and healing. Then, we know, beyond words, that the action is not wholly our own. In fact, just as the original violence was beyond words, so too words are inadequate to describe the peace that may descend upon a person who desires it. In these instances, the very word forgiveness limps.

Civic and Personal

Forgiveness has not only a personal, but a civic dimension. In the civic arena, it bears the same burden of naming the truth, mutually binding up the wounds, and moving in solidarity toward a fresh beginning. The word reconciliation may better describe this civic reality. A classic American text for reconciliation, continues to be Abraham Lincoln's Second Inaugural Address. It captures our theme in the cogent phrase: "with malice toward none, with charity toward all."

Some years ago I visited the Lincoln Memorial late one evening. In shadow and light, after the tours buses had departed, a quiet reverie hung in this marble sanctuary.[2] Climbing up the gleaming white steps and reaching the top, I stood at the base of the statuesque Lincoln. I turned left to read the Gettysburg Address, which Lincoln delivered in a short, two-minute address on November 19, 1863. On this occasion he dedicated a cemetery for the honored dead of the Battle of Gettysburg where 53,000 Confederate and Union soldiers died over the course of three blistering days in July. Despite the Union victory, Lincoln's address bore no sense of triumph. I read his solemn words chiseled in cool stone: "Four score and seven years ago,. . . .that these men may not have died in vain, ... but that we the living could usher in a new birth of freedom." It was a solemn, almost biblical, lamentation. Yet freedom was born of this lament.[3]

Then turning to the right I read on the other wall Lincoln's Second Inaugural, given sixteen months later, on March 4, 1865,[4] as the devastating Civil War drew to a close: "With malice toward none, with charity toward all, let us bind up the nation's wounds."

These two texts not only invoked the blessing of a "new birth of freedom for all," but Lincoln implied that such freedom was possible only if the blood shed not be in vain, only if all joined in binding up the wounds.

Lincoln invoked the New Testament call to forgiveness. He urged a caring, rather than a harsh, peace once the war was over. But although he believed in a soft peace, he knew it could be won only by a hard war. Relying on the Old Testament, he developed this theme of a purifying scourge in this passage of the Inaugural:

> American Slavery is one of those offences which, in the providence of God. . .He now wills to remove [through] this terrible war, as the woe due to those by whom the offence came. . . . Fondly do we hope – fervently do we pray – that this mighty scourge of war may speedily pass away. Yet if God wills that it continue, until all the wealth piled by the bondsman's two hundred and fifty years of unrequited toil shall be sunk, and until every drop of blood drawn with the lash, shall be paid by another drawn with the sword, as was said three thousand years ago, so still it must be said "the judgments of the Lord, are true and righteous altogether."[5]

Such a *fitting* scourge, such reconciliation, bears epic dimensions beyond our individual grasp. Lincoln's invocation does, however, remind us of our urgent quest for meaning and how central a vision is for the day to-day task of survival, of binding the wounds, and of reconciliation.

One hundred years after Gettysburg, Martin Luther King, Jr. reissued the vision to yet another generation of Americans. On August 28, 1963, on the steps of the Lincoln Memorial, King enthralled a throng of over 100,000 on the Mall with his vision of reconciliation. "I Have a Dream." It became the new beacon light for the Third American Revolution still being waged. King intoned:

> Five score years ago, a great American, in whose symbolic shadow we stand today, signed the Emancipation Proclamation . . . a great beacon light of hope to millions of Negro slaves who had been seared in the flames of withering injustice. . . .

> One hundred years later the Negro is still sadly crippled
> by the manacles of segregation and the chains of discrimi-
> nation. . . .
>
> I have a dream that one day on the red hills of Georgia,
> sons of former slaves and sons of former slave-owners will
> be able to sit down together at the table of brotherhood.
> . . . I have a dream. . . .

In a rising paean, King concluded:

> When we allow freedom to ring, when we let it ring from
> every village and hamlet, from every state and city, we
> will be able to speed up that day when all of God's
> children – black men and white men, Jews and Gentiles,
> Catholics and Protestants – will be able to join hands and
> to sing in the words of the old Negro spiritual, "Free at
> last, free at last, thank God Almighty, we are free at last."[6]

King's dream, an American dream, a World dream, has yet to be
realized. It calls for an experience of our common God and our
common humanity, beyond the manacles too readily imposed by
religion, gender, or skin color. The achievement of freedom is a
daily struggle in the courthouses, on the streets of America, in
our mutual relationships, in fashioning our political structures so
that they include, rather than exclude, so that caring prevails over
bigotry. It is indeed a conversion.

Reconciliation bears both epic and homely dimensions. King
had a broad, expansive dream, but it has a familiar geography –
from New York to California, from Georgia to Maine. The dream
draws fuel from the daily task of earning our bread and loving
our children and embracing our friends. Yet even daily tasks
require courage. Peace is always a risk, love leaves us vulnerable.
We may be stabbed in the back. The peacemaker, with hand
outstretched, rather than clenched in a fist, may get hurt. Those
who would be peacemakers, therefore, need the martyr's faith of
a King or a Lincoln.

The Heart of the Matter: Another Story

The realization of acceptance more often comes in mundane,
daily tasks. A few years ago I was visiting my brother Bill who,
together with his wife Lynette, owns a ten-acre family orchard in

the Yakima Valley. Bill and I were pruning some young, five-year-old cherry trees for the first time. In fact, we were determining their fruitfulness for years to come. Bill, in his quiet way, showed me how to shape the trees. The key, he said, was to select out and save five dominant limbs. These would provide the scaffolding for the other fruit-bearing branches. "I can't tell you in words which ones to cut," he said, "I just have a feel for it." As he pruned, he opened a center with five branches flaring outward round an empty center. I watched his deft trimming, the young tree taking form. Then he said, "OK, that's it, now you try one," and he strolled off to prune another tree – not even looking back. After lopping off a few branches, I told him I was fearful that I would make a mistake. Laughing lightly he said, "Cherry trees are very forgiving." Yeah, I thought, not only cherry trees, but you too. Then he explained how one cut does not last a lifetime. The tree is sturdy. Limbs grow back. The pruner has another chance next year. I thought later, perhaps that's the way forgiveness works best, in the give and take of working together, imaging a goal, but not fixated on it, in touch with the bonds of friendship and an acceptance of the reality before you.

Not a bad spirituality. The Zen of cherry-tree pruning: Quietly aware of your own center and the tree's center, take your cuts, trim the broken, the diseased, and off-centered; prune away with all the care and skill you have, confident there will be another time, another season. Central to this Zen is a commitment to a life of honesty, love and discipline. It requires a daily discipline and a willingness to suffer self-examination.

Myrna's Story

Honesty and self-examination, so necessary for bringing about lasting freedom, arise from daily care in our personal lives. Myrna offers a good example of someone willing to examine her past and to discover a pattern of subservience which blocked her freedom.

I was giving her an eight-day retreat. About the fourth day, I offered her the prayer for forgiveness printed at the end of Chapter Seven as a possible pattern for her prayer. The next day, with a fresh color in her cheeks, she reported, "I used that forgiveness prayer as you suggested. I thought I had worked through most everything. In fact, when I started this prayer, I returned to that time when I was thirteen and my older cousin Willie forced me to have sex with him. I had been over that a lot in therapy and in prayer. I have felt a cleansing in my self and in my sexuality.

"But what came to me vividly when I started this prayer was an earlier experience. I was about eight and my brother Tad seven. Tad and I were always very close. We went fishing, played hide 'n seek, played soccer together, got into the same trouble together, but I would hang back and Tad would always get into trouble by going one step farther. On this particular day, I don't know what he had done, maybe it was coming home late for dinner. Anyway my mother was mad and my father shook Tad, had him grab his ankles. Then my father took out his belt and whipped Tad two or three times in front of all of us. I remember being shocked. I was glad it wasn't me. I was angry at my dad. I was sorry for Tad. I was surprised at how my mother concurred in his punishment. Then I felt my own shame. I felt naked and exposed as if a raw nerve in our whole family was laid bare. All those moments came flooding back to me in prayer. Finally I wept. We were all implicated, each caught up in our roles. We all loved each other, but none of us could get through to the other. I didn't expect forgiveness to take that direction. God touched that raw space in myself and, not only in me, but somehow all of us together, so that we reached out and embraced each other.

"Before me lay a deeper truth about our family," Myrna went on. "You see part of the truth for me is how I cower and cringe at conflict. That's been my blind side. I don't want to get into trouble and I somehow stand back, allowing other people to play out my conflicts. I am astonished," she concluded.

Forgiveness for Myrna was not rational. It wove its way through stories. It came as a numinous gift in prayer. It erupted from her consciousness when she was ready. It was not something she achieved on her own, although prayer opened her to the possibility.

The Story of a Man with Paralysis

Here's another story of forgiveness, which releases a man from paralysis:

When Jesus returned to Capernaum after some days, it became known that he was at home. Many gathered together so that there was no longer room for them, not even around the door, and he preached the word to them. They came bringing to him a paralytic carried by four men. Unable to get near Jesus because of the crowd, the friends of the paralytic opened up the roof above him. After they had broken through, they let down the mat on which the paralytic was lying. When Jesus saw *their* faith, he said to the paralytic, "Child, your sins are forgiven."

Now some of the scribes were sitting there asking themselves, "Why does this man speak that way? He is blaspheming. Who but God alone can forgive sins?" Jesus immediately knew in his mind what they were thinking to themselves, so he said, "Why are you thinking such things in your hearts? Which is easier, to say to the paralytic, "Your sins are forgiven," or to say, "Rise, pick up your mat and walk"? But that you may know that the Son of Man has authority to forgive sins on earth" – he said to the paralytic, "I say to you, rise, pick up your mat, and go home." He rose picked up his mat at once, and went away in the sight of everyone. They were all astounded and glorified God, saying, "We have never seen anything like this." (Mark 2: 1:12, emphasis added, *NAB*)

When the question is posed which of these is easier: "Your sins are forgiven" or "Get up, pick up your mat and walk"? Don't we spontaneously give the wrong answer? Jesus takes the *toughest* choice head on: to forgive sins is *harder* than for the man with paralysis to pick up his mat and walk. To forgive is the miracle. To be restored to the fullness of our self and to be at peace with our relationships is harder than for a person with paralysis to be healed and to pick up his mat and walk. The critics ironically know what is at stake: "Only God can forgive sins," they say. Only the source of the soul can heal the soul.

The action of Jesus implies several things:

1. We need to be vulnerable enough to say: It hurts, can you help me? Those who do not acknowledge hurt won't get cured!

2. We get (a lot of) help from our friends if we are open to receiving it. Notice the phrase "When Jesus saw *their* faith."

We would expect it to read, "When Jesus saw *his* faith." But faith can not be privatized, it flows out of a community.

3. Nothing ever goes entirely right. That is, nothing ever goes the way *we* planned it. Look at the paralytic in yourself. You thought that with a little help from your friends you could see Jesus pretty easily. But *no,* when you get there he is surrounded by a crowd. Your friends are undaunted. Dramatically they strip away the tiles on the roof, lift you up, lower you down into the jam-packed room. Great entrance! All you wanted was to be able to walk again, but now you are really in a pickle, up front, center stage with all the world to see you. Not only that. You are suddenly surrounded by conflict. The Scribes and Pharisees – those smart, prickly authorities – are ready to pick and probe at you under their moral microscopes: "You are a paralytic because it's your own damn fault," they claim.

But now Jesus gazes at you and suddenly your whole body quivers with relief. He does not judge you. He does not question, "Why are you interrupting my busy schedule?" He does not look up at the roof and say: "Oh, you again." He does look at *their* faith, the faith of your friends who carried you. He accepts you, takes you by the hand, and says: "Your sins are forgiven!" His voice echoes deep within you. And the pain of previous rejections comes flooding up and flows out and now for the first time in years your body feels free and alive.

And then you hear the nit pickers squabbling about some fine point or other, but Jesus rebuffs them, sends them packing, stumbling all over themselves. Then he turns to you and says: "Get up and walk."

Now all desire transformed. In a moment the numbness gone, but the pain sharper. You feel the blood coursing through your legs and you *want* to get up and gradually you *do* get up and you wobble here and there for a few moments. And then, after you take a few steps, you are elated and you wonder why it was such a big deal. And a couple of your friends throw their arms around you, give you a big hug and congratulate you for being so brave – and you, you know they've got it all turned around because all you did was to say to *some friends who could really help you:* it hurts.

In this vignette we start to see how religion offers and mediates healing balm for our souls, yet how often religious leaders ward off such healing. Religion draws us together in a community of friends who seek and offer acceptance. Religious leaders too often offer rules and regulations, which assert their power. Once such leaders turn and understand that they too are in need of healing, they can open hearts to compassion, just as Jesus did.

Let's pause again for a while to reflect: *Where do you hurt? Name it with all honesty. Then, whom do you need to ask for help? Which of your friends takes you to God? What does God say to you? Who tries to block the action?*

Who do we need to ask for help? Sometimes we pass over the most obvious person. Or we think, "I can do it by myself." Or, oversensitive to our plight, we will not let someone else touch our mat. As you ponder these questions, you may feel paralyzed yourself. If you feel stuck, you may wish to pause a second time to consider these questions:

Who are the pharisees that pick at you the most? How do their voices reside in you? How do they block you from seeking help? Who triggers your projections (those elements in our self which we would just as soon not look at, but which we unconsciously recognize in other people who remind us of what we want to avoid)? How do you hide your self?

Honesty shapes the process of forgiveness. Often we have unconsciously developed covers for hiding the truth from ourselves and from others so some simplicity helps. In fact, the request for forgiveness is marked by simplicity:

"I did it. I'm sorry."

The divine response may be equally simple: "Go in peace, sin no more." Or if we ask forgiveness from a friend, the response might be, "Yes, it hurt. I'm sorry too for my part in the fight. I really appreciate your taking the initiative." Or our friend's response might well be nothing more than a few tears and a big hug. If we acknowledge our mistake and accept forgiveness, it breaks the cycle of shame or guilt that saps our healthy energies. We no longer waste our energies on dodging the truth. We can then focus on *being* and *doing* what we are good at.

We have yet another choice. We can choose whether to emphasize the good or the bad – not that we obscure one or the other, but we can choose which one we dwell on. In this choice, we help to construct our own reality. The good becomes *better,* the bad becomes worse. It is a simple rule of grammar about comparative adjectives. If we emphasize the bad, it does not get better. It gets *worse*.[7] Emphasizing the good tends to make things better. Grammatically, as well as psychologically and spiritually, the bad becomes *worse*, or as the cartoon character claims, *worser and worser*. And the good, fostered and appreciated, becomes *better*.

This is not to say that we hear no evil, speak no evil, nor do we seek to live in "la-la" land. We do need to acknowledge the ways in which we have injured ourselves, shamed our children, lied to others, or been caught in the web of power over others. We must admit our deceit and shabby business dealings. Only then can we accept forgiveness with a clean heart. This honesty has the salutary effect of affirming our basic goodness. If we can acknowledge that we lied when we have indeed lied, then we have a claim at least to knowing honesty when we see it. Covering up catches us up in such a muddle that we can no longer perceive our own authentic self.

Religion can help us or hinder us in seeking forgiveness. Many of my undergraduate students, if they are familiar with religion at all, find that religion blocks them from seeking God. They perceive religion as accusatory, blaming, pointing to the sin, rather than providing a welcoming community that opens the doors. They size up the Churches as more concerned about finances, power struggles over who is going to be in charge, and an overbearing tendency to correct the sin, rather than to welcome the sinner. Yet if we are going to consider spirituality in anything more than just its personal manifestations, if our journey is going to take us to our destiny, if we are serious about the communal dimensions of God's action among people, then we must examine the claims of religion.

We might start, however, with a simple examination:

Have you been hurt or even betrayed by "religious people?" Have these experiences blocked you from examining the truths of your own soul in relationship to the great religious traditions?

Do you pray through a sacred text? Have you explored how to interpret these texts using contemporary research? How might religious ritual give voice to your deepest desires?

Is your religion mature or immature? Have you explored its invitation to compassion? to building a just society?

Who opens the door to you?

Stories of Forgiveness and Freedom

The great religions encourage the way of honesty and simplicity, caution against power. They reserve their strongest condemnations for false prophets and oppressive religious leaders who block people from encountering God's mercy and love. They thrive on stories, proverbs, anecdotes, folk wisdom, and parables – no doubt because they are down-to-earth and practical. They inhabit the *real* place of *real* people.

Mark's gospel, for instance, depicts a masterful portrait of the Gerasene demoniac, a deeply troubled person. It also shows the subtle interplay between mental illness and the stigma cast by society. In this gospel Jesus not only heals the person, but breaks the chains with which society binds the victim. He implicitly extends liberation from prejudice to the community.

> When Jesus got out of the boat, at once a man from the tombs who had an unclean spirit met him. The man had been dwelling among the tombs, and no one could restrain him any longer, even with a chain. In fact, he had frequently been bound with shackles and chains, but the chains had been pulled apart by him and the shackles smashed, and no one was strong enough to subdue him. Night and day among the tombs and on the hillsides he was always crying out and bruising himself with stones. (Mark 5:1-5, *NAB*)

The author provides an almost haunting repetition of the words chains, shackles, bind, tombs, and bruising himself.[8] Efforts to restrain the demoniac were useless because his wild fury enabled him to break the bonds designed to control him. Forced to live isolated from human community, he wandered among the dead in uninhabitable places, through graveyards and mountains. As a victim of severe insanity and stigmatized by his fellow citizens, the man's real shackles lay within. Likewise, the citizens of this village are shackled within and maintain their reality so that their secure little world remains unthreatened.

Being bound in order to be controlled is hardly restricted to those suffering from severe mental disease. Nor is self-hatred unique to those considered mentally or emotionally ill. Feelings originally suppressed for fear of rejection continue to bind people internally until they are admitted, claimed, felt, and released. We have seen earlier in Martin Luther King's address how we are enslaved by our prejudices and at some deeper level yearn for that vision where we can proclaim: "free at last, free at last, thank God Almighty, we are free at last."

According to the therapist, Dr. Alexander Lowen, suppressed feelings remain stored in muscles, producing a muscular shield, a protective armor. They become structured in the body as chronic tension.[9] In a body suffering from chronic tension, spontaneity, which is the essence of self-expression, becomes impossible. The same chronic tension and stiffness affects the body politic. A threatened society continues to build its stiff armor and resist genuine freedom.

Mark's gospel continues the story:

> Catching sight of Jesus from a distance, [the demoniac] ran up and prostrated himself before him, crying out in a loud voice, "What have you to do with me, Jesus, Son of the Most High God? I adjure you by God, do not torment me!" Jesus had been saying to him, "Unclean spirit, come out of the man!" He asked him, "What is your name?" He replied, "Legion is my name. There are many of us." And he pleaded earnestly with him not to drive them away from that territory. (Mark 5:6-10)

As the story winds toward its conclusion, "Legion" is driven out into a herd of swine which then rushes down a steep bank into the sea where they are drowned. The townspeople then come out to see what has happened.

> As they approached Jesus, they caught sight of the man who had been possessed by Legion, sitting there clothed and in his right mind. And they were seized with fear.[10] ... Then they began to beg [Jesus] to leave their district. As he was getting into the boat, the man who had been possessed pleaded to remain with him. But Jesus would not permit him but told him instead, "Go home to your family and announce to them all that the Lord in his pity has done for you." Then the man went off and began to proclaim in the Decapolis what Jesus had done for him; and all were amazed. (Mark 5:10-20)

The townspeople have great difficulty in accepting this new situation. They ask Jesus to leave. By healing the familiar crazy man who roved through the tombs, Jesus has upset the natural order of things. Not only that; he has also wiped them out economically: all their pigs have been driven over the cliff.

I have always found it somewhat difficult to understand what is going on here, but here is what I make of it: At one level, by entering the Greek-speaking Decapolis, Jesus has come into foreign territory. In addition, the Jews considered pigs unclean, and no Jew would have been raising them. Further, this "mental case," within the Jewish law, meant that the person was both unclean and an outcast. Living among the tombs in contact with the dead would have further contaminated him. So for a pious Jew, this story presents at least four levels of religious impurity and hence of exclusion from temple worship and rejection by society. This man was an untouchable of the worst order.

Once healed, the man wishes to follow Jesus, but is told to remain. Some might have felt rejected anew, but not this "wild one." Now filled with a new passion, he preaches the good news of his healing to the town and to all his kinspeople. And "they were amazed." One senses that many would just as soon have wished to be non-amazed. Their tidy world was overturned, and now this wild one has not only recovered his sanity, but is crazy about the good news of his deliverance.

Part of the restoration to wholeness is that the man comes out of hiding. Jesus unmasks Legion and not only drives them out, but, as the story goes, casts them into the swine. This cleansing stirs and heals not only the demoniac but also attempts to unbind the community from its accustomed ways of shackling others. As the French philosopher Leon Bloy once said, "Wherever Jesus walked, things could never be the same again."

Women Who Hide and the Society Which Hides Them

We explored earlier in Chapter Seven how women may be especially prone, through social conditioning, to the sin of hiding. Mary Pipher, a psychologist, has vividly described how society encourages this hiding among adolescent girls. As young girls shift into adolescence and become attune to the norms of their culture, Pipher says, they become "female impersonators," who fit their whole selves into small, crowded spaces. Vibrant, confident girls become shy, doubting young women. Girls stop thinking, "Who am I? What do I want?" and start thinking, "What must I do to please others?"[11]

Pipher suggests that adolescent girls experience a pressure to deny their true selves not from parents but from the culture. Just at the time they are seeking for their identity, girls learn to hide their true self and to display only a small portion of their gifts. So early on a pattern is set. Many adult women often know how everyone in their family thinks and feels except themselves. They are great at balancing the needs of their co-workers, husbands, children and friends, but they forget to put themselves into the equation.

Pipher explains how American culture is rife with girl-hurting "isms," such as sexism, capitalism, and lookism, which is the evaluation of a person solely on the basis of appearance.[12] These isms force the young woman into hiding under a mask of selling goods through sex appeal, of pleasing others, of fitting into a stereotyped model of looking good.

Any woman who emerges from this tomb of hiding, gives birth to herself. She becomes aware that she can be known and loved by another, not as a passive reflection of patriarchy's archetype, but because she is the fully human, fully vulnerable person she has become.[13] She has become unshackled, and the community may well wish that such healing, such an unleashing, had never occurred!

If a woman can emerge from her hiding, perhaps a new concept of family can be born, a concept that does not depend upon one person in the middle who has no separate personhood of her own and seeks only to serve the others; a new concept of family that recognizes mutuality, independence, responsibility and commitment in its members. If a woman can emerge from hiding, then a new concept of society will also emerge. Leadership will be based on mutuality, recognition of individual gifts, and commitment. The burden is not on women alone to achieve this new partnership, but on all women and men working in mutuality towards this ideal. Since these values will undermine capitalism and consumerism as we know them today, we can expect massive social resistance from both men and women to these changes.

Unearthing Living Water

The Samaritan woman (John 4:1-42) likewise comes out of hiding. She wonders at how Jesus reveals "all the things which she did." In her story we see the cultural tension at work: Jews did not mingle with Samaritans, nor did strange men talk with women in public. Thus the Samaritan woman lives with a double bind. After a dialogue with Jesus in which he both encourages and challenges her to acknowledge the fullness of who she is and no longer to hide, she runs off to tell the *men:* "Come, see a man who told me all things which I did. Is not this the Christ?"(John 4:29) As a woman her voice is still muted. Even as she is bursting with joy, she asks tentatively, "Is not this the Christ?"

Traditionally this passage has been read as a story of a lascivious woman with five husbands who even now was living with a man who was not her husband. Then in the presence of Jesus who reveals who she is to herself, she wakes up to her sinfulness, repents, and runs off to tell the whole village. A closer reading, however, suggests not the sin of sensuality, but rather the sin of hiding who she is. Sensuality is but a mask for her hiding. Freed from hiding her past, she can now worship in all honesty and openness, "in spirit and in truth." (John 4:21)

Calvinism and Psychoanalysis

Much hiding occurs because both men and women are reluctant to face their weakness. Some of this reluctance has grown naturally out of a contempt for weakness, inherent in Calvinist doctrine. Calvinism also contributed to a strong sense of religious individualism. Philip Rieff has noted that within Protestant culture:[14]

> Individuals. . .tried to hide [their] sense of weakness, for they no longer felt a compelling explanation for it; nor could they use something in their system of worship to escape this now intensely personal fault. . . .The culture, always guilt-ridden, was no longer guilt-releasing. Without the remedy of grace or good works, conscience became the seat of emotional weakness rather than the sign of moral strength.[15]

In such a culture, all destinies are intensely personal. Thus the way to self-knowledge occurs by tracing a person's conduct from symptom back to the inner conditions responsible for the symptom. In the religious period (up to 1920) the symptom was called sin, Rieff explains. In the subsequent psychological period (1920 to 1950) ushered in by Freud, Rank, and Adler, the symptom was a neurosis. Redemption still came from self-revealing admission. Just as clergy made a sinner aware of sin so that one would be self-convicted, so too the psychoanalyst made the neurotic therapeutically aware of their neurosis. Neurotics, like their predecessor the sinner, were reluctant to admit their weakness. Both the sinner and the neurotic try to hide. Thus, Calvin's pastors and Freud's analysis had the difficult and thankless task of educating for self-awareness, but the admission of weakness was the beginning of emotional and spiritual strength in both the religious and the psychotherapeutic traditions.[16]

Catholic culture maintained a different tradition. The penitent palpably realized God's forgiveness through ritual and through the action of the community. Except for serious, mortal grievances, the individual did not even *do* anything. One simply presented oneself. God, through the sacraments, did the rest.[17] The Protestant critique of Catholic sacraments, that they often became magic and empty formalism, remains a healthy antidote to a tendency to manipulate the sacred in order "to manage God."[18] However, the widespread revival of ritual, often in rather bizarre settings, testifies to an urgent instinct in humans for God's forgiveness rather than merely their own. It also fulfills a longing for communities which offer mutuality, acceptance, and purpose.

Ritual Enactment

If these rituals become sheer routine, then they lose their elasticity for mediating God's forgiveness. Rituals at their best should offer recognized structures and forms so that individuals can freely enter into a space and time that welcomes the sacred. Through familiar movements and words, they draw on the stories, memories, and traditions of a people in order to enter deeper waters and experience God as ultimate acceptance. A blue light slanting through stain glass windows, incense rising to the sky, and familiar cadences flowing from a pastor enable the congregation to evoke its memories of God's liberating action in the past and to open their hearts to the future.

I would like to offer an example of a sacramental rite which arises out of a unique, five-day, silent retreat which we make available each year at Seattle University to a group of 30 students. For two days the students consider themes such as God's bountiful creation, their own gifted birth, and ways in which their own destructiveness erodes their basic goodness and healthy choices. In the twilight of the third day, students and faculty gather for a reconciliation rite with candles flickering amid the purple colors of Advent. Perhaps a simple Taize chant, "Veni, Sancte Spiritus," "Come, Holy Spirit," courses through the dark. The music flows with our hearts in rhythmic harmony. It opens the flow between God and soul. Silence is central. The ritual carves out space so that each soul can mourn or dance, lament past hurts, shed tears of joy, or recall graced friendships. Rituals enact what the soul cannot explain in words.

Then a scriptural reading. Then a simple song. Students have the opportunity for private confession or a conversation with a listener. Finally, two communal actions conclude the movements of the ritual. The leaders invite each person to select a stone from an ample supply placed in the center of the room. After selecting the stone, heavy or light, rough or smooth, bizarre or interesting, the students feel the texture, weight and the load. Then after confession or a listening conversion, they throw the stone out over the cliff into the sea. The entire action symbolizes our stony hearts and how they are made hearts of flesh by tendering them to God in the presence of another. God accepts them in compassion. The throwing enacts the freedom that comes from this interior openness. In this ritual action the primary emphasis is on a simple, rather than a belabored, naming of the sin in the presence of another. This sacramental rite harbors forgiving love.

After everyone has regathered in the large room, the leaders bless and anoint each person, individually placing hands on the shoulders or head and invoking God's blessed acceptance. This ritual, drawing on baptismal symbols, re-enacts one's radical acceptance by God. We close with a song and a sign of peace.

Largely non-verbal, the ritual provides space and silence for a depth encounter. It indicates a direction, congruent with the human-spirit rhythms: It moves from naming to forgiveness to acceptance. It enacts the saving action. The order seems important. To offer acceptance before the naming would get it backwards.

A National Ritual

Such rituals can become privatized, without touching the commonweal of the republic and without surfacing the guilt of a nation for its own destructive choices. The original Pilgrims recognized the need for communal reconciliation and thanksgiving when they gathered with Native Americans not only to celebrate the harvest, but to seek reconciliation with God for their offenses as a community during the past year. Thanksgiving Day thus remains one of the few holidays which is genuinely religious and secular. Of course, advertisers secularize it by dubbing it Turkey Day and drain away its ritual power.

We have another national ritual of reconciliation, which occurs each day in Washington, DC. A short distance from the Lincoln Memorial, two angled, black granite walls – with 58,000 names etched on them – emerge from the earth. One of the walls points back to the Lincoln Memorial, the other directs our gaze toward the Washington Monument. The Civil War. The Revolution. These were the two founding moments in our history. The third founding moment is happening in our own times. Civil Rights. A deeper integration within society of all our peoples. A dream announced, yet to be fulfilled.

The Vietnam Memorial, scoured out of the earth, welcomes the visitor with two arms. Hesitant in this hallowed ground, I descended to join the thousands who peered and searched for lost comrades or for a father or son or brother or sister. As I passed by slowly, I saw the mirror etched in the living stone surrounded by the thousands who have fallen and by those like me who were passing by. Flowers strewn, medals of valor left, bits of Army gear offered, and flags fluttering everywhere. I traced with my fingers the only name I recognized: Warren Fergusson, Jr., my second cousin, a young man I never met, knowing only his parents and how his death transformed the way his father, a federal judge in Los Angeles, sentenced those who resisted the war. Judge Fergusson began meting out community service, rather than punitive jail terms – the memory of his son guiding his compassion.

The grief, the tears, the shattered dreams, and most of all the horrible inhumanity of this war, this scar on the earth, cannot be hidden. They are – for the moment – collected here in reverence, and yet in a larger sense we cannot . . . we cannot . . .

measure this devotion. Somehow the grief envelops us. In the Civil War, most knew what they were fighting for. Meaning gave devotion. In the Vietnam War purpose evaporated. Many expired apparently in vain. Somehow the purpose of this tragedy lies within – within us and among us – those of us who remain to weep and to bind up the nation's wounds. Ignoring the wounds simply leads to another wounding, another purposeless war.[19]

As we descend into this hallowed ground, we become aware that the great peacemakers such as Lincoln, Mahatma Gandhi, Martin Luther King, Anwar Sadat, the Four Maryknoll women missionaries in El Salvador, all met a tragic, fatal end. They were martyrs for peace. In 1978 Anwar Sadat, the president of Egypt extended the hand of reconciliation to his arch enemy Menachim Begin knowing that he not only risked rejection by the Israelis but death from his bellicose critics at home. Five years later, while Sadat was reviewing the Egyptian troops passing in parade before his reviewing stand, radical fundamentalists gunned him down. Likewise, Archbishop Oscar Romero, prophet and witness to the slaughter of thousands of innocent Salvadoran peasants by the paramilitary National Guard trained in Alabama by the United States,[20] was shot and killed at the altar as he celebrated the Eucharist.

When we as a nation descend to the earth, go down between the walls, feel the losses in the stony silence, see our own faces reflected in the black granite and ponder together, we ritualize our losses and our complicity. Wordless, we yearn for reconciliation. In this hallowed ground, near this wailing wall, no tear is hidden.

To conclude our lamentation, we might pray with Lincoln as he invoked the prophet Isaiah in his Second Inaugural, just a month before the end of the Civil War:

> *Comfort, comfort my people; speak tenderly to Jerusalem and tell her this, that she has fulfilled her term of bondage that her penalty is paid; she has received from the Lord's hand double measure for all her sins.*

Endnotes

1. See Jane Smiley *A Thousand Acres*, (New York: Fawcett Columbine, 1991), a powerful novel depicting the generational wound of incest and how it infects the land.

2. As I climbed the steps, I envisioned other events occurring here, such as Marian Anderson's singing the Star-Spangled Banner here in 1939. After the Daughters of the American Revolution barred her from singing in Constitution Hall because she was Negro, Eleanor Roosevelt arranged with her friend Harold Ickes, the Secretary of the Interior, to make the Lincoln Memorial available. When Ms. Anderson sang, "The Star-Spangled Banner" it became a new song of freedom.

3. It would take us too far afield to show how this new-born freedom was embodied in the Thirteenth, Fourteenth, and Fifteenth Amendments to the Constitution right after the Civil War, how it impacted the Women's Movement leading to their right to vote in the Twentieth Amendment in 1920 and how the struggle for freedom continues in the Civil Rights Movement in the 1960s and the unheeded call for the Equal Rights Amendment in the 1970s and 80s.

4. Lincoln gave the Inaugural Address on the Front Steps, East Side, of the Capitol. At the time the dome of Capitol building was half-done, "unfinished business." The Washington Monument was a stump, interrupted by the War. The monuments imaged the "unfinished business" of freedom.

5. *Collected Works of Lincoln, VIII*, 73-74, 182, as quoted by James M. McPherson, *Abraham Lincoln and the Second American Revolution* (New York: Oxford University Press, 1991), pps. 36-37, which also includes this analysis of Lincoln's use of Scripture.

6. King, "I Have a Dream," *A Testament of Hope: the Essential Writings and Speeches of Martin Luther King, Jr.* ed. James Elvin Washington (San Francisco: HarperSan Francisco, 1986), pp. 217-220.

7. A cultural exception to this almost universal rule may be the Irish, who reportedly are "Never so happy as when they are feeling sad!"

8. See Barta, *The Gospel of Mark.*

9. Cited by Barta, *ibid.* Alexander Lowen, M.D. explored the suppression of the body and its effects upon self-identity and emotional health in a number of books; see *The Betrayal of the Body* (New York: Collier Macmillan, 1967), *Depression and the Body* (New York: Pelican Books, 1972), and *Bioenergetics* (New York: Penguin Books, 1975).

10. "They were seized with fear" and "All were amazed" are the biblical formula for any event through which people encounter God. Here this "seizure" has an ironical tone: the madman has been freed of seizures, those of the "sane" are just beginning.

11. Mary Pipher, *Reviving Ophelia: Saving the Selves of Adolescent Girls* (New York: Ballantine Books, 1994), p. 22.

12. *Ibid.*, p. 23.

13. Dunfee, "The Sin of Hiding," p. 325.

14. Philip Rieff, "The American Transference: From Calvin to Freud," *The Atlantic Monthly* (July, 1961), cited by James A. Knight in "Freud and Calvin: a Comparative Study," *A Psychiatrist Looks at Religion and Health* (Nashville: Abingdon Press, 1964), pp. 76-77.

15. Rieff, p. 107. [Pronouns changed for the sake of inclusive language.]

16. Knight, "Freud and Calvin," pp. 76-77.

17. My sister Margaret suggests that we grew up with Calvinist Catholicism!

18. Clergy and lay ministers may be prone to manage God, ostensibly to protect the people but, more importantly, to maintain their own power.

19. Wasn't the Gulf War – 150,000 Iraqis, 143 American deaths – such a war? Avowedly, we were preserving our American way of life, the flow of oil, but, according to the President, we were also vindicating the loss of the war in Vietnam – proving that we could "win a war."

20. "America Knew," *The New York Times* (November, 1993).

CHAPTER TEN

Hoping:
Exploring Mystery

Boundaries make imagination possible and give birth to hope. They distinguish a new creation from a nightmare. They differentiate mysticism from psychosis. Boundaries make hope possible because they acknowledge our humanity. They contour our yearnings and help us give flesh to our dreams. They quell the urge that we have to escape the pain and the joys of being human.[1]

A poem by Wendell Berry explores our need for boundaries and how they allow for fecund creativity:

> *Enclosing the field within bounds*
> *sets it apart from the boundless*
> *of which it was, and is, a part,*
> *and places it within care.*
> *The bounds of the field bind*
> *the mind to it. A bride*
> *adorned, the field now wears*
> *the green veil of a season's*
> *abounding. Open the gate!*
> *Open it wide, that time*
> *and hunger may come in.*[2]

Without boundaries our dreams can become destructive. I recall that during my psychotic reaction I imagined myself being called to Rome as a discerner to help straighten things out in the Vatican! Anyone who thinks they can straighten out the Vatican should register immediately that they are suffering from monstrous delusions! Such unbounded urges may arise from our preoccupation with self. They may cloak inflated desires for power and prestige.

157

We should not readily dismiss our images or dreams as delusional, however. Often they nestle a divine spark. They foster the stirrings of hope. A powerful image in my own experience occurred during a retreat outside of Rome in 1972. While at prayer in the chapel, I had an palpable sensation of a shower of camellia petals. Since I was not fully fluent in Italian, I later described the event in a group sharing with fellow retreatants as "una pioggia di rose," a rain of roses. Such symbols mediate God's presence to us. God dwells beyond our mere imagining in nameless presence.

Every conversion experience that I have ever witnessed was propelled by an image of hope. The burning bush for Moses, for instance, embodies a radical re-orienting of his feelings, memory, imagination, intellect and will. Moses began to imagine and to see and to interact differently. His perceptions shifted. He took on the viewpoint and compassion of God to "set my people free."

A conversion image comes as a gift, as a surprise, as a call, which reminds us again that it comes as a revelation. It is not a construct of our own will or a figment of our cravings. It arises from the depths of our self and yet transcends us. And it beckons us to re-orient our whole life toward a fresh vocation.

Naturally we need to interpret, to discern, to judge: whether the image-event is from God, whether it is congruent with our best nature, whether it bears seeds of creation or destruction. A mark of its healthy potential is whether or not it has boundaries; that is, whether it respects human limitations.

God as Teddy Bear

This imaging activity arises early in the development of each child. Psychologists have noticed how crucial it is for a child to be able to play with an imaginary companion. D.W. Winnicott, a child-psychoanalyst, observed the close attachment which older infants form to some special object, such as a blanket, a stuffed animal, or a toy.[3] The object, which Winnicott designated as a transitional object, provides the child with comfort and soothing. The infant assumes absolute rights over the object, which are implicitly agreed to by all the family. The infant may affectionately cuddle the object or slap it around. The object must never change, unless changed by the infant. For the infant, it gives warmth and shows a vitality of its own.

The child invests its *self* in the object by projecting its own fantasies and dreams. Psychologists use the technical term "cathected" to describe this emotional investment They also note how the object is gradually "decathected"; that is, the child's emotionally charged investment of itself in the object abates and withdraws. About the age of five, the child relegates the Teddy Bear or security blanket or Muppet doll or Barney the Dinosaur to limbo.

Occasionally when I propose this theory in my Religion and Psychology class, some students, often a young woman, will say, "No, no. I still have my Muppet doll in my room." This apparently late withdrawal indicates a nostalgia for that safe period in childhood when they were two to four years old, rather than a delayed childhood.

This transitional object phenomena, however, does not conclude with infancy or childhood. It has spread out over the whole cultural field, according to Winnicott. In fact, he says, the transitional object starts each human being off with what will always be important for them. It provides a privileged arena of personal experience which will not be challenged.[4] The privileged space prefigures the arts, religion, imaginative living, and creative scientific work.[5] In fact, Winnicott offers the provocative thesis that God is a transitional object. Certainly our image of God is extremely intimate and we invest our core *self* in such an image. If we look at the God-image as a transitional object, then we could make the following observations:

1. At the outset, the God-image must be congruent with our own personality even though our immediate family will mediate this image. The God-image will naturally have fragments of the child's father and mother, which the child idealizes.

2. The child, or later the young adult, may "cathect" with a God-image, in which the whole of one's self is invested, which provides a sanctified, privileged space – a holy space – to explore one's self and one's world.

3. In time two events dispel or "de-cathect" this God-image: A. As the person matures, the child's God-image no longer reflects an adequate projection of the Self, or B. God may

reveal God's Self to the person through a spiritual upheaval, a sudden awakening, crisis, or loving encounter.

A better understanding of this process could help teenagers to shift from a borrowed religion, that is their parents' images of God, to accepting and embracing their own personal experience of God. Children have their own relationship with God, which is often quite profound. Their own friendly, imaginative image of God may remain rather private since the God adults talk about remains foreign.[6]

David Heller, a child psychologist, explored children's images of God. He asked 40 young theologians, ages four to twelve, to name the most important thing he or she believed in. The result, he reported, was a baptism into the mysteries of childhood spirituality.[7] Jesus, Baba, HaShem (Hebrew) and My Friend God were just a few of the names the children spontaneously mentioned.

Of considerable contemporary interest, Heller says, were the children's responses to the question, "What if God were the opposite sex?" Almost without exception, the boys showed signs of agitation concerning the prospect of a female God. They were reluctant even to entertain the question, as if some all encompassing feminine force were about to descend on them. Here is Heller's conversation with nine-year-old Arthur on the issue:

Arthur: "God is a man, for sure."

Heller. "But could you make believe that God was the other sex?"

Arthur. "But God is a man!"

Heller: "But could you play, what if?"

Arthur: "If God was a. . .huh [look of astonishment]. Well, I don't know [nervous laughter]. Well, I couldn't even imagine God being a lady. No sir. Boy, that would change the whole world."

Heller speculates that Arthur's fears, and the similar fears of his male peers, may represent apprehension concerning their own feminine qualities or anxiety about the mystery of motherhood. In any case, their responses were memorable. The boys gave evidence of an undercurrent of love and fear of femininity – conflicts which were particularly difficult for them.

Girls, in contrast, Heller noted, used the same questions about God's sex as an opportunity to express their budding political views. Becky Sue, 11, for instance, saw no good reason why a girl could not be God – "or at least president of a country." Going even further, Tamara, 12, suggested that if God were a woman "there would be less violence in the world."

These responses from children suggest how the human energies of sexuality and power become invested in our God-image and consequently the huge investment we have in the unchanging quality of this "transitional object." If our experience of God matures, growing out of our own imaginative projection into personal experiences, then more and more in our early adulthood we come to encounter God in relationship. We may face a trauma in letting go of our early images of God because they are so much a part of us and our security. But as we mature spiritually, our view of God as a security blanket, as a rather infantile transitional object, recedes. We then encounter God *as God is* and ourselves *as we are* in a mutuality of giving and receiving. To encounter God as God is, however, we have to continue letting go of our "security blankets," even those which pass for being mature.

Paul Pruyser advanced Winnicott's work. He emphasized that the illusional world is an important world of play.[8] It provides an arena for the creative imagination in which feelings are not antagonistic to thinking. For the child, Pruyser observed, the transitional object has a sacred character with an elaborate ritual. An aura surrounds the Other. Certain rituals must be observed with regularity. Religion is similar, and it creates an illusory, intermediate area of experience that helps bridge inner and outer reality. It creates a bounded space of hope. If a person's own relationship with God is to mature, however, some childhood features of religion must be "decathected."

Religion can suffer from the same treatment as the Teddy Bear. It can become frozen in time and mean "only what I want it to mean." Or it can be left on a shelf and pulled down again only when I face a personal crisis. It is above all prone to distortion. It can be too realistic or it can be too narcissistic.[9] Generally, traditional Western religion in the last two centuries has tended to be too realistic; that is, it has repressed the more personalized images of God of local cultures. It spends more time on a theology of God rather than on an experience of God. On the other end of the spectrum, the view of God arising from American therapeutic-spirituality may remain too narcissistic. It may simply conform to projected needs without challenging us to let go of the bonds of our enclosed world and encounter God. In any crisis, we may dive for our religious security blanket and thereby avoid God as God is. Religion may block us from experiencing God.

Bound up in our individual self-preoccupation, we remain wrapped in despair. In this travail we do not even discover our self, but rather our self-preoccupation. God, however, seeks to break through to us through relationships or through community.[10]

An example of an image with divine power is the image of Our Lady of Guadalupe, who mediates a sacred power for the Hispanic peoples. It has not only sustained them through years of oppression, it has allowed them to claim their own heritage. In so doing, it offers hope, a tremendous liberating potential to a whole people, to *un pueblo*.[11]

Freedom or Enslavement

We must ask whether the God-image brings freedom or enslavement. Does it enable the person or community to share in the compassion of God or does it ensnare us in our own preoccupying interests?

Ruth Burrows, a contemporary English Carmelite, expressed her experience of the unseen God and how God liberated her in this way:

> Often the image would spring to my mind of myself in a little boat without oar or sail, on the vast expanse of ocean beneath a midnight sky. There was a sense of terror at the loneliness, at the dreadful depth below, at the utter helplessness of my state, but also the glorious security, unfelt though it was, of being held and controlled by the unseen God. I knew that I would rather be in that little boat with "nothing" than enjoy all that the world could offer me. I was wrapped around, clasped in mystery.[12]

Through this image Burrows both grasps and offers her own radical identity, her loneliness and helplessness, and her resulting terror. Mystery offers her glorious acceptance, even as she lets go of everything else. The vestiges of her compulsive self wash away, so that she is ruled solely by God's acceptance rather than by any tyranny of the should.

A fundamental principle of discernment is that God brings freedom. Anything else is not of God. A few years ago Fred, a Protestant chaplain who ministers to mentally disabled people in a state hospital, described to me his experience of transformation. He first drew a two-part diagram:

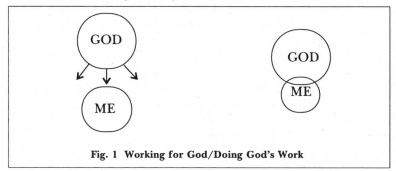

Fig. 1 Working for God/Doing God's Work

"The first image shows the old me," Fred explained. "In it I am working *for* God. I'm very busy, I'm doing lots of things, I'm generally tired, and I'm vaguely dissatisfied with the way things are going. From time to time I get angry at the patients for no apparent reason.

"The second image shows me and God in partnership. Now I'm doing God's work. It's mutual. I take time for prayer. We talk about it together. It's a peaceful time, although at times I struggle. I'm also more open with others about what's going on in my interior, especially with a spiritual director. The staff tells me, 'You're looking younger.' Or 'you seem like you've got a load off your back.' Or they report, 'the patients certainly enjoy their visits with you.' I know in my heart what's really going on. When I'm doing God's work, I still put out a lot of energy, but it's coming from the core of who I am, and it's not an effort. I'm not fighting against the goad. You know what I mean?"

I do. Fred says it so simply that, as he talks, I do a body check myself. I feel the ease in myself in following his suggestions, in shifting from working *for* God to doing God's work. I am present to Fred without straining. I share his joy, I am not thinking about my next appointment or mentally preparing tomorrow's class. In the first sketch God comes across as the boss, perhaps even a good boss, but I am working very hard and deriving my inner worth

from my external activity. In the second sketch I join with God
in partnership as an intimate.

So revelatory images give us direction. Often they break
open our perceptions in an entirely fresh way. In his novel *Report
to Greco* Nikos Kazantzakis describes such an image that bursts
upon two pilgrims. They had passed by it before, but now they
encounter it as if for the first time:

> We had toured the Holy Mountain for forty days. When,
> completing our circle, we finally returned to Daphne, the
> most unexpected, most decisive miracle was awaiting us.
> Though it was the heart of winter, there in a small, humble
> orchard was an almond tree in bloom!

> Seizing my friend's arm, I pointed to the blossoming tree.
> "Angelos," I said, "during the whole of this pilgrimage
> our hearts have been tormented by many intricate ques-
> tions. Now, behold the answer!"

> My friend riveted his blue eyes upon the flowering almond
> tree and crossed himself, as though doing obeisance be-
> fore a holy wonder-working icon. He remained speechless
> for a long moment. Then, speaking slowly, he said, "A
> poem is rising to my lips, a tiny little poem: a haiku." He
> looked again at the almond tree.

> I said to the almond tree,

> "Sister, speak to me of God."

> And the almond tree blossomed.[13]

A struggle precedes a revelation such as this. These two pilgrims
had wandered 40 days and then circled home. In all likelihood,
in their travels they shed many of their tried-and-true perceptions.
They underwent a purgation of their own self-preoccupation.
Suddenly an almond tree blossomed and simplified all the intri-
cacies of their lives. It was a wondrous icon because it opened
onto mystery. Its beauty awakened the pilgrims. They started to
see all things differently. We notice too that the image was
bounded; it brought them back to the wonders of their own world.

Earlier we said that something in our lives blocks the call to
freedom. It arrests our development. It blocks our sense of wonder. The arresting factor may be the loss of the child in us, a sadly
foreshortened sense of our desirability.[14] If we are appreciated
by others, then a sense of our goodness can awaken in us.

This awakening can occur in one of two ways: indirectly and directly. We awaken each other indirectly. Teenagers especially can spend long hours on the phone, discussing, replaying, reviewing an event which just happened. They want to know how they did, how they looked, whether they looked foolish or "cool." All such human exchange at the interpersonal level awakens our core selves by arousing our desire for the other. We feel attractive in feeling attracted. Ultimately only God can directly awaken us. Only God, "by whose desire we are desirable, can directly touch our sense of our desirability."[15]

The awakening effected by Jesus during his lifetime had to be similar to this awakening that persons do for each other. But, Jesus being without sin and thus totally possessed by his sense of being desired by God, had the maximum possible impact on his friends within the limits of person-to-person contact. The baptism of Jesus marks his radical, open reception of God and the beginning of his own ministry.

> And the holy Spirit descended upon him in bodily form like a dove. And a voice came from heaven, "You are my beloved (*agapetos*) Son; with you I am well pleased (*eudokesa*)" (Luke 3:22).

Some years ago, while I was reading this text in the original Greek, I was struck by how powerful this event must from been for Jesus. Two words in the Greek text underscore God's desire: *agapetos* and *eudokesa*. *Agapetos* means "the loved one" and has resonance with *agape*, the Christian word for love feast or banquet. "You are my son, my love feast."

Normally translators say *eudokesa* means "well-pleased," but that does not convey its depth. "Well-pleased" seems aloof, too polite. A better translation is "fully delighted." God is "fully delighted." God is bursting at the seams with love. So a translation of the whole passage could read: "You are my Child, my love feast, in whom I am fully delighted." That captures God's rapture, God's desire, God's absolute delight in us.

We cannot image God desiring anything. Yet the scene reveals God's desire for humans to become fully who they are. The dove symbolizes a new creation. It recalls the dove returning to the Ark after Noah had released it to determine whether the flood had receded (Genesis 8:8). It symbolizes God's abiding, loving, desirous Spirit in our lives.

After this event, Jesus created an entirely new hope for human existence. His presence swept the whole range of human interaction. It exhausted the possibilities of mutual awakening. He announced the Reign of God, which is nothing other than a transformation of relationships effected by God's desire for us. If God first loved us, then we are called to love one another – to become fully delighted in ourselves and in others. Jesus manifested God's delight in humanity.

With the execution of Jesus this wondrous new possibility collapsed. It seemed it could not revive – no new leader, no new politics, no new human hope. The collapse meant a terrible loss of innocence and of human expectation. Young spouses, lovers, friends know, at least in part, the nature of this loss. They had thought that this special person exhausted the possibilities, had brought their life to its limits and had taken it past all boundaries to a brand new awakening and awareness of themselves. Now it was dead.

But God was not done. God's love would not be bound by human expectations. The God who desires that love break through the bonds of enslavement broke through death itself. New life abounded. So stunned were the early Christians that all their early accounts convey a mixture of doubt and joy, of hesitancy and of wonder. That Jesus, now risen, lived among them was too good to be true. Yet something powerful, unexpected had happened to this bundle of fearful followers. Suddenly they stepped out of their fearful self-preoccupation. They became empowered by the hope, the memory, the promise of Jesus. They experienced a peace beyond all understanding. In their depths they knew God's desire for them. They knew that the very shalom of God could never leave them. Since the whole social and political existence of people had been committed in the trial of Jesus before the religious and political leaders and because this social order had been plunged with Jesus into the darkness of Golgotha, God touched the whole social and political existence and made of it a both a Gathering and a Way,[16] which are the two earliest names for the followers of Jesus. God awakened this Gathering. God launched a new Way. In this new political order the mighty would be brought low and the humble exalted.

Because of the breakthrough of God, the community cannot remain closed to new members. Otherwise it could no longer welcome fresh invitations from God. Likewise, the discovery of our desirability by God cannot remain a private event, nor the exclusive terrain of the mystic. In this released condition, we know ourselves for the first time. We know we come from the hand of God. We are desirable because desired. We are now star-bound lovers because our deepest desires are aligned with the stars from which we came.[17] We are aligned once again with our origins and our destiny.

A New Genesis: An Older Story

Astrophysics which explores the stars reminds us anew of our beginnings and the alignment of our bodies with their source. In his fascinating book *Lonely Hearts of the Cosmos,* Dennis Overbye narrates a new genesis story featuring the astro-physicists who voyage into space to trace our origins without ever leaving home:

> What could be closer to the flavor of myth than the notion that the universe did in fact appear, perhaps out of nothing; that the atoms in our bones and blood were forged in stars light-years away and billions of years ago; or that the even more ancient particles of which those atoms are composed are fossils of barely comprehensible energies and forces that existed during the first microsecond of creation? We are all artifacts of the universe, walking reminders of the ultimate mystery. We are walking dust, waking stardust.[18]

Waking stardust! Perhaps then our ancestors intuited a great truth as they gazed at the stars, the origins of their flesh, and called their yearnings for union "desires."

Ignatius and the Call of the King

The breakthrough of the divine found particular expression in the life of Ignatius of Loyola (1491-1556). Ignatius experienced his own radical acceptance by God as the call of Christ. This numinous experience came to him in the image of a gentle and gracious king. He portrayed his extraordinary experience of God as one of profound intimacy. Yet this limping ex-soldier and former courtier knew little of the language of a spousal relationship. In the world of Ignatius marriages were made for business and political reasons and had little to do with love, loyalty, fidelity, trust and commitment. But he had known the intimacy between king and vassal, lord and servant. He knew from experience the covenant between the two, how each was ready to give his life for the other. There was a bonding which made them almost one in their lives, aspirations, disappointments, and successes. In the *Spiritual Exercises* Ignatius presents Jesus as such a Lord, a gentle King who invites his followers to a companionship, characterized by intimacy and by a sharing totally in the mission of Jesus: to bring the good news of salvation, liberation, justice and peace to all peoples. In the *Spiritual Exercises* Ignatius placed this call of the King just after a person has had some experience of radical acceptance by God.

Similarly, in this book in which we are exploring the spiritual journey, we have explored our images of God immediately after the experience of conversion and forgiveness; that is, after our experience of our acceptance by God.

> Conversion,
> acceptance,
> experiencing a God who desires us
> and who fulfills our deepest desires
>   are all *one.*
> An almond tree blooms,
> and all the world is one.

Truth blossoms all at once. Only afterward, recollected in tranquillity, do we trace the petals bursting.

Carl Jung described this oneness as the union of opposites. It flows out of our acceptance of our own destructive and creative potential:

1) We face the pain of our own contribution to disorder (sin, destruction);

2) As we willingly stand in the center of the storm, we let go;

3) And we experience the holy Other, present and alive.

In all the great religions a symbol mediates this presence. In Eastern religions, as well as in medieval Christianity, this symbol takes the form of a mandala, such as a lotus flower or a rose window, a harmonious circle with the unified self radiating out from the center.

The mandala paradoxically contains male and female, earth and heaven, fire and water. It implodes with its own energy. Another representation of this dynamic unity is the uroboros, a snake wound round in a circle swallowing its own tail. The snake itself symbolizes life and fertility. The circled snake represents the eternal return of life and its wholeness.

Before the Holy a symbolic stripping seems appropriate,[19] as if the body pined to return to some originating, playful freedom. This stripping also recognizes our own fear and trembling. We uncover our self before the Self that embraces us. When Moses, for instance, envisions the Holy as a burning bush, he takes his sandals off as he nears the mystery. Coming down from the mountain, however, is just as important as going up. When Moses descends, he faces again the limitations of his own clan, his friends, and himself.

The Story of Sheila

A sacred symbol can help our decision making. The example of a woman named Sheila might help explain this point. During a retreat, she imagined herself playing in a large, flowered meadow on the slopes of Mount Rainier. She became conscious of coming into contact with her own masculine energy, which both terrified and comforted her. She felt vulnerable, open, fruitful. Later in the same retreat, she imagined a dual set of images which depicted two dimensions of her self. One showed her harried self and the other her peace-filled self. In the first, she imagined herself as a busy executive on the seventh floor of a 70-story building, working her way to the top. Busy, busy, busy. In the second she imagined herself in the midst of a warm, cellar kitchen of a large castle. In the center of the kitchen, a wise black woman kneaded the bread, peeled potatoes, listened, nodded, smelled the musty wine, attended to the movements around her. Like a black Madonna, she was silent, knowing, caring.[20] Sheila knew instinctively that the decisions she made as the harried executive could be destructive and dissipating. Those she made in the cellar kitchen in the quiet presence of the black woman brought her inner power and peace.

A talented woman with many family and community responsibilities, Sheila was highly intuitive, experienced in prayer, and uncannily aware of the dynamics of a complex community. At

times she was subject to anxiety attacks. She might let her boundaries down and become absorbed with too many commitments and
conflicts. Contemplating these two contrasting figures: the frenetic business woman and the serene black woman, helped her
to re-center herself and to shape her decisions. Gazing on the
mountain gave her strength to muster her courage. Sitting with
the black woman she poured out her conflicts and found a center
from which to move.

Abnormal Re-actions

The student of psycho-spirituality can readily see that if a person
is still governed by the compulsions, then compulsive neurotic
behavior may accompany any experience of the Holy. Those
driven by compulsions will receive the Divine in aberrant, even
bizarre, forms.[21] In fact, the initial mystic experiences of the saint
often had some of these features.

Joseph Campbell comments that both the mystic and psychotic jump into the river of life, but one has learned to swim
and the other is drowning. Is not the difference primarily that
mystic has discovered boundaries, whereas the psychotic is bound-
less? The mystic has learned how to stay afloat and to ride with
the current; the psychotic thrashes with fear, fighting the flow.[22]
If these perceptions are correct, then I believe that the positive
portions of abnormal religious experience have not been given
sufficient attention in psychiatric, or even in contemporary spiritual literature.[23]

For now, it is important to highlight how the Holy manifests
itself normally. Later we can explore how the abnormal may
intensify the normal to such a degree that it becomes distorted.
In those borderline instances, the boundaries conditions are lost,
somewhat like water which has reached the boiling point.

Implications of the Revealed God-Image

Implicit in the encounter with the Holy is a calling. An encounter
with the Holy reshuffles the self, one's world, and one's relationships; it is rooted and grounded in all that one is and is becoming.
It calls for a new integration, a fresh direction. Consequently it
carries with it a new naming. Nothing is ever the same again.

Nothing fits. New wine has burst old wineskins. So Saul becomes Paul, Simon becomes Peter, a nameless woman becomes Mary of Magdala. The encounter with the Holy carries dense implications for the course of one's vocation. All is changed, utterly changed. We cannot go home again. We are beckoned, and we yearn to share this experience with others.

This call takes time to unfold. It needs to be distinguished from ongoing compulsions and from patterns of destruction to which we are still all too prone. Winnicott's observations on "transitional objects" hold true. Over time the numinous image must be de-cathected so that the Self and God stand in relationship rather than fusion. Distinguishing these features – what is of God, what is of me, and what arises from what is contrary to God has traditionally been called the discerning of spirits.[24]

Shared Meaning: Dreaming the Possible

The discernment of spirits always happens in a community and is ultimately confirmed by it. The spirit lives and moves and breathes within us for the sake of others as well as for ourselves, and we discover these movements by sharing our depth experiences and clarifying our vision together. A shared vision orders life from within.[25] It sets boundaries, as well, to any messianic fervor we might have to do it all on our own.

Fabricating a common purpose will not do, rather a vision arises out of the generosity, virtue, and courage of a people. It cannot be imposed from without, although great leaders surface the best aspirations of a people. During the 1988 presidential campaign "this vision thing" constantly eluded George Bush. He fumbled around about "a thousand points of light," but in the end he impatiently settled for manipulation. Raising the specter of the Willie Horton story and spawning fears was easier than facing the roots of crime and challenging the national unwillingness to face our crises.[26] In the end, politicians often flee from the leader's duty to attend to the nation's better self and its deepest desires because the political cost can be so high.

Each of us faces a similar, subtle temptation which arises whenever we attempt to face the future and reflect on it. It is the temptation to try to conceive of a community and myself – based on an analysis of the present moment. This attempt may have three results: I confirm where I am already; I simply reverse directions and turn back to a previous pattern; or I extend into the future of who I am already. Nothing new breaks through.

Reverence: A Regard for Truth

Breakthroughs may come through contemplation. They may follow upon our own struggles as a blessing, rather than as a result. They are more easily recognized when they are awaited, longed for, and expected. In tribal societies a sacred vision, a graced breakthrough of Spirit into their lives, flowed from a stance of reverence.

Freud, who treated so much of what was wrong with the human psyche, was once asked to step back from his clinical work and describe a healthy person. He responded with unusual succinctness. Such a person, he said, "has the capacity to work and to love." I would add a third: a capacity for reverence. The mature person has the capacity to work, to love, and for reverence.

Reverence lacks any utilitarian agenda. It both includes and transcends love. It shapes our love; it conforms our work to the possible. From its root *revereri*, reverence means "to fear, to stand in awe of." With reverence, a person surrenders to the truth of the wholly other and, in letting go of one's own accustomed truth, quakes. A person trembles before ultimate truth and is replenished. Reverence regards the truth of the other as well as of self. It allows the other to be other, and not to be absorbed into the insatiable self.

I recall such moments of surrender to beauty when I was a boy. In the early, dewy summer's day, with the mist steaming off the Sheyenne River in North Dakota, a meadowlark's trill rose out of a waving field of wheat. Each of you can, no doubt, recall similar moments: A love shared while gazing out on the rolling, white-capped waves of a stormy sea. Or while tramping through the woods, you came upon a ring-tailed pheasant. Startled more quickly than you, it shrieked and claimed your heart.

Reverence in nature has a curative power because it stills the craving of our hearts. Through our walks in the woods or gazing with another on a rough sea, we surrender ourselves to the moment. We lose track of ourselves. In return, we receive ourselves back, replenished, restored. We have been bathed in the truth of connectedness with every creature and consequently of the truth of our own nature.

Reverence allows a stillness, invites us to the darkness of nothingness so that the truth of our being and our relatedness to all can course through us.

More than most, persons with mental illness seek this stillness, but their disease rages like a howling storm through them. Physically enfeebled, they may buy into their own powerlessness and cling to feelings of worthlessness. They are overwhelmed: "The good I will, I cannot" (Romans 7:19). They lack the hope to break the circle. They are more likely to buy into the big lie: "I cannot escape. I'm no damn good! Why does God punish me so?"

If they rely simply on their own power, this lie becomes true. But if they can move toward an attitude of reverence, acknowledging the truth of their own helplessness and relying "on a power greater than themselves," then they may upend this lie. But, without reverence they are condemned to a cycle of recriminations. They are without hope.

If the adult child of an alcoholic has lived in a chaotic childhood, then she may, largely unconsciously, seek to please everyone in order to avoid the inevitable tempest. In addition, she may become a total caregiver, running faster in order to escape the bedlam lurking within. She may be able to make intense, short-term commitments, but become paralyzed at the prospect of long-term planning. She has grown so accustomed to chaos erupting at any time that she cannot count on what will happen a month or six months from now. She attempts to smooth over differences and to suppress her anger. Even after confronting her life pattern, she may be driven in her quest for recovery. She may push herself beyond endurance in public charities or physical fitness. Or she will initiate ten superficial friendships, rather than two sustainable ones.

Once we are on that kind of track, who will stop us? Who will stop the spinning of the squirrel cage, where we are chasing our tail round and round and round? How will we still ourselves? How will we allow the space for emptiness? How will we reverence?

Valerie, a capable, young woman of 21, recounted the story of how her mother's alcoholism had affected her. She was the oldest of five children. Her mother spent many hours at the bar each day and came home only to collapse. For three years, from the time she was eleven to fourteen, Valerie became the primary caregiver for the younger children and the manager of their fragile household. Then suddenly, her mother entered AA, sobered up, and re-entered the family equation. Valerie felt displaced; she even missed the old chaos, because she felt she had had a valued role in bringing a shaking stability to the family. Now with her mother sober, all these established patterns were disrupted. Fortunately, she discovered AlaTeen, a youth group for children of alcoholics. After several months she opened up enough to share the years of pain and her current feelings of loneliness and displacement. In AlaTeen she began to acknowledge a "higher power" in her own life and to appreciate herself, not just what she could do.

Reverence contemplates the truth, which invites us to a new time and a new space. It invites us to shed old habits and to await new gifts. It breaks the cycle of self-craving and of wrestling fulfillment from others. A person infused with reverence imagines the possible and projects a grounded future.

Reverence beckons us to communion with the world. It urges us to join with others in our contemplation because only together can a vision of the whole be received. Reverence depends on communal supports, so that we can risk the loss of egotism for the sake of the self-in-relationship. In parts of the East, people embody the reverence they hold for each other through the rite of *Namaste,* a Sanskrit word meaning, "I honor in you that which is whole." It also means: "The God coursing through me, honors the God in you." On encountering each other, they bow, greet each other with the two hands joined in the traditional posture of prayer. This gesture symbolizes the reconciling of the positive and negative, the male and female, the body and mind.

Namaste calls us to reverence ourselves and others. Breath upon breath, the spirit, yearning for the healing of our planet and of ruptured relationships, unfolds among us.[27] We will return to this theme of Spirit and of healing the planet in solidarity with others. In the next chapter we describe the need for a mentor figure to help us discern the movements of this Spirit and to guide us in our journey, which can be both terrific and terrifying.

Healing and Curing

Both religion and psychology offer hope. The purpose of religious healing is not that I get in touch with my self, but that I experience God, that I accept this free gift of relationship in my life. Within this relationship I necessarily grasp and accept myself as well, just as God accepts me. Though this divine acceptance carries with it self-acceptance, the latter is not the focus. Herein lies the radical difference between religion and psychology. If I simply "get in touch with myself," I run the risk of gazing on my own broken mirror or even of adoring my self. The language may be more sophisticated, but it is still idolatry, worshipping something other than God. Like any idolatry, in self-idolatry we are then condemned to the endless cravings of our very self, and the self can hardly satisfy its own desires for fulfillment. Then like Narcissus enraptured by his own beauty reflected in the pool, we drown.

Another difference between psychology and religion is that religion addresses the whole person and mobilizes all the resources – inner and outer – for the sake of wholeness. Religion may mediate healing; psychology tends to focus more on curing.

Healing addresses the whole person; curing addresses the disease or the dysfunctional system. Healing always considers the structure of relationships. Curing may be temporary if deeper healing does not occur. Until recently many modern medical practitioners, who had become increasingly specialized, had lost sight of the need for healing and focused on the cure of the disease. Exceptions to this occurred, of course: nurses, internists, family doctors, and specialists who considered the web of influences on the disease and enabled lifestyle changes as well.

A person may be healed, but not cured. A father on his death bed, for instance, may be reconciled to an estranged son. The disease from which he suffers, may or may not have been caused by a broken heart, but it still runs its course. Had the reconciliation occurred earlier, a cure might also have happened. Who is to say? The tragedy of the road not taken remains. Healing concerns itself with reconciliation, with the restoration of relationships, and deepening, often through suffering, our appreciation for the interconnected fabric of life.

Religion itself has been crippled because we have come to dissociate belief from faith. We think of belief as a way of thinking, but the original intent, in Anglo Saxon at least, was not to describe a way of thinking but a way of acting. Be-lief comes from the old Anglo-Saxon *be,* which means by, and *lief,* which means life. Belief then is what we live by. Psychology, by grappling with human life-issues and struggles, can enliven our be-liefs.

To conclude then, hope needs boundaries. It has a fondness for sacred times and sacred places, despite its acknowledgment that the sacred permeates all of creation. Enclosure provides care. It offers space for spousal fecundity. Boundaries respect human limitations and allow hope to blossom.

> *The people craving for vision,*
> *perish in blinding space,*
> > *Lusting in the night, restless for the dawn,*
> > *discovering only their own appetites.*
> *Then a dim light contours the horizon*
> *and hope rounds the Earth.*

Endnotes

1. See Lynch, *Images of Hope.* Lynch calls the urge for living without boundaries the heresy of "angelism." Its antidote, he says, is an imagination grounded in the Incarnation.

2. Wendell Berry, *Sabbaths, IX* (San Francisco: North Point Press, 1987), p. 18.

3. D.W. Winnicott, *Therapeutic Consultations in Child Psychiatry* (New York: Basic Books, 1971), pp. 1-25.

4. *Ibid.,* p. 12.

5. *Ibid.,* p. 14.

6. Robert Coles, *The Spiritual Life of Children* (Boston: Houghton Mifflin, 1990).

7. David Heller, "The Children's God," *Psychology Today* (December, 1985): 22-27.

8. See also Ana-Maria Rizzuto, *The Birth of the Living God* (Chicago: University of Chicago Press, 1979), pp. 87-108; 109-129.

9. Pruyser uses the term "autistic," but I prefer to use "narcissistic," since it has more immediate resonances with the general reader.

10. For an excellent, contemporary treatment of the Christian images of God see Elizabeth Johnson, "Feminist Theology and Critical Discourse about God," *She Who Is* (New York: Crossroad Publishing Co., 1992), pp. 18-57.

11. See Jeanette Rodriquez, *Our Lady of Guadalupe: Faith and Empowerment Among Mexican-American Women* (Austin: University of Texas Press, 1994).

12. Ruth Burrows, *Before the Living God* (Denville, NJ: Dimension Books, 1981), p. 82.

13. Nikos Kazantzakis, *Report to Greco* (New York: Simon and Schuster, 1965), p. 234.

14. Sebastian Moore, *Let This Mind Be in You: The Quest for Identity through Oedipus to Christ* (New York: Harper & Row, 1985), p. 117.

15. *Ibid.*

16. *Ekklesia* and *Ho hodos* Acts of the Apostles 9:2; 18:26; 19, 9,23; 22:4; 24:14,22.

17. Recall that the etymology of "desire" is *de + sidus,* concerning the stars.

18. Dennis Overbye, *Lonely Hearts of the Cosmos: the Story of the Scientific Quest for the Secret of the Universe* (New York: HarperCollins Publishers, 1991), p. 3.

19. We need further exploration of the dynamics and differences of these numinous experiences, especially with regard to gender differences. See the writings of women mystics such as Evelyn Underhill and Julian of Norwich.

20. Students of the *Spiritual Exercises* will recognize these two images as fruits of "The Contemplation on the Two Standards."

21. This truth follows the old Latin dictum that each person receives an experience according to their own capacity. *Quidquid recipitur per modum recipientes recipitur.*

22. This truncated analysis does not include the poignant situation of those subject to chronic mental illness, often due largely to disease or chemical imbalance.

23. See *The Fires of Desire: Erotic Energies and the Spiritual Quest,* Fredrica R. Halligan and John J. Shea (eds.) (New York: Crossroad, 1992) for the papers given at Fordham University on this topic. The novelist Flannery O'Connor also has some telling portraits, describing transforming religious experience, which appear to be abnormal on a psychological scale.

24. A sequel to this current book would amplify the process of discerning spirits and the cost of discipleship.

25. Lynch, *Images of Hope,* p. 86.

26. See Donald L. Barlett and James B. Steele, *America, What Went Wrong?* (Kansas City, Mo: Andrews & McMeel, 1992).

27. The word medicine shares the same Sanskrit root as meditate and mediate. Formerly, the medical practitioner had the capacity to meditate on the patient and to mediate healing power. Similar to the admonition to physicians to heal themselves was Bernard of Clairvaux's caution to his monks, not to preach until they were healed themselves, lest they pollute the fresh springs of God's grace with their own infection.

PART FOUR

Discerning the Way

Since then, at an uncertain hour,
Agony returns;
And till my ghastly tale is told,
This heart within me burns.

I pass, like night, from land to land;
I have strong power of speech;
That moment that his face I see,
I know the man that must hear me:
To him my tale I teach.[1]

− Samuel Taylor Coleridge,
The Rime of the Ancient Mariner

CHAPTER ELEVEN

Spiritguide

The searing vision of the Ancient Mariner gripped him and fueled his tale, so that he told it over and over to any ready listener. A fever for redemption courses through his story. Although he confesses to his crime of killing the albatross, no one grants forgiveness. Consequently he never enters into the wedding feast, never celebrates deliverance, never marks new life after death. We have met such people on our front stoop. Most often we hurry on. When we stop to listen, however, we are caught up and gripped not only by the Ancient Mariner, but by our own untold tale as well. We reach out and grasp for a spiritguide to listen to our tale.

The journey is long. Our hearts grow weary. At times we are confused, so we pause and seek direction. We need guides for the next leg of the journey, someone to hear and interpret our story lest our confusion totally muddle us. A great Sufi sage Jalaluddin Rumi said: "Whoever travels without a guide needs two hundred years for two day's journey." The West, of course, remains highly suspicious of gurus or sages unless they have scientific credentials. It also has a phobia of discipline as an infringement on one's freedom. Yet the West is now taking to Eastern disciplines such as Yoga or Zen. The Zen master will tell you that "one is most free when one is most disciplined." Discipline makes one free.

The West, however, places such a high value on individual freedom that it pays a cost in isolation and alienation. The mystic tradition in both the East and the West, however, implies a surrender to the Transcendent, not to some sage or guru, no matter how wise that person might be. In fact, the genuine gurus "know that they do not know" and encourage inner freedom even as they insist on the discipline of the way. The Jews called such a discipline *halakhah* or the way to walk. The Hindus call it *Marga* (way), the Chinese, *Tao* (way); and the Hindu Vedantins spoke of *Brahmacarya,* or walking in the Brahma. As we have seen the early Christians called themselves *People of the Way.*[2]

A spiritguide conveys a sacred place wherein the person can openly share his or her innermost spirit. A spiritguide harbors dreams, longings, desires, abject fears, and a dread of abandonment. As listener, a spiritguide attends to our doldrums. She has seen the shadow of the albatross. She knows the freedom of forgiveness.

St. Teresa of Avila, who suffered for many years at the hands of inept spiritual directors, said that given a choice between a guide who was pious and one who was knowledgeable, she would readily select the knowledgeable one. No doubt she was affirming her need for a person who would not only listen to her and understand her, but who would understand the ways of God and how God offers reconciliation with a soul. She knew from rough experience that such knowledge had little to do with pious palliatives.

Spirituality has had a long tradition of a spiritual father or a spiritual mother. Such a spiritguide is the best guard against deception. The term "spiritual" may be misleading since it has kinship with ethereal, ghostly, living in another realm from the ordinary. I am using "spiritual" here to mean one who is "spirit-filled." It implies someone who can guide because he or she has experienced the spirit. Such knowledge is not linear; it does not fit into clear and distinct ideas. Often, the better guides are those who know with clarity "what they do not know." They acknowledge their limitations and appreciate their strengths. They flow with the ways of the spirit, which can never be neatly pinned. They relish their own humanity as they grow humble, sensitive, and grounded. Since they are emptied of egotism, they have the capacity to care for others.

Caring

The most basic meaning of *caring* is to grieve, to experience sorrow, to cry out with. The word *care* finds its roots in the Old

High German *Kara* which means lament, as in *Kar-freitag*, (Compassion Friday) the old German word for Good Friday. This is striking in that we tend to think of caring as an attitude of the strong toward the weak. Yet more properly understood, a caring person enters into the pain of another and is simply present. Hence, a caring spiritual director allows a person to be present to the core of who he or she is before God.

A psychotherapist ideally conveys a similar sense of caring. Psychotherapy utilizes the relationship between client and therapist, the transference, so that the client can experience and clarify how he or she relates to others and explore choices which might enhance interaction with others. Clear boundaries are established: the therapeutic hour of 50 minutes helps clients to know their boundaries and to respect those of the therapist. Because of these clear parameters, clients know that this hour is safe. They can explore painful, wrenching issues, and then it is over for a few days. Normally this relationship does not and should not extend into any other realm of the client's world. It is a safe playground. When regression for the sake of the ego occurs, clients can play out behaviors within safe boundaries, largely without consequences, and then, from the options they have explored, they can choose mature, congruent behaviors. Effective psychotherapists are not only knowledgeable, but they communicate trust by their *caring* for the patient.

Psychotherapists ideally focus on the person, rather than on the problem. Like the spiritual director, a skilled, caring psychotherapist will acknowledge that life is a mystery to be lived, rather than a problem to be solved. Respecting the depths of a person allows space and freedom for significant problem solving and for healing to occur.

Psychotherapists may find themselves confronted with emotions of an extremely violent and primitive kind which they themselves find disturbing. If they remain calm in the face of abuse, they will usually find it possible to track, understand, and empathize with their clients' feelings. This stance enables clients to name actual childhood experiences, interpret, and re-frame them.

Thus, if clients accuse the therapist of neglect or rejection, the therapist might say: "I'm sure that you have felt rejected in this way by other people before me. Can you remember when you first felt as you are feeling now?" In this way, it is often possible to disclose a history of repeated patterns of hope followed by disappointment and to explore with clients that it is because their hopes are so exaggerated that they are always doomed to failure.[3]

Whereas psychotherapy capitalizes on the therapeutic relationship between therapist and client, spiritual direction explores the relationship between the directee and God. This relationship to God, however, encompasses all of the person. Consequently, it manifests itself in all the directee's relationships, and within spiritual direction these other relationships may need exploration, discernment, and active choices. Hence, if other relationships are destructive, then the relationship with God probably reflects this. The reverse could also be true. In the first instance, the person may need to shift for a while from spiritual direction to a therapeutic context; in the second, a person may need to let go of problem solving to allow space for contemplation.

Case Study: Eric

Some years ago Eric, a young married man, came to me for spiritual direction. Five years before he had been in a Jesuit novitiate for 14 months. Subsequently, during a long sojourn in Thailand he had trained in Zen meditation, and now he often frequented a Benedictine monastery for one or two day retreats. He felt "very close to God" during these monastic weekends, but increasingly he grew irritated that God seemed so distant during the rest of his life. He thought that perhaps he needed to spend a longer time in a monastic setting.

Within a short time it emerged that he and his wife Rose were having periodic conflicts and arguments. She wanted to "work things out," talk on a regular basis, and surface their differences. He got confused in these confrontations. He needed time to think. When he came home from work, he needed some breathing room or just wanted to be by himself for a while. When they did get into an argument, he felt an impulse to run, to get as far away as possible. Going to the monastery calmed him.

I suggested that perhaps God was calling him in a new way, inviting him to accept the full range of who he was. Did he ever feel angry?

Initially, he said, "No, I wasn't angry." But at the next session he described how his mother had never allowed him to be angry and that his father, when he was drinking, would go into a rage. He had learned early that being angry was dangerous. Now these old wounds shaped Eric's pattern of escape, and his arguments with his wife Rose were triggering earlier traumas.

I asked him if his centering prayer, his familiarity with Zen, might help him to stay present to Rose – to face the emptiness, to acknowledge his feelings of abandonment, of fear, of anger, rather than to run from them. We also talked about how he could negotiate and establish some regular times with Rose so that he might claim his need for a time out to think things over. After a few months of difficult struggle, he and Rose were communicating regularly and at a much deeper level. They had agreed to talk through their issues and conflicts *after* Eric had had some time out to reflect on and think through how he was feeling. My sense was that Eric's long acquaintance with prayer and the practice of Zen enabled him to stay with his relationship with Rose rather than run from it. Facing these early childhood traumas still triggered anxiety, but now he could name their origin, calm himself and focus on Rose. He was walking into the darkness with love.

Confronting his anxiety felt for Eric like confronting death itself. It conjured up his primal fears of abandonment, which he had successfully repressed by running, by hard work, and at times by mediation. If he were to encounter Rose for who she was, however, he could no longer run from this side of himself. He had to turn and contemplate the self he had become.

Eric had to give himself up to the risks of the world and allow himself to be engulfed and used up. In some way he had to pay with life and consent daily to die to old, so-called safe patterns. Otherwise he would end up as though dead in trying to avoid life and death. "Fear of life," Ernest Becker once explained, "leads to excessive fear of death."[4] And the denial of death can mask all our choices.

Eric had been denying life by fleeing to the monastery. More specifically he was fleeing from his anger and his anxiety about being angry.[5] The God with whom he had become familiar and intimate at an earlier stage in his life had now become an idol – an escape from life.

In another few months, Eric came to a surprising awareness. Almost overnight, his relationship with God changed. Now he sensed God's presence throughout the day. At times he was moved to tears at the kindness of Rose, or the beauty of an elderly woman or of a rare flower, or a strange, crooked tree. "I no longer need to go to the monastery; it was a painful death, but I sense God all around me."

This vignette, which covered a short span of time, should not suggest that Eric's transition was easy. His years of prayerful discipline, his fidelity to his wife, their deep and mutual care for each other, all harbored a space for this breakthrough to occur rather quickly. They both had walked through much pain together. In our sessions, Eric and I had begun by focusing on his relationship with God, until it became obvious that something major was blocking his prayer life. Then, even though our conversations shifted to his conflicts with Rose and to his early childhood traumas, the matrix for our conversation remained his spiritual life, of which these other relationships were a vital part. In the end we returned and affirmed how his relationship with God had undergone a profound shift.

Especially in a person's middle years, a spiritguide may help a person face the shadow side or the weaker aspects which had been repressed but now may surge up for attention.[6] If a person has had pathological anxiety and guilt, unhealthy dependencies, and animosities in earlier years, these will prevent one from examining the real issues at mid-life. With a spiritguide to mirror these turbulent interior depths, the person can face the pain, and the self may flower with new strengths. The person, just as Eric did, may then plunge into life with a fresh vigor, enthusiasm, and confidence because he or she is no longer pouring energy into protecting one's weak side. These foibles can now be laughed at, rejoiced with, and open bridges towards others who are weary of protecting their own frailties.

Mentoring

We can now describe more fully the characteristics of a contemporary adult mentor, which will often overlap with what we have described as a spiritguide.

Mentors help mediate the identity of their mentoree and to explore their intimacy needs and expressions. Mentors allow a safe space, an ever-widening space for the playful and disciplined expression of "who I am" and "who I am in relationship." As the mentoree moves from *self* to Other, he lets go of the supports, history and patterns which have allowed him until now to "be *self*." At the same time he is not a *self* in isolation. The *self* is always mediated by others. As he grows in self-knowledge, he takes on the role of mediating himself.

A good mentor rejoices that my Self comes from me rather than from her. A good mentor promotes freedom. To do so she needs purification lest she cling to her own agenda and impose her own projections.

Mentors play the fourfold role of 1) repository of memory, 2) assistant in imagination; 3) a diviner of desires – asking with regularity "what do you want?" "who do you desire?" and 4) decipherer – listening for the differences, asking questions and clarifying. "Out of these desires you have named, which one is central to who you are?"

Mentors also know that the ordination of our desires is incomplete until we surrender to "the wholly other," who is God. All else are "inordinate" desires. The mentoree may confuse the mentor with God and wish to surrender to him or her. Manipulative mentors can play into this dynamic and encourage a cult of personality. Then the person surrenders responsibility to an idealized figure. All their desires are spent on clay feet idols. They circle endlessly, shoring up inadequacies and dreading transformation. They make a bargain: "I'll idolize you, if I don't have to change."

Authentic mentors reverence the person before them. They know that no external answer will suffice. Beyond being present and trusting, they can be interactive. They can surrender to the truth of this person before them. They can surrender their need to control, to direct, to offer the right answer and to receive back a coloration and nuancing of their own interior. They thus provide places apart so that the mentoree can explore his shadow side and embrace all of who he is.

The psychological intimacy between a mentor and mentoree or between a therapist and client has great potential for exploitation, manipulation, and self-aggrandizement. Without appropriate boundaries, trust will be destroyed. The mentor, as the power figure in this relationship, has the sacred obligation to maintain clear boundaries.

A Story: My Mentor, Dr. Z

I first met him on my second day in the psych ward. Dr. Zieverink, the attending psychiatrist, had bright eyes, a quick smile, a beard, and a rumpled suit. I eyed him suspiciously. He asked me how I was feeling, how I was doing. I was evasive. He checked for side effects on the medication I was taking. I wanted to know how soon I would get out of here. He was evasive: "It takes time, a few weeks, a few months. Each person is different."

From those unlikely beginnings, he became the most significant mentor figure I had in my 30's. Often we do not choose our mentor figures. They happen to us.

Over time I grew to know Dr. Z better. After two years of intensive therapy, I would stop back for a friendly, informal visit about once a year. By then he was a brisk, generous man in his 40s, married for several years to another prominent professional, the father of two children, and chief of psychiatry at a major hospital. In addition to his therapeutic practice, he was a skilled organizer. He was a major player in pushing through reforms in state law for insurance policies and health care for people with mental illness.

In his therapy he operated out of a psychoanalytic psychotherapy model, but was flexible, highly interactive, and intuitive. By disposition humanistic, he had imbibed the wit and intelligence of his Jesuit teachers. Fresh, buoyant, his optimism flowed out of an assessment based on study, tests, and personal interaction: "Fifty percent of the population have problems and are working on them; the other fifty percent of the population have problems and are doing nothing about them." I tended to filter his views and reduce his lengthy life discourses down to a few pithy adages. He was eager to learn from his patients. "I know more about you than I do about myself – that is the nature of it. We've spent a lot of time together."

Dr. Z needed no crutches, so he did not rely on jargon. He conveyed a sense of competency, even bravado. He had a broad range of goals for himself. "Life is short. You realize that when you hit 40. You have to make choices. Plan for what you really want to do."

"So what do you want to do?" he would ask me.

Then he would listen. Really listen. Interactively listen. So that by the end I could claim for myself: this is who I am and this is what I wish to do and these are the people I would like to do it with.

Always interested and interesting, he was thoroughly committed to the care of patients. He stretched himself mentally, spirituality, and was personally available. Well-focused, intent, then off in a rush.

Holistic Centers

Mentoring often occurs in a community context. Students, young business professionals, housewives may rely on a slightly older person for their initiation into learning, for entering a profession or for carrying for children. Some health centers provide mentoring on a temporary basis.

Prior to modern drug therapy, there were sanitariums in the countryside for illnesses such as tuberculosis. Clean air and living in harmony with nature were the prescription for restoring the balance needed for good health. Do we not need new sanitariums – healing centers cleansed of pollution, awake to people's spirituality, freed of sullied relationships, which could address the violence we wreak on ourselves and others? Within these centers a certain amount of mentoring is needed.

Early healing practices arose out of communities. They did not isolate the patient, but rather included him or her through elaborate healing rituals. Stark exceptions proved the rule. In cultures, such as the Inuit on the Bering Sea, when a person realized that they were about to die, they might seek refuge in the wilderness or trek out to an ice floe and die in solitude.

The example of the rites of healing in the ancient Greco-Roman world may assist us in visualizing new healing centers.[7] In ancient Greece healing occurred in large medical/religious shrines to which people journeyed from miles around. Healing always involved some sacred mediation of the gods. Shrines to Asklepios, the god of healing, were pervasive through Asia Minor, Greece and later the Roman empire. Most often, these shrines, such as the one at Epidauros outside Athens, had a beautiful natural setting, chambers for the sick in which healers cared for the sick, instructed them in their dreams, and led them through a ritual healing labyrinth. Integral to the healing centers was a wondrous amphitheater where the plays of Aeschylus and Sophocles heightened awareness of the social conflicts and cleansed the emotions (catharsis). Votive offerings attest to the efficacy of these ancient healing centers. These ancient shrines suggest the following features for holistic healing:

1) *Ritual:* The community mediates healing and wisdom through ritual, which included prayer, dream-therapy, chants, and entering into an inner journey by going down into the darkness of the labyrinth. Our own contemporary rituals, however, cannot simply borrow from the past. It makes little sense to fly to high priced institutes in California to indulge in rituals borrowed from other cultures. Rather healing rituals need to develop and flow from our own lived context and our ongoing relationships.

2) *Imagination and dreams:* Drama played a cathartic role in ancient Greece by purging the emotions. Strolls through graceful gardens and autumn woods rested the soul. No TV pacifiers! Imaging gods who heal was central. Dreams accessed a person's spirituality, which was an integral resource for interior healing.

3) *Family Care:* After acute care by professionals, families or friends become the primary health caregivers.

4) *Best available medicines:* Medications, scientific practice, herbs, appropriate technology were central to the healing process at the Greek shrines.

5) *Environment:* In beautiful mountain valleys, Physician-healers, dramas, flowing water, dream therapy, and religious ritual combined to treat the whole person. Even though specialization seems inevitable in our own complex, urban conditions, a contemporary version of holistic medicine is becoming the norm more and more.

6) *Peace-making:* Much illness results from warring nations, tribes, and families. Besides the physical wounds, psychic scarring passes from generation to generation. To cite just one example, $3 to $5 billion dollars a year is spent in the United States on medical expenses for battered women. In addition to treatment for abused women and children, men need help and training for how to handle their anger. Institutes for peace are needed to learn how to wage peace,

rather than war. We could paraphrase Paul VI: "If you want health, work for justice."[8]

God's Work of Art

Mentors, who help us on the Way, have skills which resemble art more than science. They follow the pathways of intuition, imagination, and quirky chance, rather than rigorous testing and controlled experimentation. Sensitive mentors have an aesthetic grasp of the whole. They intuit that we grow by cooperating with and surrendering to the Artist who creates and heals us, and by attending to the delicate weave of all of our relationships.

Since a mentor might not readily be available, we can ask questions of our own spirit, such as the following:

> Who listens to me? Who cares for me? Who will mediate forgiveness and acceptance? Who embodies the energies of my spirit?
>
> What guidance do I find for this inner journey? What myths? How do I avoid being inflated by my delusions?
>
> How do traditional religious rituals help or hinder me from encountering the numinous or the Holy One in my life? How do I discover the peacemaker in myself?

Jesus as Mentor

Throughout his ministry Jesus of Nazareth formed around himself a band of disciples, people who were intrigued with what he was doing and left everything to follow him.[9] This group was not limited to the Twelve. The disciples spent time going around with Jesus on his itinerant ministry. They listened to his preaching, witnessed his conflicts and his acts of power, and enjoyed his table companionship, at times helping out. During his agonizing last hours, many deserted him; by all accounts some of the women disciples kept vigil with him to the end and even after.

To get at the interior reality of what it meant to follow Jesus, it is helpful to compare it with the following of other leaders at that time. It was not unusual in first century Palestine for a rabbi to have disciples who attached themselves to him for the purpose of learning interpretation of the Torah. In such cases, the disciples followed the teacher, which meant that pupils literally "walked behind" their Teacher on the road.

Discipleship with Jesus was quite different. According to Elizabeth Johnson, it had five features:

1) Being a disciple of Jesus depended first of all on his call. Unlike the custom of a pupil approaching a rabbi and asking to study with him, the pattern was reversed. Jesus chose his own disciples, often people with seemingly little to recommend them, and sometimes with obvious disqualifying characteristics. The response of the person called was given in all freedom. The call was sheer gift. Some responded "no."

2) Jesus' call to a person was "follow me" (Mk 1:17). Joining his band meant binding oneself in a spirit of allegiance to this person. It involved a willingness to share with him his uncertain and perilous destiny. This again is distinct to Jesus; other rabbis had disciples for a limited time. The disciple of Jesus bonded and committed to his person for a lifetime.

3) Discipleship with Jesus involved an extraordinary demand: that the response be total. One had to abandon everything else. Parents and family ties, nets and other means of livelihood, religious duties such as burying the dead, wealth, social status, pious custom – all are suitable payment for this pearl of great price. Nothing superseded the commitment. Discipleship meant radical transformation so that one turned from egocentricity to letting go, from self-interest to self-gift.

4) Jesus's own mission differed radically from the usual rabbi. He proclaimed the nearness of God's powerful and loving reign and reached out in a healing, liberating way to overturn oppression and to reconcile sinners and to welcome outcasts into God's reign which was already breaking out. Jesus made his disciples co-workers, even sending them out on their own to preach, to heal, to drive out the demons that held people in bondage.

5) Breaking all previous ties introduced the disciple to an open communal life. No one was a follower in isolation, but was supported and challenged by others with a similar commitment. For all of the inevitable tensions which arose, the ideal of their interaction with one another was mutual love. The

norm for leadership among them was service, taking the last place, rather than the culturally prevalent mode of domination. They never became an elite over against the great unwashed "outside" but associated with all comers, sharing (sometimes to their chagrin) the joy and feasting of Jesus' table companionship with tax collectors and sinners.[10]

So, although we could affirm that Jesus was a mentor, he burst the bounds and transforms our understanding of this role. More accurately he invited people to discipleship. He enjoined them to love one another "as I have loved you so that your joy might be complete." Then go and spread the good news.

In our own life's journey we reach a stage where there is nothing more to say. We face another juncture where all we can do is fall forward into love itself. We step out onto a bridge which has not been built, a path which we do not see, and reach for an embrace for which we yearn but may not feel. In the following vignette an abbot invites a disciple to such surrender:

> *Abbot Lot went to see Abbot Joseph and said: "Father, according as I am able, I keep my little rule, and my little fast, my prayer, meditation and contemplative silence; and according as I am able I strive to cleanse my heart of bad thoughts: now what more should I do?"*
>
> *The elder rose up in reply and stretched out his hands to heaven, and his fingers became like lamps of fire. He said: "Why not become all flame?"*[11]

Endnotes

1. Ernest Hartley Coleridge, ed., *Coleridge: Poetical Works* (London: Oxford University Press, 1912, 1967), p. 208.

2. These two paragraphs represent a summary from Paulos Mar Gregorios *A Light Too Bright the Enlightenment Today* (New York: State University of New York, 1992), p. 222.

3. Anthony Storr, *The Art of Psychotherapy* (New York: Methuen, 1980), p. 90.

4. Ernest Becker, *The Denial of Death* (New York: The Free Press, 1973).

5. See Carol Tavris, *Anger: The Misunderstood Emotion* rev. ed. (New York: A Touchstone Book, 1982, 1989).

6. Levinson, *The Seasons of a Man's Life* , pp. 198-208.

7. For an extensive treatment of the Asklepian tradition see my article: Patrick J. Howell, S.J., "Psycho-Spiritual Sources of Healing the Human Heart," in *Suffering and Healing in Our Day*, Francis A. Eigo, O.S.A., ed. (Villanova: Proceedings of the Theology Institute of Villanova University, 1990), pp. 95-136.

8. In an address to the United Nations, October, 1965, Paul VI said: "If you want peace, work for justice."

9. The following description of discipleship is drawn from Elizabeth A Johnson, CSJ, "Discipleship: Root Model of the Life Called Religious," *Review for Religious* 42 (Nov./Dec., 1983): 864-872.

10. *Ibid.*, pp. 865-867.

11. *The Wisdom of the Desert: Sayings from the Desert Fathers of the Fourth Century*, trans. by Thomas Merton from *Verba Seniorum* (New York: New Directions, 1960), p. 50.

CHAPTER TWELVE

As Sure as the Dawn

One decision, sometimes made without thought of the future, may determine the course of one's life. The Hindus call it *karma*. Thornton Wilder called it chance. Wilder explored this mystery of human destiny in *The Bridge of San Luis Rey*, the story of how people's lives, from a diversity of paths, intersected in one tragic moment on a bridge. What forces or factors, what influences, what decisions and whose, determine the course of my life?

Whether or not one believes with Shakespeare that "there's a divinity that shapes our ends, rough-hew them how we will," we are fascinated by the mysterious play of forces that determine the course of every human life.

All of us have many feelings, promptings, and desires which point to a certain destiny. At times we are greatly confused as we attempt to sort out our desires and motivations, especially when faced with an important decision. We are beset by an interior, contradictory dialogue which goes something like this:

"What is best?"

"I could do this." "Or I could do that." "On the other hand. . . ."

"It's never been done before?" "I've always done it this way."

"Yes, I can do it." "But it's scary. I'm afraid."

"People will criticize me." "I think God wants this for me."

"But this will give me security and then I can begin helping others more."

Such dialogue can paralyze us. And we sense we are drawn right back to an earlier struggle (Chapter Three) to identify our deepest desires and to rough-hew a direction.

In this final chapter, we ask how we make such life decisions? How do we center ourselves and find our way through our conflicting desires to a decision that flows in harmony with our Source? How do we tell whether the promptings we experience are of God or if they are the spirit of destruction trapping us? At first glance, it is not always easy to distinguish them.[1] Many people have been helped, however, by a process of discernment which attends to their interior responses. Within the context of their relationships, they reflect on how God might be inviting, challenging, guiding, even seducing them.

Discernment

Discernment derives from the Latin *cernere*, which has sired an interesting family of verbs such as *to cut, to sift,* and *to discern* as well as adjectives such as *shear, certain.* Its Latin origins suggest a sifting out in order to arrive at certainty. The Greek relative of *cernere* is *krinein* meaning to separate, to decide, to judge. Thus a hypo-*crite* is one who *overly cuts* and, in Greek, hypocrite describes an actor who feigns emotion of one sort or another. The Greek origins of discernment suggest that excessive *cutting*, always looking for nuances, may make a caricature of life without ever entering into it. Genuine discernment steers clear of such a trap.

These roots suggest we can arrive at truth sufficiently to act on it, but we must be careful not to overextend the process. By *over cutting*, by exploring every possible option, we become *hypocrites*, not so much interested in the truth, as in our own comfort. We can become so caught up in the process of discernment that we never risk deciding and then acting on our decisions.

Most people can point to some time, some circumstance, where they made a key choice and it made all the difference. They may also wonder at how they lucked out. They fell into something, they'll explain. They admit that healing came as a gift which had little to do with their own efforts. Had it been accessible to their own efforts, they would have opted for it long before. The choice, such as they made, might be called situating themselves in the near occasion of grace. They risked a friendship with a person who was not only fun but wise. They took a risk and invested their life savings in a shaky business. They quit a secure job in order to follow their life vocation. They entered a sanctuary, prayed wordlessly, wept, and discovered a deep truth.

These are near occasions of grace. They are the flip side of near occasions of sin, which Catholic moralists formerly used to describe the dangers and temptations to the soul. When people choose the near occasions of grace, they receive a blessing beyond their ken. They plunge into a new life that they know is right even though they dread it.

A Method of Discernment

"Okay, okay, that's all well and good," you say, "but these principles of yours remain rather ethereal. Aren't there some concrete norms which could help me in my decision-making?"

There are, at least for me, but you will need to test them out based on your own experience of Spirit. Here are mine in a nutshell:

1. *Be in the Present.* The present, right here and now, touches eternity. It is the crucible in which we hold the past, the center from which we project and foresee the future. When you are fully in the present, you are in the presence of the eternal encompassing both past and future.

2. *Be grateful.* "For all that has been, thanks. For all that will be, yes." Appreciation draws us out of our self-centeredness and wonderfully nourishes our self. The Lord loves a grateful heart.

3. *Be of service.* Share your own giftedness. Do not wait until you have it all together. Help some of those who needs are immediate, tangible, and different from yours. Serve out of your abundance rather than your scarcity.

4. *Appreciate nature.* When you walk through a woods with the sun dipping in the west, you relish God's abundance. A gaze at the stars gives us a sense of scale. Our problems then seem pretty puny. Or as the ocean water foam sweeps across our feet, we connect with the sea from which we came and all other living creatures. Nature gives you time to get in touch with what you really want to do.

5. *Attend to your body.* Our bodies turn imagination to a shape and give to airy nothing a local habitation and a name. They deserve respect. They are the first to inform us when we are abusing our self. Listen to your body. It is a wealth of wisdom. If you are regularly getting sick, your body may be shouting at you to slow down, to take a break, or to stop and change directions.

6. *Play the fool, without giving just cause.* Accept mistakes. Be ridiculous. Look silly. Without risking something, we cannot achieve it. That means making mistakes and not fitting in. Normal is not all that it's cracked up to be.

7. *Forgive others, accept forgiveness.* Forgiveness is an extension of faith. It not only repairs the damage, it jump starts our growth. Apologize. Forgive. Make reparation. Clutching to your hurts is an albatross around your neck. If you knew you were going to die tomorrow, who would you call or write to? Do it.

8. *Reverence yourself, your friends, your world.* It is all a miracle. It comes from God.

These eight attitudes form the essential backdrop for discernment. We need now to attend to our interior movements. We need to sift our own healthy desires from our cravings, and our own self-centered desires from the healing, enlivening motions of the Spirit. What follows then are two prenotes and then some guidelines for such a discernment.

Two prenotes:

1) Evil embraces evil. For a person going from bad to worse in a gross and evil way, an interior motion toward continuing evil causes pleasure, and it comes heavily disguised as a good. Not surprising. In the movie *The Godfather,* we see the dark descent of the Mafia figure Michael Coreolone who becomes more and more entrapped until he orders the killing of his enemies, including his brother-in-law, while he is attending the baptism of his godson.

2) It logically follows, secondly, that a motion toward the good, for such an evil person, causes turmoil and confusion and

shame. Charles Colson, one of Nixon's lawyers in the Watergate scandal, has given testimony to this wrenching process.

So before we even start the discernment, we are making at least two assumptions: a) that the person has an underlying orientation toward the good, and b) that he or she has at least an inchoate awareness of God, as the wellspring and destiny of one's life.

An Image for Discernment

To provide a context for our discernment, we might image ourselves flowing with the stream of life, somewhat at risk because we remain oblivious to the undercurrents shaping our course. Now we have traversed a few minor rapids and gained some skill in flowing with the mainstream, and we are appreciating the pristine beauty of the trip itself. We drift toward a critical juncture. We reach a point where we experience strong resistance or difficulty or dryness in our spiritual journey. Assuming that we have already determined the main direction of our lives towards God, we can expect two possible interpretations of our interior movements:

1) Either we are fighting *against* the current, stubbornly pursuing our own selfish ends and direction – without attention, without reverence, let alone service, to God our Source. We may be dragged down by pride, riches, and the amassing of honors. We have taken on too much luggage. All these not only tend to inflate our ego, but threaten to drown our genuine, vulnerable self. We have substituted goods for the Good. We are unable to flow with our ultimate, life-giving Source;

2) or, the second interpretation is that we are indeed flowing with the Source of our being, surely hesitant at times, but largely in the mainstream, making choices that arise out of who I am, out of my limited reality, out of my commitments and responsibilities as a human being. If that is the case, then two sub-principles are needed:

a) If such a person feels at peace from the beginning to the end of the decision process, then the action flows with and toward God.

b) If a person, however, feels uneasy, unquiet, agitated, then two things may be occurring:

   i) Some back eddy of selfishness may still need purification; we may be clutching to some old hurt or excessively protecting our vulnerability and resisting the challenge of the good; or

   ii) it is the wrong choice.

These interior movements are subtle; we can deceive ourselves because, somewhat like a spinning whirlpool, we get sucked down into our delusions. We need the help of a confidant or spiritguide to lend us a hand and to remind us of our center.

Guiding Values

The remedy for our sluggish ways may come to us as a surprise. We will no doubt say, "Why didn't I see that? I knew it all along. I just didn't realize it. How could I have been so blind?"

Never mind. God's time is not our time. But we can adopt some attitudes:

A) *Simplicity of heart.* Do I live with simplicity, no longer hiding myself? Do I seek more and more to live with an open heart? Do I cling to self or to others? Do I reverence people for who they are? Am I aware of and welcome my own sexuality and vulnerability? Am I also conscious of lurking shadows, back eddies, which may seek to suck me in or cause me to panic so that I manipulate others? Can I receive love as well as give it?

B) *Poverty of spirit.* Can I travel lightly and without excess baggage? Do I reverence things for what they are and not give them divine power? Or do I make idols out of them, as if money or riches or a long life or a short life or a sculpted, lean body or a pampered, comfortable life could "save me"?

C) *Humility.* Do I strive daily to name honestly who I am and my own gifts and to channel them and share them in the service of others? Can I accept help from others? Such humility shares the perspective of Irenaeus, the second century spiritual commentator: "the glory of God is the human person fully alive." Humility includes being fully alive. It does not sprout from a groveling denial of my talents or obscuring my core identity. It is not the false humility of the devious Uriah Heep sketched by Charles Dickens' *David Copperfield.* Heep professed, "I'm just a 'umble man," but his fake humility masked his crafty greed. Genuine humility opens us to the Ground of our Being who rejoices and laughs with us, who links us in solidarity with the Earth and with other creatures.

Principles for Life Choices

By now I hope it might be evident that the very structure of this book gives the basic dynamic principles for making a life choice. In fact, each chapter might be seen as a signpost along the course which we are charting. Taken together they offer the guiding principles for discernment. So we are now in a position to recapitulate our discussion in order to provide a systematic outline for discernment.

We are confident, too, that the reader will have sought to internalize the process and will see the futility of using these principles as external rules. There are no short cuts to holiness (except those which God provides), and the quest lasts a lifetime. The way to holiness ensures joy, but it often delivers tough, painful jolts. It thrives on love, withers on duty. Ultimately it comes as a gift because we are creatures of a loving Creator.

We can say then that the structure of discernment embodies the following features:

1) We may find ourselves cast adrift. We hunger for meaning, but it eludes us. One young man expressed the futility of his life saying, "I am face down in an inch of water and drowning." We face the ultimate choice of life or death (Chapter Two).

2) In the beginning was desire (Chapter Three). We are restless until we rest in God. But for now, it is not all that clear. Sated by a consumerist culture, fueled by the insecurities of

a nation whose imperial tentacles wrap the globe, and clouded by our own early fears of abandonment, our deepest desires are embroiled with our cravings. Freud called our instincts a "seething cauldron" and urged that they be governed by reason and science. That is a start, but it is inadequate. Few people can shoulder this hearty stoicism anyway. We do know, however, that our desires need attending to. They point us toward God.

3) The God beyond all naming elicits our desires and spices our actions (Chapter Four). Yet to name the mystery reduces the irreducible mystery. The Jewish practice reverences the mystery by never naming God's name. It indicates God by the tetragrammaton YHWH, four letters signifying the name of Yahweh, which are never pronounced aloud. Thus silence reverences God. In public readings in the synagogue, the reader substitutes "adonai, lord" for YHWH. Nonetheless, in order to talk of God, we need to name. We named God as Source and invited you to flow with its evocative power. Better yet, allow God to name God's self to you.

4) Drawing near to these waters, actually plunging into them, requires faith (Chapter Five). Faith is the courage to accept acceptance. We never stand outside this faith. If we could, we would then page through a mail-order catalogue and request that an order for faith be sent to our mailing address.

We live and breathe and have our being in faith. Faith is a matter of heart. Faith invites life's abundance. Without faith, we simply seek our own comfort. We are too easily satisfied with wealth and power and these, like blobs of cholesterol, gradually choke our heart. So faith accepts God's acceptance of us. In faith we choose Love and share Love.

5) A loving God invites us to accept all of who we are. God's acceptance allows our self-acceptance. Even those darkened, musty corners of hatred, omission, infidelity, lying, and manipulation can now see the light of day. We loosen and let go in God's love, and we are relieved and grateful (Chapter Six).

From the vantage of God, who is freeing love and loving freedom, we grasp how we we are born into the hells around us and how we later contributed to them. As children of freeing love, we can struggle together to build a realm of peace and justice. We can confront the causes of injustice – racism, sexism, consumerism, militarism, deceit in offices of public trust, imperialism – which undermine God's reign. We see more clearly how we are both children and parents of these "isms" (Chapter Six). Service of others and of the Earth no longer burdens, but rather gladdens our hearts.

6) We also looked at how shame and stigma operate (Chapter Seven). They mask our feelings of inadequacies. They hide our fears and self-hatred. They allow society itself to be safe from intrusions by God. They bolster religious elites and they identify intruders as outcasts. Above all, they block us from making choices which flow from our deepest desires, from our union with God.

7) God breaks through. A gentle whisper gladdens our hearts (Chapter Eight).

8) We move, more and more openly, toward accepting others, just as we ourselves have been accepted. Such acceptance makes forgiveness possible (Chapter Nine). Within this rooted identity I have a choice to make: Can I embrace loving freedom and freeing love? I discern. I choose how I will serve (in the context of the particularity of myself within the history of my relationships.) In effect, I consider three things: vocation, location, and audience in which my gifts will flourish.

Out of a free and mutual relationship with God, a woman or a man asks, "How do I follow you, [God]?" This question is the crucial touchstone of discipleship:

How can I work with you? But then I discover that the question is not enough. I move into the very mystery of God. I discover and begin to live out the strategy of God. So my choices flow out of simplicity and honesty. I no longer am bound by possessions, prestige, and pride. We can sketch this conclusion in the following diagram of guiding values:

Simplicity	vs.	Possessiveness
Truth	vs.	Prestige
Groundedness	vs.	Pride
Fig. 2 Discernment Criteria		

9) We move on. Hope is not hope unless it is grounded in the real. Hope flourishes when bounded; it accepts limitations because it knows the fruitfulness of husbanding one's resources. It avoids the headiness of being a Messiah, of doing it all by myself, or of seeking salvation through pride, prestige or possessions (Chapter Ten).

10) And finally, no one makes this journey on their own, and a discernment always occurs in community. Spiritguides can, therefore, help sift out truth from delusion, playfulness from compulsivity. They enlarge our horizons. They help us discern our desires and to imagine the possible. With their aid, we grow more and more conscious of the Source in our hearts who is our ultimate spiritguide (Chapter Eleven). We can now sketch a diagram of the stages of the soul's growth:

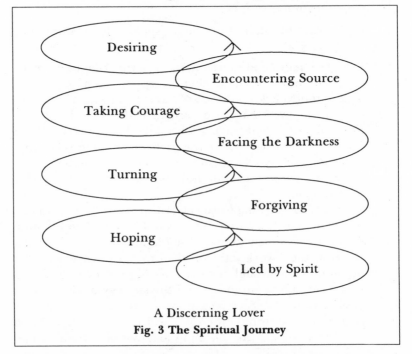

A Discerning Lover
Fig. 3 The Spiritual Journey

In order to portray these stages in the growth of a soul, we might image it as a three-dimensional double spiral or a helix. Such an image might show how the stages occur simultaneously. *Desiring,* for instance, is already a form of *Encountering God,* and being *Led by Spirit* enables us to become *Discerning Lovers*. The double spiral would show that the spiritual journey has as many shapes and contours as there are individuals who take up the quest.

William James observed two types of believers: the once born and the twice born. Each experienced the conversion process quite differently, although their eventual orientation could be the same destiny. James compared these two conversions to the well-known medical phenomenon of *lysis* and *crisis*. In *lysis* a patient experiences a gradual decline of a disease and grows steadily and progressively better (or steadily worse). In contrast, *crisis* marks a decisive moment in a disease. Up until a key moment, it hung in the balance whether the patient would survive or not. James suggested that the "once born" experience *lysis;* the twice born *crisis*. Obviously this book focuses on the latter.[2]

By one estimate 20% of the population are smooth evolvers (lysis) and the other 80% have to experience major upheavals (crisis) at certain times in life.[3] In a recent article in *The Atlantic,* Winifred Gallagher disputes this claim. She says, "the overwhelming majority of people, the surveys shows, accomplish the task of coming to terms with the realities of middle age through a long, gentle process – not an acute, painful crisis."[4] I have been using the term crisis as a crucial turning point calling for perceptions, judgments and decisions which are new, even threatening, for the individual. Gallagher uses the term more narrowly with descriptors such as acute, painful, dramatic, short-term. She is also talking only about mid-life crisis. The crisis-conversion model I have been describing could happen at any time in one's life.

In any case, we all have a lot to learn from each other. The lysis-conversion models a certain solidity, a naturalness with the ordinary rhythms and changes of life. It suggests an image of waving fields of grain, golden brown – open and expectant, ripening gradually before an azure sky. The crisis-conversion models an urgency about God in our lives. It looks at the lightning crackle. It acknowledges the thundering storms that can suddenly cloud the skies, the wind and hail that can level a ripening field, and the bolts that, in a moment, shake the earth and a person's heart. Those who have suffered from alcoholism, mental illness, the violence of concentration camps, the ravage of war, rape know instinctively what I mean. Both lysis and crisis experiences are valid; both enhance the other. One without the other would be either too placid or too dreadful.

The Challenge of Change

We cannot count on this sort of change; we cannot make it happen. It comes as a great boon. Usually change – when it occurs at all – follows long and arduous trying. The turning point, however, may be sudden and critical. Perhaps in memory, we even focus our story round an event which becomes prototypical of a chain of events that happened over a longer period. I know I do that. For rhetorical purposes I can shape a gradual change into a critical change.

Personality change follows a change in action. We begin by trying on a different behavior; gradually it becomes habitual. A simple example illustrates how difficult it might be: When I sit and fold my hands together, my right thumb naturally wraps over my left thumb. When I try the reverse, wrapping my left thumb over my right thumb, my hands feel awkward, out of sync. My awkwardness over such a simple physical change enables me to see how profound and difficult trying out a new psychological stance or a deeper social commitment to justice might be. Instinctively, I know that I cannot do it alone, although sheer will power might carry me for a few days. I know that in some instances I need professional assistance and that I will need the support of friends. Above all, I need the humility to ask for help.

The sequence for transformation, according to Allen Wheelis, is first suffering, then [desire,] insight, will, action, and finally change.[5] Nobody can do it for us. We create ourselves. Or rather with God's help, we co-create ourselves. Grace, which is God's motion within us, pervades the enterprise from beginning to end. Though we have focused primarily on the first four factors – suffering, desire, insight, and will, action is paramount. As one of my own mentors bluntly oversimplified it, "Insight is crap. Nobody ever changed because of an insight. Without action nothing changes." Without action we chase insights like children running after butterflies with holes in their nets.

Individual and Social Conversion

My own caution about these twelve chapters is that their focus has perhaps been too narrowly on the solitary journey of the individual without enough emphasis on the social dimension of conversion and the role of community, especially friends, in this transformation. Such an emphasis has been a matter of perspective, and perhaps personal experience, rather than conviction. I am convinced that the social and personal dimensions of conversion are intertwined. We are social creatures. As social persons, we advance along twin poles – social and personal. We journey together. Such a pilgrimage is best made in the sporting company of other pilgrims – by no means like-minded – entertaining and edifying each other through life stories. Without solidarity we ride the latest fad. Without solidarity we get caught up in our own religiosity. Without solidarity, we become deluded by shadows of ourselves. Without civic responsibility, we surrender to the despair of the self alone.

A Closing Vision

I sometimes think that salvation (both social and personal) means simply that when I die at least one other person will be willing to present me to God and say, "Here's my friend, Patrick. He's a good man."

These introductions will be but the beginning of an infinite mutuality. Friendship begetting friendship. Lovers welcoming lovers. A celebration of all that we have been and all that we are becoming in the company of others.

Perhaps it is a good sign that I can already think of a couple hundred people that I am eager to introduce. In fact, once I am through the door myself, I think of the scene, in a down home sort of way:

"Howdy, God. I'd like you to meet my friends, Chris, Peter, and Pat.

"And I'd like you to meet my good friends Terri and Joe and their children Ben, Kevin and Katie.

"And my parents, Joe and Virginia, and my brothers and sisters and their families. All 39 of them.

"And several scores of Jesuits.

"The Institute for Theological Studies at Seattle University.

"My colleagues Gary and Mike and Jeanette.

"The pastoral studies students at Santa Clara.

"And all the folks whose stories illuminate this journey:

Sarabel and Lillian and Barbie from the psych ward, my undergraduate students from Religion and Psychology, and the wonderful, generous ITS students, little Jenny sipping tea with her tough grandmother, Betty who slit her wrists, the woman with leprosy at Molokai, Bill who first met You on the mountain and had a tough time coming down, gregarious Mark who's now a social worker caring for mental patients, the police officers in Portland, and Carmen who gave up hating her body and started to enjoy life, and Sheila who helped me encounter Your wisdom as a black madonna.

Myrna who faced her shame and accepted Your healing,

Tom, the courageous Vietnam veteran,

Valerie who first encountered You through Alateen,

Eric, who sought You in Thailand and Benedictine monasteries, and found You in Rose.

And Dr. Z. . . .And. . . .Well, I'd like You to meet all my friends. No, reason to cut it short, I understand You've got lots of time."[6] So I'd like to look around, but since I understand You have an eternity or two, I'd also like You to meet some of the many who made this book possible:

The Jesuits of Seattle University; Seattle University for my sabbatical in 1992-93; Loretta, James, Marianne, Sharon, Katherine, Phil, Mike, Jeanette, and Annette & Gwen of the Institute for Theological Studies; Jesuit House, Gonzaga University, for summer writing; The Jesuit School of Theology, Berkeley; The Bannan Foundation of Santa Clara University; Ryan Sawyer, word-processing; Jerry Cobb, SJ, Jim Harbaugh, SJ, and Margaret Zidon, who read the book and discerned the heart; Sarah Smiley for caring and diligent editing; Sheed & Ward who took a risk."

"Well, that's it. I guess now it's Your turn."

Endnotes

1. See Jacqueline S. Bergan and Marie Schwan, *Freedom: a Guide Prayer* (Take and Receive Series) (Winona, MN: St. Mary's Press, 1988), pp. 136-141 for an explanation of Christian Discernment and for a prayerful method of discernment.

2. I was drawn into exploring this difference by students in my course "Psychological Issues in Spirituality," (Santa Clara University, Winter Quarter, 1993).

3. John R. Quinn, "Scandals in the Church: Reflections at Paschaltide," *America* (April 10, 1993): 4.

4. Winifred Gallagher, "Midlife Myths," *The Atlantic* 271 (May, 1993): 51-55, 58-62ff.

5. Allen Wheelis, *How People Change* (San Francisco: Harper & Row, 1973), p. 102. I have added desire to his list.

6. I believe the communion of saints begins now. See Gerard Manley Hopkins, "As kingfishers catch fire, dragonflies draw flame," *The Poetical Works of Gerard Manley Hopkins,* p. 141.

Seven Guideposts for a Healing Spirituality

After several years of pastoral counseling and spiritual direction, I have summarized seven guideposts for a healing spirituality.

1) Pain strips away false cares or aimless cravings. It may paradoxically, like birth pangs, mark the beginning of new life. The medical profession used to speak of two ways to recover from a bodily disease – one gradual and the other abrupt: *lysis* and *crisis.*[1] Similarly, in the spiritual realm there are also two ways in which inner unification may occur, one gradual, the other abrupt.[2] A *crisis* shakes us loose from our ruts, untethers us from our usual moorings, and sets us off on a trip. A *lysis* marks the gradual, day-by-day improvement in a person's health.

St. Paul perhaps exemplifies the most dramatic conversion in Christian history. Yet after his crisis of falling to the ground, being blinded by light, and being accepted by Ananias, he had an extended period – perhaps as long as seven years – in Arabia to ponder this shattering event before he began his public ministry. No doubt, he had instructors to assist him. He had a crisis followed by a lysis.

The crisis may accelerate the conversion, but does not guarantee it. Not everyone experiences a *crisis*, but all are called to *lysis;* that is, to ongoing daily conversion to inner truth and spiritual reality.

2) People going through a major life change need transition time. Just as fields, depleted of nutrients, need to lie fallow, people

need a time out, a hallowing time, a desert time.[3] They often
need a guide to help them stay in this arid emptiness so that they
can abide the anxiety and not take flight into the frenzy of activity.
It is a meager diet of locusts and honey, a time in the wilderness,
which may take any of a number of different forms: camping for
an extended time in the forests, working with AIDS patients,
taking a seminar in Jungian psychology, carpentering alongside
others to build homes for the poor, making a retreat in a Benedictine monastery, or pruning trees in a cherry orchard.

**3) People on a journey tell stories through which they grasp who
they are.** Telling stories shapes a living text. They help us see the
past so that we can imagine a pathway toward our individual and
collective future. Chaucer demonstrated this well in *The Canterbury
Tales.* In this class journey, 33 pilgrims exchange stories as they
wend their way to the shrine of Thomas á Beckett to pay homage
to the saint who assisted in their healing.

　　Stories from the heart illumine where we have been and cast
a light on the next step. They are not recipes for how to cook up
a spirituality. Rather, they cast light on an apparently obscure
path and invite people to continue even when the next step
appears to be impossible.

4) People change through (sufficiently honest) relationships.
Friendship makes it possible to hear the voice of honesty so that
truth may quicken the heart. As one wag put it, "The truth will
set you free, but first it will make you miserable." Good friends
encourage us to face the truth. An honest relationship emerges
in time and cannot be rushed. It is woven with strands of stories,
convivial meals, and challenging conflicts. It emerges from lives
shared. It not only heals, but bonds us together *for* life and *through*
life. Such a friend accepts us as we are, loves us as we are, com-
munes with our spirit as we are and suggests the healing mystery
which dwells among us and beckons.

**5) Hope makes it possible to get up in the morning and to take
the next step. Hope gives meaning to the present.** A shrewd
observer of humanity once said, "If you want to be a millionaire,
sell a product everyone needs, but if you want to be a billionaire,
sell hope." The adage carries a contradiction. You cannot package
hope, but everyone longs for it. Without concrete, realizable hope,

we flounder in the slough of despair; we cannot go forward because we are mired in our present misery.

6) God creates; both Creator and created are meant to live in relationship. We begin with a truth: I am created. Therefore, I have to start by accepting something, namely that I am human. I am not a carrot, nor a peacock, nor shoe leather, nor a goat. I am human. So I need to accept and to learn what it is to be human. I need to discover and appreciate my body, my feelings, my sexual energy; my capacity for learning and wisdom; my desires and gifts for friendships and for love; my openness and destiny to Spirit.[4] Accepting creaturehood presumes that God is not some distinct, remote personage or idea, but acts lovingly, in relationship, and through all of creation. The Creator and created live in mutual relationship.

Trusting this relationship I respond to my Creator out of who I am. I respond as Patrick, not as Monica, not as Jerry, not as Chris, not as Jennifer, but as Patrick. That's who I am. And I need especially to get to know myself and especially myself *in* relationship. For some, this acceptance may mean having to accept that "I have had one heart attack." Or "I have lost my best friend to a senseless, tragic death." Or " I have a bipolar disease with which I can barely cope at times." Or "I live day to day on food stamps, and my family and I live in a rat-infested ghetto." For others, it may mean accepting, "I have received an extraordinary inheritance." "I have a talent for leadership – even though I'm scared spitless by it." Acceptance does not mean complacency, nor that I have to "like" where I am; it means turning face front into my entire reality.

7) Love overflows into service.
The medieval teachers said that "Love is diffusive of itself." It spills over; it fills its surroundings. It pervades a community which breaks bread together, shares forgiveness, and seeks justice in the face of evil together. A person radically accepted by another naturally wishes to share that acceptance, that gift of love with others.

Endnotes

1. William James, *Varieties of Religious Experience* (Cambridge, Mass.: Harvard University Press, 1985), pp. 152-153. James applied this distinction to the spiritual life: *Crisis* – the decisive moment in a disease; *Lysis* – the gradual decline of a disease.

2. This time differential for transformation – whether eruptively or over a longer period of time – occurs in the distinction that James makes between a *twice-born* and a *once-born* religious experience. James, *Varieties of Religious Experience*, pp. 74, 139.

3. William Bridges, *Transitions: Making Sense of Life's Changes* (Redding, Mass.: Addison-Wesley, 1980).

4. I am indebted to Fr. Howard Gray, S.J. for some of these images, drawn from a three-day workshop on *The Spiritual Exercises*, Colombiere College, Clarkstown, MI (June, 1985).